Annual Review of Addictions and Offender Counseling

Best Practices

Annual Review of Addictions and Offender Counseling

Best Practices

Edited by
STEPHEN SOUTHERN

RESOURCE *Publications* · Eugene, Oregon

ANNUAL REVIEW OF ADDICTIONS AND OFFENDER COUNSELING
Best Practices

Resource Publications
An Imprint of Wipf and Stock Publishers
199 W. 8th Ave., Suite 3
Eugene, OR 97401

www.wipfandstock.com

ISBN 13: 978-1-62032-938-2

Manufactured in the U.S.A.

Contents

1

Editorial

The *Annual Review of Addictions and Offender Counseling: Best Practices* represents a labor of love. It was incubated in the editorial board meetings of the *Journal of Addictions and Offender Counseling (JAOC)*, which I have been privileged to edit. *JAOC* receives each year interesting and informative manuscripts describing innovations and creative approaches to addictions and offender counseling. In addition, our journal readers and members of the International Association of Addictions and Offender Counselors (IAAOC) submit excellent manuscripts, which address significant professional issues in our profession, as well as useful literature reviews.

The Executive Board of IAAOC has encouraged us to return to the original mission of *JAOC* in which we endeavor to publish primarily research findings. Yet, having so few pages in our journal would result in a failure to cover adequately all the innovations in clinical practice and developments in the profession. The IAAOC Board authorized me to develop this *Annual Review* so we can continue to offer our members and all counseling professionals information about best practices in our field. With the help of my outstanding editorial assistant, Kate Hilton, we would like to offer this collection of best practices in addiction and offender counseling.

Keith Morgen has agreed to serve as editor of *Annual Review*. He has included a Call for Papers so that Volume 2 of the review offers ongoing coverage of evidence-based practices, creative programs, innovations in clinical practice and emerging professional issues. The following chapters are included in the first volume of the *Annual Review of Addictions and Offender Counseling.*

Evidenced-Based Practices in Addictions Counseling: A Long Overdue Discussion for IAAOC and How the New Annual Review Can Support the Endeavor

KEITH MORGEN

It is time for papers that specifically state what was done, how it was done, why it was done (i.e., what is the science behind the intervention), and most importantly, how you can implement the same practice in your setting.

Best Practices in Offender Rehabilitation: Reviews from the Field

STEPHEN SOUTHERN

Offender counseling has been affected by the movement toward empirically supported treatment, especially applications of cognitive behavior therapy. Best practices in offender rehabilitation take into account contexts and needs of clients based on particular problems, populations, and settings.

Codependency: A Critical Review and Proposed Feminist-Based Model for Assessment and Treatment

VIRGINIA A. KELLY, ELIZABETH S. MICELI, LESLIE V. HAMMER, JAMES M. McGINN, & EMILY KEUPER

Using the model described here, with a heightened sensitivity to and understanding of the gender issues raised, may provide the practicing counselor with a structure from which to base work with a codependent client

Forgiving Betrayals: A Treatment Model for Couples Affected by Addiction

KAYLEE K. VANCE, ANDREW P. DAIRE, & JENNIFER M. JOHNSON

In treating the relationship as a vital component of addiction treatment, clinicians are also treating the individual and preventing relapse, which may also result in preventing the destruction of the relationship.

Diminishing Relationship Discord While Practicing Motivational Interviewing and Cognitive Behavior Therapy

MELANIE M. IARUSSI

Diminishing discord and enhancing client engagement are common challenges for counselors, especially those who work with involuntary clients in addiction and offender counseling. MI is an approach that can help counselors accomplish these tasks to increase the likelihood of positive client outcomes. In addition, many counselors currently practice CBT when working with these populations and adding MI may be a valuable addition to their repertoire of skills, especially considering the preliminary evidence that a synergistic effect may occur when MI and CBT are paired.

Treatment of Alcohol Abuse among College Students: A New Look at REBT

EDWARD WAHESH & JANE E. MYERS

By placing the emphasis of counseling on the beliefs that create the problems, rather than on reducing the quantity of alcohol use, the client was empowered to make widespread and deep change in his life. This change also may be long lasting because the client has developed skills to identify and dispute irrational thinking in the future.

Voices of Substance Abuse Professionals: Hurricane Katrina and Post-disaster

TIM S. VANDERGAST & PAMELA S. LASSITER

One goal of the present study was to provide a voice for substance abuse treatment professionals who experienced professional and personal challenges while serving clients during this turbulent moment in U.S. history. Findings indicated that 12-18 months after Hurricanes Katrina and Rita, participants remained in the thick of a long term, complex, professional and personal recovery process . . . The importance of self-care, both post-disaster and long-term emerged from the current study.

Voices of Recovery: An Investigative Study of the Effectiveness of Gender-Sensitive Substance Abuse Treatment

Telsie A. Davis & Catherine Y. Chang

It is our belief that through the offering of respect-of-person, empowerment, access to information, women-only therapy opportunities, and mixed-gender groups once women have sobriety and support, women will be able to experience successful treatment outcomes such as insight, positive coping skills, empowered behavior, and re-engagement with family that have often alluded this underserved population.

Counseling the Female Sexual Offender: Integrating a Trauma Focus into Treatment

Matther J. Paylo, Stephanie Kinch, & Victoria E. Kress

Counselors often treat female sexual offenders with a traditional approach, which focuses only on the sexual offense. This offense-only approach discounts or at least minimizes the impacts of a trauma history and its impact on the offending behavior (Strickland, 2008). A trauma-focus may be helpful in minimizing reoffending behaviors . . . With an existent working alliance, a set of coping skills, and some understanding of the impact of trauma, the counselor can more effectively engage the individual in cognitive restructuring related to her offense(s)/victimization.

Mental Health Court Goals and Practices: A Staff Perspective

Katie Ellis, Leanne Fiftal Alarid, & Michael Tapia

Future research regarding MHC staff may wish to consider the referral process, quality staff communication between agencies, providing timely access to treatment services, and providing that treatment for a long enough duration so that, ultimately, clients remain stable long after the MHC experience ends.

Stephen Southern and Kate Hilton
Department of Psychology & Counseling
Mississippi College
Clinton, Mississippi

2

Call for Papers

Annual Review of Addictions and Offender Counseling:
Best Practices—2014
Submissions due July 1, 2013

The International Association of Addictions and Offender Counselors presents a new publication, *Annual Review of Addictions and Offender Counseling: Best Practices*, that publishes papers focused on empirically-based practices (EBPs) in addictions and offender counseling. The monograph publishes once per year (March) and is peer-reviewed.

Papers are now being solicited for the March, 2014 issue. Areas (focused on addictions and/or offender counseling) of interest include:

- Meta-analyses demonstrating an EBP or validating an already established EBP
- Counseling intervention research utilizing a control and/or treatment comparison group
- Specific strategies for promoting the use of EBPs in community-based settings
- Counseling practice guidelines based on science and theory and that include decision-making flow diagrams. These papers should be specific and contain information and supplemental materials (in article or available by contacting author) so that the material disseminated can be applied to the reader's practice setting.
- Creative and innovative practices from clinicians in the field

We welcome papers developed from a recent American Counseling Association Conference presentation or an entirely original work. At least one member of the authorship team must be an IAAOC member.

Papers may be no longer than 15 pages in length (not counting title page, 50-word abstract, references, tables/figures). Papers must adhere to the guidelines of the Publication Manual of the American Psychological Association (6th edition).

Submissions and inquiries regarding the submission process should be directed to the Editor:

Keith Morgen, Ph.D., LPC, NCC
Editor, *Annual Review of Best Practices in Addictions and Offender Counseling*
Assistant Professor of Counseling & Psychology
Centenary College
Hackettstown, New Jersey
morgenk@centenarycollege.edu

3

Evidenced-Based Practices in Addictions Counseling

A Long Overdue Discussion for IAAOC and How the New Annual Review Can Support the Endeavor

KEITH MORGEN[1]

This brief paper reviews the state of evidenced-based practices (EBPs) in addictions counseling, challenges for the addictions counseling profession in advancing the use of EBPs, and how the new *Annual Review of Best Practices in Addictions and Offender Counseling* can help the International Association of Addiction and Offender Counselors (IAAOC) integrate EBPs into addictions counseling education, training, supervision, and practice.

Major institutes and organizations such as the Institute of Medicine (2005), National Institute on Drug Abuse (NIDA, 2004), and National Quality Forum (2005) all recommend substance use disorder (SUD) treatments that employ EBPs. Myriad treatment principles (e.g., Center for Substance Abuse Treatment, 2006; NIDA, 2009), meta-analyses (e.g., Dutra et al., 2008; Pearson et al., 2012), clinical studies (e.g., McCarty et al., 2007) and clinical practice guidelines (e.g., Management of Substance Use Disorders Working Group of the Department of Veterans Affairs / Department of Defense, 2009) direct SUD practitioners on how to effec-

1. Keith Morgen, Department of Counseling & Psychology, Centenary College; President-Elect, International Association of Addictions and Offender Counselors. Correspondence concerning this article should be addressed to Keith Morgen. Email: morgenk@centenarycollege.edu

tively work with SUDs using EBPs. Unfortunately, as underscored by the Institute of Medicine (2005) and Wisdom et al. (2006), the EBPs do not typically reach the SUD treatment population. This is particularly a problem for community based organizations that lack the size and resources of larger medical centers and major clinical trials (Forman, Bovasso, & Woody, 2001; Lundgren et al., 2011). Consequently, the *Annual Review of Best Practices in Addictions and Offender Counseling* serves a critical need in the dissemination of the "how-to steps" required for the implementation of EBPs within addictions counseling practice and training. This paper will address the state of EBPs within addictions counseling and ways this annual review can strengthen the use of EBPs within addictions counseling.

EBPs: What We Know

The SUD treatment field has established several EBPs. Each EBP is comprehensive in scope and practice and can be interpreted in multiple ways. Table 1 briefly reviews a *selection* of the most common EBPs and a sample of the research/publications available to demonstrate effectiveness and guide practice. There are many more examples of EBPs. Counselors are encouraged to consult websites of such agencies as the Institute for Research, Education & Training in Addiction (http://ireta.org/), the Substance Abuse and Mental Health Administration (http://www .samhsa.gov/ebpwebguide/index.asp) or the Knowledge Application Program of the Substance Abuse and Mental Health Services Administration (http://www.kap.samhsa.gov/products/manuals/tips/index.htm) for EBP guidelines and research. Four common EBPs will briefly be discussed below with resources outlined in Table 1. The resources demonstrate just a small selection of the wealth of counseling guidance for understanding and implementing these EBPs in addictions counseling practice.

Cognitive Behavioral Therapy (CBT)

CBT is one of the most extensively studied treatment models with countless articles demonstrating CBT effectiveness in a multitude of clinical areas, including SUDs. In brief, CBT employs the theory that learning and thought processes lead to the development and maintenance of substance use. CBT works by adjusting these thought and behavioral processes.

Motivational Interviewing (MI)

MI is a brief and direct intervention where clients explore obstacles for change. MI-based counseling is non-judgmental in the process of helping patients exploring substance use behaviors.

Behavioral Couples Therapy (BCT)

BCT works to improve the quality of the marital/couples relationship affected by substance use by one or both partners. BCT helps the couple re-establish trust and improve communication.

Contingency Management / Community Reinforcement (CM)

CM works through the principles of reinforcement for non-substance behaviors (e.g., negative urine screen). These reinforcements, such as vouchers, can be traded for products consistent with a drug-free life. CM has been used with success in the treatment of cocaine and alcohol dependence.

EBPs and Dissemination: Where We are Now

Early difficulties in strengthening SUD treatment services led the Center for Substance Abuse Treatment to create the Addiction Technology Transfer Centers (ATTC) in the early 1990s. ATTCs consist of offices across the nation that are charged with training SUD clinicians and programs as well as developing mechanisms to disseminate and implement best practices in SUD treatment. Out of this work came the *Change Book* (ATTC, 2004) which guides programs through the process of implementing EBPs.

EBP dissemination is also supported through ATTC collaboration with the National Institute on Drug Abuse Clinical Trials Network and the Substance Abuse and Mental Health Services Administration (SAMHSA) to develop the Blending Initiative (www.attcnetwork.org) that uses three components to facilitate the implementation of EBPs. First, regional blending conferences allow researchers, practitioners, directors, and policy-makers to discuss SUD treatment science and practice. Second, partnerships with state agencies help disseminate EBPs. Third, blending teams devise treatment tools (e.g., DVDs, manuals, trainings) based on science for implementation as soon as possible. Despite the wealth of resources available at such sites as NIDA, SAMHSA, and ATTC, as well as the recent research on the process of implementing EBPs (e.g., Aarons, 2006; Flynn & Simpson, 2009), the impact of these resources on SUD treatment quality is still questionable (McCarty et al., 2007).

EBPs and Dissemination: Where We Can Go

Over a ten-year period (1998–2007), out of the 1,139 counseling research articles published in all ACA journals, only 6% explored counseling intervention effectiveness (Ray et al., 2011). More relevant to SUD and IAAOC, a review of the articles published in the *Journal of Addictions and Offender Counseling* (JAOC) between 2000 and 2012 found a limited number of clinical studies had a "best practices" focus (as opposed to simply describing a technique or intervention). Of those that did touch upon best practices, most focused on instrument validation and usage (e.g., Laux, Piazza, Saylers, & Roseman, 2012) or establishing the state of the addictions counseling profession and the need for higher quality services and training (e.g., Campbell, Daood, Catlin, & Abelson, 2005).

The addictions counseling profession is in a state of transition in regard to requirements for training, education, and licensure/certification (Alcoholism & Drug Abuse Weekly, 2012; Morgen, 2012; Morgen, Miller, & Stretch, 2012). Consequently, this annual review should become both required reading and a desired forum for disseminating high-quality EBPs for addictions counseling education, training, practice, and supervision. Thus, the question becomes *how* to improve upon the 6% statistic (as cited by Ray et al., 2011) and provide a consistent stream of EBP literature that is readily applicable to addictions counseling educators, supervisors, and practitioners? Two recommendations for potential contributors to this annual review are discussed below.

IAAOC Should Have a Stronger Voice in the EBP Discussion

What is missing from the addictions counseling literature originating from IAAOC/ACA, and what is present in the addictions treatment literature originating from other professional bodies such as Division 50 (Addictions) of the American Psychological Association or the College on Problems of Drug Dependence, is the use of meta-analyses to establish EBPs and validate current EBPs. For example, no meta-analysis studies were found in *JAOC* between 2000 and 2012 when using a PsychInfo database search for the term "meta-analysis." Perhaps this finding (in part) is due to IAAOC scholars publishing those papers in other addiction journals (e.g., *Journal of Substance Abuse Treatment*). Regardless, addictions counseling needs to join in the debate on EBPs and how they are utilized in a discipline as diverse as addictions counseling. Consequently, this annual review could work in collaboration with scholars publishing meta-analyses in *JAOC*. For instance, EBPs that were demonstrated as effective via meta-analyses in *JAOC* could be presented in a clinical guidelines format in the *Annual Review*. Ideally, the same scholars who wrote the meta-analysis would also write the clinical guidelines in the *Annual Review*. This way, science and practice are blended for use by our readers.

EBPs are Only as Good as They are Applicable

Lundgren et al. (2011) found that the educational-level of the clinician was related to degree of acceptance for evidenced-based addictions training, with higher educated clinicians desiring the evidenced-based training. Since the addictions counseling profession consists of clinicians with degrees ranging from associates to doctoral, the dissemination of EBP material must be easily digested by all parties. Too often, counseling practice papers offer general overviews of procedures with vague directions and goals. If a counselor proposes a new best practice, it is the responsibility of that counselor to provide resources for the implementation and evaluation of that practice. Thus, papers submitted to this annual review should provide resources (whether in the review or as supplemental material available by contacting the author). If successful, IAAOC—through the annual review—could eventually produce a resources site similar to SAMHSA where EBP manuals, guidelines, and training resources are available for use by members. IAAOC already has the foundational infrastructure for this task through the excellent early work of the "Cutting-Edge" Techniques Committee.

Conclusion

The era of "show-and-tell" studies where counseling techniques are vaguely described is over. It is time for papers that specifically state what was done, how it was done, why it was done (i.e., what is the science be-hind the intervention), and most importantly, how *you* can implement the same practice in your setting. When we train counselors in research practices, we stress that the methods section of the research paper must be written so that another scholar could replicate the original study to validate findings. It is time that addictions counseling adopts a similar perspective for disseminating counseling practices material. Hopefully, this annual review provides a mechanism for accomplishing that goal.

References

Aarons, G. A. (2006). Transformational and transactional leadership: Association with attitudes toward evidence-based practice. *Psychiatric Services, 57*, 1162–1168.

Addiction Technology Transfer Centers. (2004). *The change book: A blueprint for technology transfer.* Kansas City, MO: ATTC National Office.

Alcoholism & Drug Abuse Weekly. (March 5, 2012). Counselor rules to be set by states (pp 1-3). Vol. 24, Number 10.

Beck, A.T., Liese, B.S., Newman, C.F., Wright, F.D. (1993). *Cognitive therapy of substance abuse.* New York: Guilford.

Budney, A.J., & Higgins, S.T. (1998). *A community reinforcement plus vouchers approach: Treating cocaine addiction.* Rockville, MD: National Institute on Drug Abuse, U.S. Department of Health and Human Services, National Institutes of Health.

Campbell, T. C., Daood, C., Catlin, L., & Abelson, A. (2005). Integration of research and practice in substance use disorder treatment: Findings from focus groups of clinicians, researchers, educators, administrators, and policy makers. *Journal of Addictions & Offender Counseling, 26*(1), 4-14.

Caroll, K. (1998). *A cognitive-behavioral approach: Treating cocaine addiction.* Rockville, MD: National Institute on Drug Abuse, U.S. Department of Health and Human Services, National Institutes of Health.

Center for Substance Abuse Treatment. (2006). *Addiction counseling competencies: The knowledge, skills, and attitudes of professional practice.* Technical Assistance Publication (TAP) Series 21. DHHS Publication No. (SMA) 06-4171. Rockville, MD: Substance Abuse and Mental Health Services Administration.

Dutra, L., Stathopoulou, G., Basden, S. L., Leyro, T. M., Powers, M. B., & Otto, M. W. (2008). A meta-analytic review of psychosocial interventions for substance use disorders. *American Journal of Psychiatry, 165*, 179–187.

Flynn, P. M., & Simpson, D. D. (2009). Adoption and implementation of evidence-based treatment. In P. M. Miller (Ed.), *Evidence-based addiction treatment* (pp. 419–437). San Diego, CA: Elsevier.

Forman R.F, Bovasso G, Woody G. (2001). Staff beliefs about addiction treatment. *Journal of Substance Abuse Treatment, 21*, 1–9.

Higgins, S. T., Heil, S. H., Dantona, R., Donham, R., Matthews, M., & Badger, G. J. (2007). Effects of varying the monetary value of voucher-based incentives on abstinence achieved during and following treatment among cocaine-dependent outpatients. *Addiction, 102*(2), 271-281. doi:10.1111/j.1360-0443.2006.01664.x.

Higgins, S. T., Heil, S. H., & Lussier, J. (2004). Clinical implications of reinforcement as a determinant of substance use disorders. *Annual Review of Psychology, 55*(1), 431-461. doi:10.1146/annurev.psych.55.090902.142033.

Institute of Medicine. (2005). *Improving the quality of health care for mental and substance abuse conditions: Quality chasm series.* Washington, DC: The National Academy Press.

Kadden, R., Caroll, K., Donovan, D., Cooney, N., Monti, P., Abrams, D., Litt, M., & Hester, R. (2003). *Cognitive-behavioral coping skills therapy manual: A clinical research guide for therapists treating individuals with alcohol abuse and dependence.* Rockville, MD: National Institute on Alcoholism and Alcohol Abuse, U.S. Department of Health and Human Services, National Institutes of Health.

Laux, J. M., Piazza, N. J., Salyers, K., & Roseman, C. P. (2012). The Substance Abuse Subtle Screening Inventory-3 and Stages of Change: A screening validity study. *Journal of Addictions & Offender Counseling, 33*(2), 82-92.

Lundahl, B., & Burke, B. L. (2009). The effectiveness and applicability of motivational interviewing: a practice-friendly review of four meta-analyses. *Journal of Clinical Psychology, 65*(11), 1232-1245. doi:10.1002/jclp.20638.

Lundgren, L., Amodeo, M., Krull, I., Chassler, D., Weidenfeld, R., de Saxe Zerden, L., & . . . Beltrame, C. (2011). Addiction treatment provider attitudes on staff capacity and evidence-based clinical training: results from a national study. *American Journal on Addictions, 20*(3), 271-284. doi:10.1111/j.1521-0391.2011.00127.x.

Lussier, J., Heil, S. H., Mongeon, J. A., Badger, G. J., & Higgins, S. T. (2006). A meta-analysis of voucher-based reinforcement therapy for substance use disorders. *Addiction, 101*(2), 192-203. doi:10.1111/j.1360-0443.2006.01311.x.

Magill, M., & Ray, L. A. (2009). Cognitive–behavioral treatment with adult alcohol and illicit drug users: A meta-analysis of randomized controlled trials. *Journal of Studies on Alcohol and Drugs, 70*, 516–527.

Management of Substance Use Disorders Working Group. (2009). VA/DOD clinical practice guideline for management of substance use disorders (Version 2.1). Washington, DC, Department of Veterans Affairs and the Department of Defense.

McCarty, D., Gustafson, D. H., Wisdom, J. P., Ford, J., Choi, D., Molfenter, T, & Cotter, F. (2007). The Network for the Improvement of Addiction Treatment (NIATx): Enhancing access and retention. *Drug and Alcohol Dependence, 88*, 138–145.

Morgen, K. (2012, March). The need for recalibration of how states define addiction counseling competency. Paper presented as part of the panel Suggestions for Integrating Addictions Counseling into the Licensed Professional Counselor Licensure Process at the American Counseling Association Annual Conference & Exposition, San Francisco, CA.

Morgen, K., Miller, G., & Stretch, L.S. (2012). Addiction counseling licensure issues for licensed professional counselors. *The Professional Counselor: Research and Practice, 2*(1), 58-65.

Moyers, T. B., & Martin, T. (2006). Therapist influence on client language during motivational interviewing sessions. *Journal of Substance Abuse Treatment, 30*(3), 245-251. doi:10.1016/j.jsat.2005.12.003.

Moyers, T. B., Martin, T., Christopher, P. J., Houck, J. M., Tonigan, J., & Amrhein, P. C. (2007). Client language as a mediator of motivational interviewing efficacy: Where is the evidence? *Alcoholism: Clinical and Experimental Research, 31*(Suppl 3), 40S-47S.

Moyers, T. B., Miller, W. R., & Hendrickson, S. L. (2005). How does Motivational Interviewing work? Therapist interpersonal skill predicts client involvement within Motivational Interviewing sessions. *Journal of Consulting and Clinical Psychology, 73*(4), 590-598. doi:10.1037/0022-006X.73.4.590.

National Institute on Drug Abuse. (2004). Report of the blue ribbon task force on health services research at the National Institute on Drug Abuse. Bethesda, MD: U.S. Department of Health and Human Services, National Institutes of Health.

National Institute on Drug Abuse. (2009). Principles of drug addiction treatment: A research-based guide. Bethesda, MD: U.S. Department of Health and Human Services, National Institutes of Health.

National Quality Forum. (2005). *Evidenced-based treatment practices for substance use disorders.* Washington, DC: author.

O'Farrell, T., & Fals-Stewart, W. (2006). *Behavioral couples therapy for alcoholism and drug abuse*. New York: Guilford.

Pearson, F.S., Prendergast, M.L., Podus, D., Vazan, P., Greenwell, L., & Hamilton, Z. (2012). Meta-analyses of seven of the National Institute on Drug Abuse's principles of drug addiction treatment. *Journal of Substance Abuse Treatment, 43*, 1-11.

Powers, M. B., Vedel, E., & Emmelkamp, P. G. (2008). Behavioral couples therapy (BCT) for alcohol and drug use disorders: A meta-analysis. *Clinical Psychology Review, 28*(6), 952-962. doi:10.1016/j.cpr.2008.02.002.

Ray, D. C., Hull, D. M., Thacker, A. J., Pace, L. S., Swan, K. L., Carlson, S. E., & Sullivan, J. M. (2011). Research in counseling: A 10-year review to inform practice. *Journal of Counseling & Development, 89*(3), 349-359.

Wisdom, J. P., Ford, J. H., Hayes, R. A., Edmundson, E., Hoffman, K., & McCarty, D. (2006). Addiction treatment agencies' use of data: A qualitative assessment. Journal of *Behavioral Health Services & Research, 33*, 394–407.

Table 1: Selection of EBPs and Resources

Cognitive-Behavioral Therapy	
Source	Summary
Magill & Ray (2009)	Meta-analyzed 53 controlled trials of cognitive-behavioral treatment (CBT) for adults diagnosed with SUDs. 58% of SUD patients receiving CBT services demonstrated better treatment outcomes than SUD treatment patients in a comparison condition. 79% of SUD patients in CBT treatment reported substance-use reduction rates above the median as compared to those on a treatment wait-list or no treatment control group. CBT treatment effects diminished over time, with somewhat weakened effects appearing between the six-month and nine-month follow-up and becoming much more diminished following 12-months post-CBT treatment.
Beck, Liese, Newman, & Wright (1993)	Details Beck's cognitive model and how it relates to addiction. Text covers case formulation, management of the therapeutic relationship, and the structure of the therapy sessions. Reviews cognitive skills for patient education regarding the treatment model and managing cravings. Specific cognitive and behavioral strategies and techniques are described in detail.
Carroll (1998)	Available from National Institute on Drug Abuse The manual provides a CBT model for cocaine use disorder, focused on: Basic Principles of CBT Craving Motivation for cocaine abstinence Cocaine refusal skills Problem solving Case management
Kadden et al. (2003)	Available from National Institute on Alcohol Abuse & Alcoholism The manual contains material for 22 sessions; 8 required sessions and 14 elective sessions. Each participant receives a total of 12 sessions composed of a fixed set of core sessions and several elective sessions chosen for the individual patient. CBT topics for treating alcohol use disorder focused on: Coping skills Craving Managing alcohol thoughts Problem solving Alcohol refusal skills Dealing with a lapse

Motivational-Interviewing	
Source	Summary
Lundahl & Burke (2009)	Review of four meta-analyses of MI (Burke, Arkowitz & Menchola, 2003; Hettema, Steele, & Miller, 2005; Lundhahl, Tollefson, Kunz, Brownell, & Burke, 2009; Vasilaki, Hosier, & Cox, 2006). MI was found an effective alcohol use disorders treatment, showing outcomes equivalent or better than other treatments (success rates between 0% and 20% better than other treatment) and significantly better than no treatment controls (success rates between 10% and 20% better than no treatment). MI was also found an effective treatment for illicit drugs (marijuana, cocaine, heroin) with MI demonstrating effectiveness equal to or better than other established treatments.
Moyers & Martin (2006)	Project examined 38 motivational enhancement therapy sessions from Project MATCH (Matching Alcoholism Treatments to Client Heterogeneity) to investigate the relationship between therapist behaviors and client speech. Conditional probabilities calculated between MI-consistent (MICO) therapist behaviors, MI-inconsistent (MIIN) therapist behaviors, and immediately subsequent client speech. MICO behaviors more likely to be followed by self-motivational statements. MIIN behaviors more likely to be followed by client resistance.
Moyers, Miller, & Hendrickson (2005)	Investigated 103 unique MI sessions for substance abuse. Therapist interpersonal skills positively associated with client cooperation, disclosure and affect expression.
Moyers, Martin, Christopher, Houck, Tonigan, & Amrhein (2007)	Examined 38 sessions from Project MATCH and 45 sessions from the New Mexico site in Project MATCH. Behaviors consistent with MI (MICO) were significantly likely to be followed by client Change Talk (CT). Behaviors inconsistent with MI (MIIN) were significantly likely to be followed by Counterchange Talk (CCT).

Behavioral Couples Therapy (BCT)	
Source	Summary
Powers, Vedel, & Emmelkamp (2008)	12 randomized clinical BCT trials (8 for alcohol, 4 for other substances) BCT produced better outcomes than control conditions regarding relationship quality at post-treatment and follow-up phases BCT produced good outcomes regarding substance use at follow-up phase
O'Farrell & Fals-Stewart (2006)	Practice guide for implementation of BCT with alcohol or illicit drug issues
Contingency Management (CM) / Community Reinforcement	
Budney & Higgins (1998)	Available from National Institute on Drug Abuse The manual provides a CM/Community Reinforcement model using vouchers for cocaine use disorder, focused on: Cocaine refusal skills Lifestyle changes
Higgins et al. (2007); Higgins, Heil, & Lussier (2004); Lussier et al (2006)	Series of studies showing how voucher-based CM produced positive outcomes with cocaine use disorders

4

Best Practices in Offender Rehabilitation

Reviews from the Field

STEPHEN SOUTHERN[1]

Concerns by state and Federal governments regarding efficacy of correctional treatment have stimulated significant attention for evidence based practice. Offender counseling has been affected by the movement toward empirically supported treatment, especially applications of cognitive behavior therapy. Best practices in offender rehabilitation take into account contexts and needs of clients based on particular problems, populations, and settings.

State and Federal governments exercise control over the budgets that fund much of correctional treatment, including offender rehabilitation. Naturally, funding sources expect agencies and institutions to produce good results as evidenced by reductions in offending, recidivism, and progression from juvenile delinquency to adult criminality. Empirically supported treatments, especially involving applications of cognitive behavior therapy (CBT), therapeutic community (TC), and family eco-

1. Stephen Southern, Department of Psychology and Counseling, Mississippi College. Correspondence concerning this article should be directed to Stephen Southern, Department of Psychology and Counseling, Box 4013, Mississippi College, Clinton, MS 39058 (Email: Southern@mc.edu).

logical therapy approaches, contribute to enhanced accountability and credibility of offender counseling and rehabilitation.

Offender Rehabilitation

Wormith and colleagues (2007) provided a definition of the term:

> ... *rehabilitation* refers to a broad array of psychosocial programs and services that are designed to assist offenders in addressing a range of needs related to their offending behavior and in achieving a more productive and satisfying lifestyle (p.880).

Offender rehabilitation includes a wide range of community-based and institutional programs intended to intervene in the progression of offending behaviors and restore the individual to a course of normal development and community contribution. These approaches assert there is more to rehabilitation than incapacitating the offender in prison or delaying reoccurrence of offender behavior. Recidivism is not a unitary construct with many components including re-offense, arrest, conviction, and re-incarceration (Wormith et al., 2007). Nevertheless, recidivism remains an important marker of beneficial outcomes from rehabilitation efforts.

Global or macro approaches to assessing outcomes in offender rehabilitation focused on recidivism rates after particular groups of offenders received community or institutional treatment for varying amounts of time. For example, one approach to determining effects of offender rehabilitation might involve monitoring the rates of returnees to a juvenile treatment facility according to months served in the institution. A better approach to evaluating outcomes involves comparing the effects of a targeted intervention to another treatment package, frequently involving treatment as usual. A more helpful, microscopic approach to monitoring rehabilitation efforts incorporates a dismantling of the treatment package with meaningful comparisons between treatment and control groups and determining which treatment components are generating beneficial changes in offender behaviors of interest.

The microscopic approach responds to characteristics of offenders and treatments and addresses the classic challenge in psychotherapy research offered by Paul (1967): "*What* treatment, by *whom*, is more effective for *this* individual with *that* specific problem and under *which* set of circumstances" (p. 111). Addressing Paul's challenge, clinical researchers began to accumulate evidence of the effectiveness of particular interventions in specific settings for identified populations presenting targeted problems.

What Works

A large scale study of recidivism showed that two-thirds of offenders released from 15 states in 1994 were re-arrested within 3 years of discharge (U.S. Department of Justice, 2006). Cognitive-based correctional programs reduced recidivism beyond the effects of incarceration by 6%, while therapeutic communities contributed to a 6% reduction in rates over 300 evaluations of programs conducted over a 35 year period (Aos, Miller, & Drake, 2006). Cognitive-behavioral treatment programs in prisons reduced recidivism rates of sex offenders by 15% (Aos et al., 2006).

Cognitive-behavioral programs for offenders are typically highly structured and offered in a small group, manualized treatment modality (Wilson, Bouffard, & MacKenzie, 2005). The programs focus on challenging cognitive distortions that contribute to relapse or reoffense. CBT alters criminogenic thought processes and the maladaptive and antisocial behaviors that follow. The treatment programs are skill-building in that offenders learn adaptive and prosocial approaches to appraising stressful and other challenging situations. There is an emphasis upon counteracting dysfunctional cognitions through behavior experiments and homework. Offenders may develop metacognitive skills in self-observation and self-awareness as they engage in decision-making and problem-solving. One of the dominant cognitive-behavioral programs for offenders is moral reconation therapy (MRT).

MRT integrated cognitive-behavioral skill-building with systematic application of Kohlberg's (1976) theory of moral development (Little & Robinson, 1988). Offenders attending 1-2 hour group sessions complete homework exercises and discuss moral problems that are best resolved through empathy, delayed gratification, and group conscience. Meta-analyses have established that MRT reduces recidivism for a variety of offenses including offenders with history of substance use disorders (Wilson et al., 2005).

Meta-Analyses and Major Reviews

Between 1985 and 2005, 52 meta-analyses on correctional treatment were reported (McGuire, 2005). Although there are some problems in interpreting and generalizing from meta-analyses, it is clear that some specific treatments were effective in reducing recidivism. The average effect size of approximately .10 reflected some beneficial outcomes with particular effect sizes ranging from -.09 (suggesting an iatrogenic or negative outcome) to .38 when program services addressed principles of risk, need, responsivity, and other contextual factors (Andrews & Bonta, 2003; McGuire, 2002; McGuire, 2005; Wormith et al, 2007). Cognitive-behavioral treatments produced the best effects, especially when the programs targeted specific problems or addressed the needs of particular populations including youthful offender, substance abusing offenders, and sex offenders. The meta-analyses answered the challenge of "what works for whom" and established a foundation for transferring effective treatments to the field.

A major generalization has arisen from the transfer of treatment outcome studies to the field. The principles of risk, need, and responsivity determine the extent to which treatment integrity correlates with beneficial treatment outcome (Andrews, Bonta, & Hoge, 1990; Andrews, Bonta, & Wormith, 2006; Andrews & Dowden, 2005; Wormith et al., 2007). That is, the potential effectiveness of a given correctional treatment is largely a function of whether programs target high-risk populations, address specific criminogenic needs, and incorporate measurable cognitive-behavioral interventions. Meta-analyses and careful attentions to the contextual details of interventions contradicted Martinson's (1974) famous assertion that "nothing works." While there have been great advanced in determining what works, even the evidenced based treatments of multisystemic therapy and cognitive skills training can be improved through precision in implementation and evaluation (Littell, Popa, & Forsythe, 2006).

A meta-analysis of 129 studies (Parhar, Wormith, Derkzen, & Beauregard, 2008) established that coercion in treatment fails to produce beneficial outcomes in institutional and community treatments. Mandated treatment, especially in institutional settings is ineffective. Voluntary treatment in any setting produced significant effect sizes ranging from .08 to .24. It appears that benefit from participation in a potentially important treatment involves freedom of choice in the decision to become engaged in the treatment process. This calls into question the regular practice of court-mandated treatment. Early identification and treatment of troubled youths promises to intervene in the progression of offender behavior that may result in court-mandated and involuntary treatment in institutional settings.

Adolescent Offenders and Juvenile Justice

The evolution of offender behavior is well understood (e.g., Wilson & Hernnstein, 1985). Counseling programs for adolescents typically emphasize prevention rather than rehabilitation. Primary prevention efforts address strengths and skills that shape adolescents away from conduct problems or delinquent behaviors. An anti-bullying program conducted with middle school students is an example of primary prevention. Secondary prevention refers to early identification and intervention of adolescents who present characteristics known to be associated with risk for developing a major problem such as substance abuse or violence. In secondary prevention, professionals conduct screening to identify at risk adolescents who may benefit from programs designed to reduce risk factors or increase protective factors (Doran, Luczak, Bekman, Koutsenok, & Brown, 2012). Tertiary prevention programs include various offender rehabilitation interventions, similar to those offered in community and institutional settings to adult offenders. However, there is less focus on recidivism and more emphasis upon reducing the progression of the problem behavior into a fully developed disorder.

In juvenile justice settings, most interventions represent secondary prevention or tertiary prevention (i.e., rehabilitation). Primary prevention is practiced in community settings, especially schools, recreational, and youth care centers. Prevention programs are frequently based on large-scale studies which must be "localized" to reflect culturally relevant concerns and practices (Reese & Vera, 2007). Juvenile justice professionals and other who work with adolescents in community settings must be muliticulturally competent and committed as advocates to social justice for poor and ethnic minority groups.

Punishment Versus Skill Building

Findings from meta-analytic studies and research reviews support observations that punitive juvenile justice policies and perspectives are being replaced with evidence-based interventions and restorative principles (Merlo & Benekos, 2010). While juvenile delinquents were historically afforded opportunities for rehabilitation and diverted from the punishment oriented adult system, the justice model or "law and order" policies of the last few decades exposed developing youth to incarceration, incapacitation, and deterrence models of corrections (Hinton, Sims, Adams, & West, 2007). Programs that "get tough on juvenile offenders," such as boot camps and "Scared Straight" interventions are now recognized as ineffective and potentially harmful to young offenders and community members (Howell, 2003). Young offenders are in the process of development. Their emerging lifestyles can be altered and they can develop the skills needed to contribute to society. Prevention and rehabilitation efforts replace punishment and justice oriented corrections with young offenders.

Gains in juvenile offender rehabilitation have been afforded by comprehensive strategies intended to translate research findings into practical techniques and diffuse "best practices" among institutional and community programs ready for change (Howell, 2003). Federal clearinghouses provided since the 1990s by the Office of Juvenile Justice and Delinquency Prevention (OJJDP) facilitate access to promising and effective programs for implementation and training.

Adolescent Substance Abuse Treatment

Adolescent substance abuse is a major risk factor in the pathogenesis of conduct disorder, delinquency, and adult offending (Doran et al., 2012). School and community samples estimate adolescent substance use disorders (SUD) at 6–10% of the population in a given setting. Estimates of SUD range from 33–41% of adolescents in mental health systems and 62-81% of juvenile justice systems (Doran et al., 2012). Substance use disorders in adolescents reflect shared risk factors with mood and conduct disorders, ADHD, learning disabilities, and various types of aggression. Identification and treatment of SUD reduce the likelihood of delinquency, recidivism, and institutionalization (Doran et al., 2012).

There is etiological overlap among substance use disorders, delinquency, psychiatric disorders, and violence (Doran et al., 2012). Neurotoxic effects of drug exposure interact with parenting and family problems to produce problems in brain development leading to cognitive, psychological, and social deficits. Common pathways for adolescent substance use and conduct disorders include exaggeration in normative impulsivity, risk taking, and poor decision making. Continued use of substances may reflect dysfunctional coping, lack of parental monitoring, and differential association with deviant peers who are also engaged in SUD. Increasing impairment of inhibitory and executive functions occur as ongoing substance use produces damage to brain structures and neurocognitive deficits in reasoning, memory, and learning, frequently with emotional distress. In this manner, substance use and conduct disorders evolve into adult criminal behavior and aggression (Doran et al., 2012). Effective treatment of adolescent SUD may prevent youths from engaging in adult offending and the cycles of relapse likely to lead to institutionalization.

Treatment of adolescent substance use disorders involves developmentally appropriate interventions that take into account comorbid problems (e.g., mood disorder or ADHD) and focus on risk reduction rather than punishment of offender behavior (Doran et al., 2012). Greenwood (2008) identified strategies for treating adolescents in secure settings. Interventions should target problem behaviors that can be changed such as problem-solving, substance refusal, and social skills. Effective interventions are evidence-based and tailored to address individual needs. Institutional care should provide services to the adolescents presenting the highest risks, including those with fully developed SUD. Consistent implementation of comprehensive treatment packages conducted by qualified mental health providers produces the most positive outcomes. Implementation of best practices is difficult when the institution focuses primarily on public safety, punishment, and institutional control of adolescent offender behavior.

Treatment programs for adolescent SUD and delinquency are not all equally effective. Community-based treatment of SUD and aggressive behavior emphasize family approaches and comprehensive care (Doran et al., 2012). Effective institutional programs target SUD and delinquent conduct in skill building groups and individual therapy for comorbid conditions (Doran et al., 2012). CBT, motivational enhancement therapy

(MET; brief therapy focused on motivational interviewing), and contingency management (CM; or positive behavior support) represent evidence-based best practices for institutional settings (Doran et al., 2012).

CM is based on operant conditioning principles in which behavior is viewed as a function of contingent consequences. In institutional settings, positive behavior support or incentive programs can be implemented in the classroom, residential unit, or campus-wide. CM programs not only address behavior management issues of the institution, but also contribute to the effectiveness of problem-solving in the therapeutic community. Rewards are administered for targeted behaviors, such as compliance or abstinence, and withheld for failure to earn adequate points or tokens over a specified period of time. CM is well-established as an effective treatment for adult and adolescent SUD (Doran et al., 2012).

Motivational interviewing (MI; Miller & Rollnick, 2002) increases motivation to change by matching treatment to the level of ambivalence versus commitment presented by a client. MET involves therapists engaging in empathy and other relationship building skills and collaboratively assisting clients in recognizing discrepancies between their current behaviors and goals. MET improves engagement of adolescents in voluntary treatment and prepares youths to take advantage of other interventions in the treatment package. MET has demonstrable effectiveness in a wide range of community settings (including medical and mental health settings), as well as institutions (Doran et al., 2012).

CBT represents an essential component of any adolescent substance use disorder treatment. Juvenile offenders presenting substance abuse problems also benefit from family therapy, especially in outpatient and community settings, and individual therapy in secure settings (Doran et al., 2012). Family based approaches include attention to several dynamics and contexts.

Family Based Approaches

Sexton and Alexander (2002) described some early family-based counseling interventions evaluated from the perspective of the principles of empirically supported interventions. They concluded that existing empirically supported interventions improved family functioning in general and produced some specific effects in reducing drug use and recidivism. In meta-analytic and large scale reviews in that time, there were statistically significant effect sizes for improvement of global family problems, as well as delinquent conduct of children and problem solving and communication skills within the family system. Four family therapy approaches were identified as effective for treating substance abuse and delinquency: functional family therapy (FFT; Alexander & Parsons, 1973), multidimensional family therapy (MDFT; Liddle, 1995), multisystemic therapy (MST; Henggeler et al., 1999), and structural family therapy (SFT; Szapocznik & Kurtines, 1989). Each of these evidence-based approaches addressed individual factors and salient relational contexts in family, peer, school, and neighborhood contexts (Hinton, Sheperis, & Sims, 2003). The family therapy interventions produced immediate beneficial effects that were maintained at follow-up.

MST is an excellent example of an evidence-based best practice in family therapy (Sheidow & Woodford, 2003). During the 1990s, a series of randomized clinical trials established the effectiveness of this "family-ecological systems approach" (Henggeler, 1999). MST focuses on the strengths of family members and engages them as collaborators with the treatment team. Realistic goals are established for overcoming the problem behaviors of the youth and others in the family system. Interventions are conducted in the home in order to remove barriers to services delivery. Clinicians are available on call 24 hours per day; therefore, caseloads are kept small. There is a focus on maintaining developmentally appropriate behaviors by finding the fit between the identified problems and their broad systemic context. Sequences of behavior are targeted for well-defined, action-oriented interventions. There must be continuous efforts by the family members and treatment team. All stakeholders are held accountable for attainment of goals. MST interventions are subjected to ongoing evaluations. The team plans for maintenance and generalization of treatment gains in order to help troubled youths and their families avoid relapse and recidivism. MST has become a very popular approach in community corrections.

Youth Villages is a private nonprofit organization dedicated to helping emotionally and behaviorally troubled children and their families live successfully outside psychiatric and juvenile justice facilities. They offer intensive in-home and wraparound services in order to achieve mental health, substance abuse treatment, and juvenile justice goals. Youth Villages (2013) Multisystem Therapy programs engages the family members, as well as teachers, social workers, neighbors, peers, extended family members and other stakeholders in a comprehensive systemic treatment process. Their programs provide intensive, 24 hour support services over three to five-month periods. Carefully developed treatment plans are implemented and monitored using MST's quality assurance protocols. This application of the developmentally-oriented, family ecological approach has been designated a highly effective program by the Substance Abuse and Mental Health Services Administration (SAMHSA), which maintains the National Registry of Evidence-based Programs and Practices (SAMSHA, 2013).

MST, FFT, and other developmentally-oriented ecological models have demonstrated good results in helping adolescent offenders and their families escape the cycles of relapse that lead from adolescent substance abuse to adult substance use disorders and adult offending. Implementation of effective components of treatment for adolescent substance abuse and delinquency can help young persons avoid relapse and incarceration. Adult offenders who continue to present substance use disorders benefit from particular treatments targeting relapse and recidivism.

Treatment of Adult Substance Use Disorders

There is a very high prevalence of substance use disorders among offenders; therefore, substance abuse treatment is a cornerstone of offender rehabilitation (Wormith et al., 2007). Meta-analytic studies established a reduction in recidivism for incarcerated substance-abuse offenders ranging from 5.3–6.9% (Aos et al., 2006; Wormith et al., 2007). According to meta-analytic studies (Aos et al., 2006; Wormith et al., 2007), cumulative data regarding effects of treatment for substance use disorders indicated that institutional treatment prepared inmates for follow-up in community. Prison based programs prepared inmates for effective aftercare. The combination of prison and community treatments produced the best results in terms of reducing risk of relapse for substance use disorders and drug-related reoffense (Wexler, Predergast, & Melnick, 2004; Wormith et al., 2007).

A recent review of the literature on effective substance abuse treatment programs established some generalizations. Bahr, Masters, and Taylor (2012) identified some common features in treating substance use disorders in incarcerated prisoners, parolees, and probationers. The most effective interventions incorporated cognitive-behavioral interventions and therapeutic communities. Drug courts were also effective in reducing rates of drug abuse relapse and reoffense. Treatment gains were more likely to be maintained when there was an effective aftercare program. CM, in which offenders received inducements to participate, improved effectiveness of various interventions. The most effective treatments were intensive interventions that specifically targeted characteristics of high-risk offenders. Boot camp programs were not effective for juvenile and adult offender populations (Bahr et al., 2012).

Pharmacological treatment has been included in care for drug and alcohol abuse and dependence (Bahr et al., 2012). Some drugs used to treat addiction are agonists in that they produce pharmacological responses viewed less harmful than the substances they replace. Traditionally, use of methadone to treat heroin addiction fits this model. The second approach to treatment involves use of an antagonist to counteract the effects of a targeted drug of abuse or to reduce craving. Naltrexone is an opioid antagonist that has been used effectively with opiates, cocaine, and alcohol dependence. Two other pharmacological treatments have been more effective. Topiramate is an antiseizure medication shown to be effective in hard reduction in the treatment of alcohol dependence. Use of topiramate resulted in fewer drinks per day, fewer heavy drinking binges, and more days abstinent (Baltieri, Daro, Ribeiro, & de Andrade, 2008). Buprenorphine treatment has been effective with opiate and cocaine abstinence. The best results of pharmacological treatment included detoxification treatment and substance abuse counseling (Bahr et al., 2012). Many addiction treatment professionals would argue against pharmacological treatment, preferring instead the therapeutic power of a recovery group, such as Alcoholics Anonymous (AA), or the evidence based approach of the therapeutic community.

TC is a common prison-based psychosocial treatment for substance use disorders. The TC model emphasizes open communication between staff and inmates, consensus building as an approach to problem resolution, and focus on recovery from addiction. Institutional TC programs also reduced prison misconduct, suggesting that important character traits and offender behaviors were being changed through participation in the group-oriented experience (French & Gendreau, 2006). Therapeutic communities teach important problem solving and social skills that generalize from the prison environment to community settings.

TC interventions have proven to be effective while intensive supervision, intermediate sanctions, educational programs (i.e., drug awareness), boot camps, and process-oriented groups were shown to be ineffective (Wormith et al., 2007). In fact, insight-oriented and discussion groups for high risk offenders actually contributed to higher rates of drug use and recidivism (Wormith et al., 2007). Effective components of TC treatment for substance use disorders among incarcerated offenders include motivation to become engaged in the treatment process, adherence to the treatment model by staff members, and an institutional climate that favored offender rehabilitation.

An extension of the TC model effectively integrated cognitive-behavioral interventions (including skills training) with creative arts involvement, developmentally organized treatment, and minority cultural sensitivity (Watson, Bisesi, Tanamly, & Mai, 2003). The Comprehensive Residential Education, Arts, and Substance Abuse Treatment (CREASAT) model reflects an integrative approach to constructing an effective treatment package. The CREASAT model takes advantage of adolescent readiness to learn skills that compete with drug use and to use artistic expression as a means for communication as coping skills are being acquired. A similar logic applies to applications of experiential therapy and play therapy with juvenile offenders.

Criminal Justice Drug Abuse Treatment Studies (CJ-DATS)

CJ-DATS is a national multisite research program designed to improve treatment outcomes for offenders who re-enter the community following institutional treatment or incarceration. The participants in the CJ-DATS reflect the severity of issues in the multiproblem population (Fletcher, Lehman, Wexler, & Melnick, 2007). The study participants presented serious drug problems, extensive criminal histories, and severe mental health problems. This combination of needs decreases the likelihood of a successful transition to community supervision. Incarcerated offenders with substance use disorders had the highest rates of co-occurring mental disorders, relationship problems, and poor health practices. They rarely receive adequate treatment in the community and remain at high risk for reoffense and recidivism. There were problems of unemployment, homelessness, and intimate partner violence. These offenders experienced high rates of HIV infection, tuberculosis, hepatitis, and other infectious diseases. Many of the CJ-DATS participants were survivors of sexual abuse and family violence.

CJ-DATS attempted to improve means for assessing and monitoring juvenile and adult offenders presenting substance use disorders. There were 10 participating research centers investigating multiple treatment approaches, which attempted to integrate transition from addiction treatment to community re-entry. This integrative approach to community supervision addressed criminal behavior, relapse prevention, and mental health care. The innovative approaches produced the best outcomes, especially for the highest risk offenders (Fletcher et al., 2007).

Female Offenders and Gender-Responsive Treatment

Researchers have noted that female offenders differ from male offenders in the pathways to criminal behavior, nature and seriousness of their offenses, their adjustment to prison or institutional settings, and risk of relapse (Van Voorhis, Wright, Salisbury, & Bauman, 2010; Wright, Van Voorhis, Salisbury, & Bauman, 2012). The National Institute of Corrections entered into an agreement with the University of Cincinnati to improve classification of female offenders (Van Voorhis et al., 2010). Together these parties implemented research initiatives with the Colorado Department of Corrections and various project sites to determine effective, gender-responsive treatments for women in community and institutional settings (Van Voorhis et al., 2010).

Although most female offenders are nonviolent, increasing numbers of female offenders are being placed in prisons and institutional settings due to "get tough" justice policies, especially the war on drugs. There has been a "boom" in the imprisonment of women with the number of female offenders increasing sixfold and the rate of their imprisonment per 100,000 citizens exceeding the rates of the incarceration of men (Wallace, Conner, & Dass-Brailsford, 2011). Most women who enter the justice system have committed drug related offenses, forgery or fraud, and minor property offenses (Wright et al., 2012). Frequently, these offenses are associated with running away from home, dealing with poverty and economic marginalization, and falling under the influence of male offenders or deviant peers.

Many of the women offenders were victims of emotional, physical, and sexual abuse in their families of origin, in their intimate relationships, and on the street (Wright et al., 2012). Approximately, 77–90% of incarcerated inmates report extensive histories of abuse trauma (Messina, Grella, Burdon, & Prendergast, 2007). Therefore, they present with multiproblem histories including abuse trauma, substance use disorders, mental illness, and unstable and abusive relationships (Van Voorhis et al., 2010; Wolf & Shi, 2010; Wright et al., 2012). History of victimization appears to affect involvement in criminal behavior by increasing stress and mental health problems, as well as substance abuse as a maladaptive coping response (Anumba, Dematteo, & Heilbrun, 2012). Accessing social resources such as employment, healthcare, and contact with healthy, noncriminal peers, buffer or insulate some of the female offenders from an ongoing pattern of criminal conduct (Anumba et al., 2012).

While women present fewer security problems in jails and prisons and generally respond well to community corrections, they are often subjected to harsh conditions and offender treatment programs designed to manage male offenders and deter violent conduct. Women are more likely than men to be victimized by inmates and staff members (Wallace et. al, 2011). Their adjustment problems in prison represent misunderstood sequelae of unresolved life trauma.

Female offenders in adult prisons and juvenile justice residential facilities require gender-responsive treatment. They require less security and appear to benefit from a residential environment focused on treatment and rehabilitation. Correctional officers must be trained in communication and relationship-building skills because the female offenders typically need to talk to work things out and to engage in healing relationships (Covington & Bloom, 2006). Women's treatment programs include therapeutic community, women-only groups, and content focused on women's issues including victimization, self injury, unhealthy relationships, and parenting.

Basically, gender responsive programming in institutions address their particular criminogenic needs such as abuse histories, untreated mental illness (especially post-traumatic stress disorder), intimate partner violence and coercion, drug abuse, vocational and housing problems, parental stress and lack of parenting skills, and safety in the community (Wright et al., 2012). Effective cognitive-behavioral interventions enlist fewer confrontational and rational techniques and more emotional and relational approaches (Matthews & Hubbard, 2008). Cognitive behavioral interventions address self-deprecation and depressive thinking and emphasize strengths in relationships with others.

Treatment of substance use disorders and mental health problems should also be gender responsive. It is clear that trauma plays a prominent role in the pathways that lead women to incarceration. Trauma-informed services educate women about abuse and trauma so they are able to identify maladaptive coping techniques, disrupt repetition of life trauma, avoid ongoing victimization, and develop healthy coping and interpersonal skills (Van Voorhis et al., 2010; Wright et al., 2012). There are several gender-responsive, evidence based treatment programs, which have been implemented in institutional and community settings. The programs are comprehensive in terms of addressing women's needs and integrative with regarding to blending offender rehabilitation, substance use disorder treatment, and mental health treatment.

Evidence-based, gender specific treatment for women include Beyond Trauma (Covington, 2003) and Helping Women Recover (Covington, 2008); Forever Free (Hall, Prendergast, Wellisch, Patten, & Cao, 2004); Dialectical Behavior Therapy (Linehan, 1993); and Seeking Safety (Najavits, 2002). Each of these programs has been researched with sufficient positive outcome data to designate them as best practices for women (Wright et al., 2012). Seeking Safety (Najavits, 2002) is a good example of an evidence-based treatment program that can be implemented in institutional or community settings, conducted by trained staff members, and maintained after re-entry to the family and community systems.

Seeking Safety (Najavits 2002, 2009) is a comprehensive, manualized treatment program, originally designed for women who were experiencing co-morbid substance use and mental disorders arising from trauma in life. There are cognitive, behavioral, interpersonal, and case management components with individual and group treatment modalities. Seeking Safety topics include maintaining sense of safety throughout the treatment process, establishing grounding of emotions, taking good care on oneself, recognizing "red and green flags" in terms of relapse risk, maintaining compassion, sustaining honesty, integrating splits in the self, setting relationship boundaries, coping with triggers, and engaging in healing and self-nurturing. Staff members are trained in the implementation of the evidence-based approach and tools are available for monitoring treatment adherence and fidelity. Seeking Safety has produced beneficial outcomes in a variety of institutional and community settings.

A recent review of outcome research regarding the effects of correctional-based programs for female inmates (Tripodi, Bledsoe, Kim, & Bender, 2011), established that gender responsive treatment is effective in reducing substance use disorders, diminishing symptoms of trauma, and reducing risk of relapse. Interventions targeting HIV prevention and parenting skill improvement were not clearly effective. Nevertheless, individually tailored programs targeting female offender needs have demonstrated a wide range of beneficial outcomes, including reduction of reoffense and recidivism. Community programs can be effective in concurrent treatment of substance use disorders and offender behavior by addressing underlying trauma and improving boundaries in relationships.

Intimate Partner Violence

As many as 98% of incarcerated women report a recent history of intimate partner violence (Lynch, Fritch, & Health, 2012). Consequently, they lacked community support for effective reentry and risk revictimization and relapse in treatment for substance use and mental health disorders. Women who were abused prior to incarceration presented several diagnoses including post-traumatic stress disorder, depression, self injurious behaviors, suicidality, and risky sexual practices (Lynch et al., 2012).

Having a history of intimate partner violence increased the likelihood that female offenders would seek treatment for mental health, substance abuse, and family problems (Lynch et al., 2012). Some of the women indicated a need for treatment of current relational aggression, as well as abuse extending from adult relationships to adolescent dating to childhood abuse. Duration of childhood sexual abuse, experiencing multiple episodes of intimate partner violence, and recent history of relational violence increased risk of serious mental health problems at intake (Lynch et al., 2012). From the feminist lens, victims of physical and sexual abuse by men were more likely to engage in drug use and offender behavior, resulting in their incarceration with a male-oriented correctional system. They may not receive mental health treatment or gender-responsive programming; therefore, they return to abusive relationships in a violent culture, reoffend, and repeat cycles of revictimization and recidivism.

One of the problems in treating intimate partner violence is that women sometimes initiate relational aggression or engage in violent exchanges with a partner. Even if their behaviors are intended to be preemptive or protective of oneself or children, women are increasingly treated as perpetrators of intimate partner violence given arrest policies in many jurisdictions (Miller, Gregory, & Iovanni, 2005). Then, they are subjected to ineffective treatment programs designed to treat abusive men such as the Duluth model. The one-treatment-fits-all or gender-neutral approach obscures the power imbalance in relationships and the coercive tactics used by men to control their female partners (Miller, Gregory, & Iovanni, 2005). Women who engage in violence in conflictual relationships require specialized treatment for victims and offenders. However, they do not benefit from treatment programs designed for men. Women affected by intimate partner violence would be better served by consciousness-raising in groups, education for relational boundaries, and support for establishing non-offending survival and coping skills.

A common denominator in the evolution of offender behavior in women is a history of emotional, physical, and/or sexual abuse by a male partner, resulting in increased risk for substance use and mental health disorders. Female offenders may engage in criminal behavior as maladaptive survival mechanisms for relational and societal violence. Childhood physical and sexual abuse is very prominent in the histories of women incarcerated in prisons. Gender-responsive treatment promises to help women in institutional and community settings. Similarly, men who perpetrate intimate partner violence require gender-specific programming that reveals abusive and coercive patterns. Successful treatment of sex offending, in particular, could reduce victimization and the cycle of violence.

Sex Offending

The treatment of sex offenders, increasingly by means of cognitive-behavioral approaches, produces beneficial outcomes according to several meta-analyses (Craig et al., 2003; Losel & Schumucker, 2005; Wormith et al., 2007). However, a major follow-up study measuring the effects of a cognitive-behavioral program over eight years failed to identify maintenance of initial gains (Marques, Wiederanders, Day, Nelson, & van Ommeren, 2005). Marques and colleagues (2005) concluded that their model failed to attend adequately to the "individualizing" of treatment through attention to risk, need, and responsivity in treatment planning and aftercare arrangements, including relapse prevention and case management. Methodological problems, including lack of follow-up of treatment drop-outs, confound some of the initial positive effects of cognitive-behavioral treatment of sex offenders (Wormith et al., 2007).

When Risk-Need-Responsivity (RNR) principles were applied to a meta-analysis involving 23 recidivism outcome studies (Hanson, Bourgon, Helmus, & Hodgson, 2009), recidivism rates for adolescent and adult sexual reoffense were as low as 10.9%, while general recidivism for all criminal offenses were 31.8% compared to 48.3% for a comparison group. The effects were strongest for cognitive-behavioral interventions that targeted specifically patterns of sexual offense recidivism in moderate-high risk offenders.

The research literature on the efficacy of sex offender treatment confronts the old approach in offender rehabilitation: "One treatment fits all." According to a review of meta-analyses and major studies (Wormith et al., 2007), specialized treatment of sex offenders involves careful attention to individual cycles in relapse and targeting high risk offenders for the most intensive treatments. Furthermore, special programs are needed for sex offenders with mental disorders and intellectual limitations. Overall, sex offenders need assistance with self-regulation of urges and challenging of thinking errors. In addition, this population benefits from interventions intended to increase victim empathy and to encourage the development of "good lives" (Marshall et al., 2005). Wormith et al. (2007) recommend attention to positive psychology principles of hope, health, well-being, and meaning-making. Positive approaches to increasing offender happiness and planning for a meaningful life, while applicable to most offenders, are especially relevant to counteracting the shame implicit in committing sex offenses.

Training of Providers and Translational Research

The National Institute of Corrections (2004) urges use of motivational interviewing techniques by all members of the treatment team (Hartzler & Espinoza, 2011). MI is an evidence-based treatment technique, originally developed for treating resistant addictive disorders and now viewed as generally effective for all offender populations. MI is based upon transtheoretical therapy in which a particular caregiver response is matched to the stage of change presented by the client (Miller & Rollnick, 2002; Prochaska & DiClemente, 1982). There are four basic principles for effective MI: expressing empathy for the client's perspective, developing a discrepancy between the client's values and behaviors, defusing or "rolling with" client resistance, and supporting the client's increasing readiness for action and self-efficacy expectations (Hartzler & Espinoza, 2011).

Training sessions in the use of MI as brief as two days have proven to be helpful in changing caregiver behaviors toward difficult juvenile clients (Hartzler & Espinoza, 2011). Nearly 80% of juvenile justice staff members achieved proficiency, with lesser educated staff members presenting the lowest skills levels realizing the best outcomes. The training not only prepared the personnel for effective use of the evidence-based MI, but also enhanced their positive attitudes and behaviors associated with care. It is practical and possible to teach the most effective interventions to staff members at all levels.

Probation officers can learn the principles of RNR (Andrews et al., 2006; Andrews & Dowden, 2005; Hanson et al., 2009; Wormith et al., 2007), essential to individualizing treatment, and cognitive-behavioral interventions for community supervision (Bonta et al., 2011). In this evidence-based approach, procriminal attitudes of probationers were targeted for change. The RNR model of offender rehabilitation matches the style and mode of interventions to the abilities and motivations of the individual probationer. Their needs are addressed by focused cognitive-behavioral techniques. Probation officers must be trained to work with clients on a one-to-one basis. They require training in the concepts of core correctional practice through classroom instruction in manualized treatment. The probation officers received supervision in the skills needed to facilitate meaningful behavior changes. Bonta and colleagues (2011) established that intensive training and supervision of probation officers produced significant reductions in recidivism rates for members of their caseloads when compared to probationers receiving traditional community supervision.

FFT (Alexander & Parsons, 1973) has proven to be a very effective treatment for juvenile delinquency and substance abuse. It extends the educational model of primary and secondary prevention, including early identification and treatment, to comprehensive offender rehabilitation. Translational research (Tashiro & Mortensen, 2006) and the Diffusion

Innovation Model (Rogers, 1983) were used to develop and localize the FFT approach, conduct outcome research and disseminate findings, and engage in continuous quality improvement (Duncan, Davey, & Davey, 2011).

Translating research findings into meaningful treatment options enhanced the portability and potential effectiveness of FFT as it was diffused in a variety of settings. A Delphi study of clinicians and administrators (Duncan et al., 2011) established that FFT could be applied in agencies dealing with mental illness, probation, and removal of children from the family home. The researchers determined that clinicians could be taught effective FFT practices for working with voluntary clients. Coerced families, many of whom were participating because of legal obligations, did not receive maximum benefit from the appropriately trained staff members. The match between the organizational culture and the strengths-oriented approach of FFT was highlighted. Practical considerations such as excessive paperwork and scheduling problems also diluted or diminished the efficacy of FFT.

Similarly, MST, a family therapy approach focusing on a conduct disordered youth's social ecology (family, peers, school, neighborhood, and community) has been adapted through translational research for implementation as a highly effective program in over 30 states (SAMSHA, 2013). Using subject matter experts as consultants in adaptation and implementation and "cultural advisors," MST has been implemented successfully in eight countries: Australia, Canada, Denmark, Ireland, Netherlands, New Zealand, Norway, and Sweden. The translational research process involves a series of steps designed to ensure treatment fidelity, while "localizing" and making culturally appropriate the interventions for reducing externalizing behaviors in delinquent youths (Schoenwald, Heiblum, Saldana, & Henggeler, 2008).

In order to implement abroad the best practices of MST, several steps were taken (Schoenwald et al., 2008). It was essential to engage the social services sector of the governments hosting MST programs. Identifying and collaborating with stakeholders in these countries made possible the translation and transport of the innovation. It was necessary to understand and conform to legal, social, and cultural standards of the host countries. In keeping with the findings of MST Services (n.d.), MST care providers in the international programs did not need to be Master's degree trained clinicians. Paraprofessionals could develop clinical acumen necessary to faithfully implement the MST programs in their home countries. Anecdotal reports established the value of local consultants and cultural advisors in minimizing cultural and social barriers to full program implementation. The training materials were translated from English as needed, while the protocols and interventions were tweaked to become more culturally relevant. Transport of MST to other countries generally required a longer duration of treatment in order to reach the required intensity or "dose" of therapy needed to change problem behaviors. On-call and work week standards were modified to reflect the preferences and expectations of care providers in their home countries, which differed from the work practices in the United States. Cultural advisors and supervisors guided the clinical services delivery through each unique version of MST in the eight countries served (Schoenwald et al., 2008).

Clinical services delivery of MST in foreign countries involves transporting the evidence-supported, site-specific MST *Program Goals and Guidelines* (Edwards, Schoenwald, Henggeler, & Strother, 2001) to their governments and mental health systems by translating concepts and protocols and tweaking protocols, while maintaining adherence to core MST standards and quality assurance guidelines (MST Services, n.d.). Henggeler (1999) and colleagues have managed to diffuse their highly effective program through ongoing support by MST Services, a licensed provider and consultation effort organized through the Medical University of South Carolina. Implementation tracking, provider feedback, program evaluation, and "training the trainer" programs are offered by the MST Institute (n.d.), which guides best practices established by a 45-site NIMH funded study of the transport of MST findings and an increasing number of network partners.

Summary

Evidence-based models of family therapy approaches, such as MST and FFT, promise to break cycles of offending by intervening in the evolution of adolescent problems into adult criminal conduct. Such rehabilitation efforts are guided by manualized treatment resources, which must be localized to reflect the needs of youths and their families in the community context. The programs have been implemented internationally through careful attention to translation research, innovation diffusion, and training of staff members in culturally relevant and sensitive interventions.

MI and community interventions based on the RNR model (Hanson et al., 2009) shift the focus from incarceration and control of offenders toward individually tailored treatment programs in the least restrictive environments. In this manner, offender rehabilitation genuinely addresses criminogenic factors and treatment needs such as family dysfunction and abuse, while maintaining adherence to empirically supported interventions.

Best practices in offender rehabilitation include attention to high risk offenders from vulnerable populations such as delinquent youths, women, survivors of interpersonal violence, and substance abusers. Effective rehabilitation requires systematic attention to the RNR model of care. The principles of risk, need, and responsivity determine the limits of treatment in producing beneficial outcomes with diverse problems, populations, and settings (Andrews et al., 1990; Andrews et al., 2006; Andrews & Dowden, 2005; Wormith et al., 2007). Multisite clinical trials and treatment transfer research has established that the potential effectiveness of a given correctional intervention is largely a function of whether programs target high-risk populations, address specific criminogenic needs, and incorporate measurable cognitive-behavioral interventions.

From the perspective of addressing societal violence, it is important to consider the needs of special populations and characteristics of effective treatments for these groups. Successful treatment of sex offenders could protect women and children from the pain and shame that contributes to the pathogenesis of offender behavior in youths and women. When RNR principles were applied in the design of cognitive behavioral treatments for adolescent and adult sex offenders, recidivism rates were meaningfully reduced (Hanson et al., 2009). The key to effective treatment of sex offenders is the individualizing of treatment, rather than adopting a one-treatment-fits-all approach. Female and adolescent offenders, many of whom may have been victimized by sex offenders and family violence perpetrators, require specialized services, as well.

Gender responsive treatment takes into account the abuse histories and life traumas of women, who are increasingly incarcerated in the misguided rush to punishment and deterrence of recent decades in criminal justice policy. Most incarcerated women required well-integrated treatment services that address concurrently offender recidivism, underlying abuse and trauma, and mental and substance use disorders. There are several evidence-based programs that have been proven to be effective in community and institutional settings including Beyond Trauma (Covington, 2003); Helping Women Recover (Covington, 2008); Forever Free (Hall, Prendergast, Wellisch, Patten, & Cao, 2004); Dialectical Behavior Therapy (Linehan, 1993); and Seeking Safety (Najavits, 2002). Review of effective treatments for female and adolescent offenders identified the lowest common denominator in offender rehabilitation: comprehensive intervention in the progression of substance use disorders. Substance abuse and dependence represent the pathways by which most offenders enter into a life of crime and continue a pattern of relapse resulting in severe criminal justice consequences including incarceration.

Adolescent substance abuse is a major risk factor in the pathogenesis of conduct disorder, delinquency, and adult offending (Doran et al, 2012). Treatment of adolescent substance use disorders involves developmentally appropriate interventions that take into account comorbid problems (e.g., mood disorder or ADHD) and focus on risk reduction rather than punishment. Effective treatments for adolescents include cognitive-behavioral treatments and family-based ecological therapies. There is a very high prevalence of substance use disorders among adult offenders; therefore, substance abuse treatment is a cornerstone of offender rehabilitation (Wormith et al., 2007). Evidence based treatments for adult substance dependence include TC, CM, pharmacological treatment, and cognitive-behavioral intervention. The most effective treatments were intensive interventions that specifically targeted characteristics of high-risk offenders. Boot camp programs and interventions involving offender coercion were not effective for adult or adolescent offender populations (Bahr et al., 2012).

Lessons can be learned from the review of effective interventions in offender rehabilitation. Evidence based treatment has firmly established the parameters of care for governmental authorities, agency administrators, and results oriented clinicians and stakeholders. Decision-making in offender rehabilitation must take into account the cumulative evidence regarding effectiveness of particular interventions for special populations who present high risk and specific needs. Treatments can be matched with criminogenic risks and underlying needs to reduce pain and suffering of offenders and protect society from harm. Evidence based treatments should be adapted and localized to fit the resources and cultural expectations of the sites in which they will be implemented. Research can be translated into effective protocols and interventions and staff members, even paraprofessionals, can be adequately trained at low cost to adhere to empirically validated approaches.

Nevertheless, there will always be innovations in treatment approaches within offender rehabilitation. Each of the evidence based therapies included in this review originated in the clinical experiences of sensitive and creative clinicians. There were cultural and contextual factors that afforded opportunities to explore, implement, and evaluate new treatments. Evidence based approaches are adapted and made new each time they are implemented. Any effective treatment program requires an individualized treatment plan, which takes into account the whole person and their needs in a hopefully increasingly healthy and productive lifestyle.

Recent developments in offender rehabilitation incorporate aspects of positive psychology and indigenous, non-Western approaches to care. The belief that criminal behavior is a product of cognitive, emotional, and mental deficits guided offender rehabilitation for nearly five decades (e.g., Wilson & Herrnstein, 1985); yet, treatment programs based on the offender-deficits model have realized varied success in reducing recidivism. Offender rehabilitation appears ready for a paradigm shift from a deficit-focused to a strength-based model. Treatments with women and adolescent offenders, particularly in family therapy and community corrections, point to the increasing relevance of building on strengths and pursuing positive outcomes such as healthy relationships and happiness. The foundation for a shift in perspective in offender rehabilitation can be found in positive psychology (Wormith et al, 2007). Assisting offenders to build meaningful lifestyles and embrace spirituality and values may represent the future of offender rehabilitation.

The Future of Offender Rehabilitation

Lawmakers, criminal justice professionals, and offender counselors will likely continue to rely upon evidence-based treatment, especially in school, prison, and other institutional settings. The evidence-based approaches are especially relevant in agencies and government departments in which funds are scarce and only empirically supported interventions can be justified to stakeholders and citizens. Nevertheless, there are some promising innovations in offender rehabilitation which deserve ongoing review and investigation.

Himmelstein (2011) described some promising meditation techniques used with incarcerated offenders. Transcendental Meditation (TM) has been used with good results for years. The technique involves the repetition of key words (i.e., a mantra) for 15-20 minutes twice daily. TM has produced a combination of alertness with physiological relaxation in inmates. It is one of the most researched meditation techniques (Himmelstein, 2011).

Mindfulness-based stress reduction (Samuelson, Carmody, Kabat-Zinn, & Bratt, 2007) has been implemented with prison inmates producing beneficial cognitive changes, relaxation, self-control, and relapse prevention. The technique involves focusing on one's breath during sitting medication, conducting a body scan while lying down, and practicing various Hatha yoga postures. A related technique is called *Vipassana*, which means insight. Vipassana meditation or mindfulness meditation has been implemented as a workshop or retreat within the prison setting (Bowen, et al., 2006; Himmelstein, 2011).

Mindfulness meditation involves focus on breathing and achieving freedom from distracting thoughts. In the Vipassana retreats, participants do not speak for 10 days and they agree to follow moral precepts: abstaining from violence, lying, stealing, sexual misconduct, and intoxication. In this manner, the inmate establishes an internal coherence that affords reflection and freedom from urges associated with re-offense (Himmelstein, 2011).

Mindfulness meditation, mindfulness-based stress reduction, and TM produce statistically and clinically significant outcomes in psychological and behavioral indicators, reductions in recidivism, and increases in well-being. Inmates were less hostile and demanding, more self-controlled, and less troubled by mental illness and substance use disorders (Bowen et al, 2006; Himmelstein, 2011; Samuelson et al., 2007). These results are promising and deserving of additional consideration even though such Eastern practices do not fit the typical punishment-oriented prison culture. Similarly, study of sacred texts, prayer, chanting or singing, and other disciplines from Judeo-Christian and Muslin faith traditions should be explored in institutional settings.

References

Alexander, J.F., & Parsons, B.V. (1973). Short term behavior interventions with delinquent families: Impact on family processes and recidivism. *Journal of Abnormal Psychology, 81*, 219-225.

Andrews, D.A., & Bonta, J. (2003). *The psychology of criminal conduct* (3rd ed.). Cincinnati, OH: Anderson.

Andrews, D.A., Bonta, J., & Hoge, R.D. (1990). Classification for effective rehabilitation: Rediscovering psychology. *Criminal Justice and Behavior, 17*, 19-52.

Andrews, D.A., Bonta, J., & Wormith, J.S. (2006). The recent past and near future of risk and/or need assessment. *Crime & Delinquency, 52*, 7-27.

Andrews, D.A., & Dowden, C. (2005). Managing correctional treatment for reduced recidivism: A meta-analytic review of program integrity. *Legal and Criminological Psychology, 10*, 173-187.

Anumba, N., Dematteo, D., & Heilbrun, K. (2012). Social functioning, victimization and mental health among female offenders. *Criminal Justice and Behavior, 39*, 1204-1218. doi: 10.1177/0093854812443489

Aos, S., Miller, M., & Drake, E. (2006). *Evidence-based adult corrections programs: What works and what does not.* Olympia: Washington State Institute for Public Policy.

Bahr, S.J., Masters, A.L., & Taylor, B.M. (2012). What works in substance abuse treatment programs for offenders? *The Prison Journal, 92*, 155-174. doi: 10.1177/0032885512438836

Baltieri, D.A., Daro, F.R., Ribeiro, P.L., & de Andrade, A.G. (2008). Comparing topmiramate with naltrexone in the treatment of alcohol dependence. *Addiction, 103*, 2035-2044.

Bonta, J., Bourgon, G., Rugge, T., Scott, T., Yessine, A.K., Gutierrez, L., & Li, J. (2011). An experimental demonstration of training probation officers in evidence-based community supervision. *Criminal Justice and Behavior, 38*, 1127-1148. doi: 10.1177/0093854811420678

Bowen, S., Witkiewitz, K., Dillworth, T.M., Chawla, N., Simpson, T.L., Ostafin, B.D. ... Marlatt, G.A. (2006). Mindfulness meditation and substance use in an incarcerated population. *Journal of Addictive Behaviors, 20*, 343-347.

Covington, S. (2003). *Beyond trauma: A healing journey for women.* Center City, MN: Hazeldon.

Covington, S. (2008). *Helping women recover: A program for treating substance abuse. Special edition for use in the criminal justice system.* San Francisco: Jossey-Bass.

Covington, S., & Bloom, B. (2006). Gender responsive treatment and services in correctional settings. *Women and Therapy, 29*, 9-33.

Craig, L. A., Browne, K. D., & Stringer, I. (2003). Treatment and sexual offense recidivism. *Trauma, Violence, & Abuse, 4*, 70-89.

Doran, N., Luczak, S.E., Bekman, N., Koutsenok, I., & Brown, S.A. (2012). Adolescent substance use and aggression. *Criminal Justice and Behavior, 39*, 748-769. doi:10.1177/0093854812437022

Duncan, T.M., Davey, M., & Davey, A. (2011). Transporting functional family therapy to community-based programs. *The Family Journal: Counseling and Therapy for Couples and Families, 19*, 41-46. doi: 10.1177/1066480710387269

Edwards, D.L., Schoenwald, S.K., Henggeler, S.W., & Strother, K.B. (2001). A multi-level perspective on the implementation of Multisystemic Therapy (MST): Attempting dissemination with fidelity. In G.A. Bernfeld, D.P. Farrington, & A.W. Leschied (Eds.), *Offender rehabilitation in practice: Implementing and evaluating effective programs* (pp. 97-120). London: Wiley.

Fletcher, B.W., Lehman, W.E.K., Wexler, H.K., & Melnick, G. (2007). Who participates in the Criminal Justice Drug Abuse Treatment Studies (CJ-DATS)? *The Prison Journal, 87*, 25-57. doi: 10.1177/0032885506299037

French, S. A., & Gendreau, P. (2006). Reducing prison misconduct: What works. *Criminal Justice and Behavior, 33*, 185-218.

Greenwood, P. (2008). Prevention and intervention programs for juvenile offenders. *The Future of Children, 18*, 185-211.

Hall, E., Prendergast, M., Wellisch, J., Patten, M., & Cao, Y. (2004). Treating drug-using women prisoners: An outcome evaluation of the Forever Free program. *Prison Journal, 84*, 81-105.

Hanson, R.K., Bourgon, g., Helmus, L., & Hodgson, S. (2009). The principles of effective correctional treatment also apply to sex offenders: A meta-analysis. *Criminal Justice and Behavior, 36*, 865-891. doi: 10.1177/0093854809338545

Hartzler, B., & Espinoza, E.M. (2011). Moving criminal justice organizations toward adoption of evidence-based practice via advanced workshop training in motivational interviewing: A research note. *Criminal Justice Policy Review, 22*, 235-253. doi: 10.1177/0887403410371372

Henggeler, S.W. (1999). Multisystemic therapy: An overview of clinical procedures, outcomes, and policy implications. *Child Psychology & Psychiatry Review, 4*, 2-10.

Himmelstein, S. (2011). Meditation research: The state of the art in correctional settings. *International Journal of Offender Therapy and Comparative Criminology, 55*, 646-661. doi: 10.1177/0306624X10364485

Hinton, W.J., Sheperis, C., & Sims, P. (2003). Family-based approaches to juvenile delinquency: A review of the literature. *The Family Journal, 11*, 167-173. doi: 10.1177/1066480702250156

Hinton, W.J., Sims, P.L., Adams, M.A., & West, C. (2007). Juvenile justice: A system divided. *Criminal Justice Policy Review, 18*, 466-483. doi: 10.1177/0887403407304578

Howell, J.C. (2003). Diffusing research into practice using the comprehensive strategy for serious, violent, and chronic juvenile offenders. *Youth Violence and Juvenile Justice, 1*, 219-245. doi: 10.1177/1541204003001003001

Kohlberg, L. (1976). Moral stages and moralization: The cognitive-developmental approach. In T. Lickona (Ed.), *Moral development and behavior* (pp. 31-55). New York: Holt, Rinehart, & Winston.

Liddle, H.A. (1995). Conceptual and clinical dimensions of a multidimensional, multisystems engagement strategy in family-based adolescent treatment. *Psychotherapy: Theory, Research and Practice, 32*, 39-58.

Linehan, M. (1993). *Cognitive behavioral therapy for borderline personality disorder.* New York: Guilford.

Little, G.L., & Robinson, K.D. (1988). Moral reconation therapy: A systematic step-by-step treatment system for treatment-resistant clients. *Psychological Reports, 62*, 135-151.

Littell, J. H., Popa, M., & Forsythe, B. (2006). Multisystemic therapy for social, emotional, and behavioral problems in youth aged 10-17. *The Cochrane Database of Systematic Reviews, Issue 1.* New York: John Wiley.

Losel, F., & Schmucker, M. (2005). The effectiveness of treatment for sexual offenders: A comprehensive meta-analysis. *Journal of Experimental Criminology, 1,* 117-146.

Lynch, S.M., Fritch, A., & Heath, N.M. (2012). Looking beneath the surface: The nature of incarcerated women's experiences of interpersonal violence, treatment needs, and mental health. *Feminist Criminology, 7,* 381-400. doi: 10.1177/1557085112439224

Marques, J. K., Wiederanders, M., Day, D. M., Nelson, C., & van Ommeren, A. (2005). Effects of a relapse prevention program on sexual recidivism: Final results from California's Sex Offender Treatment and Evaluation Project (SOTEP). *Sexual Abuse: A Journal of Research and Treatment, 17,* 79-107.

Marshall, W. L., Ward, T., Mann, R. E., Moulden, H., Fernandez, Y. M., Serran, G., et al. (2005). Working positively with sexual offenders: Maximizing the effectiveness of treatment. *Journal of Interpersonal Violence, 20,* 1096-1114.

Martinson, R. (1974). What works? Questions and answers about prison reform. *The Public Interest, 35,* 22-54.

Matthews, B., & Hubbard, D.J. (2008). Moving ahead: Five essential elements for working effectively with girls. *Journal of Criminal Justice, 36,* 494-502.

McGuire, R.J. (2002). *Evidence-based programming today.* Boston: International Community Corrections Association.

McGuire, R.J. (2005). *Meta-analytic reviews of offender treatment, 1985-2005.* Liverpool, UK: University of Liverpool.

Merlo, A.V., & Benekos, P.J. (2010). Is punitive juvenile justice policy declining in the United States? A critique of emerging initiatives. *Youth Justice, 10,* 3-24. doi: 10.1177/1473225409356740

Messina, N., Grella, C., Burdon, W., & Prendergast, M. (2007). Childhood adverse events and current traumatic distress: A comparison of men and women drug-dependent prisoners. *Criminal Justice and Behavior, 34,* 1385-1401.

Miller, S.L., Gregory, C., & Iovanni, L. (2005). One size fits all? A gender-neutral approach to a gender-specific problem: Contrasting batterer treatment programs for male and female offenders. *Criminal Justice Policy Review, 16,* 336-359. doi: 10.1177/0887403404273944

Miller, W.R., & Rollnick, S. (Eds.). (2002). *Motivational interviewing: Preparing people to change addictive behavior* (2nd ed.). New York: Guilford.

MST Institute. (n.d.). Welcome to the MST Institute Website. Retrieved from www.mstinstitute.org/

MST Services. (n.d.). *MST: Breaking the cycle of criminal behavior by keeping teens at home, in school and out of trouble.* Retrieved from mstservices.com/

Najavits, L.M. (2002). *Seeking safety: A treatment manual for PTSD and substance abuse.* New York: Guilford.

Najavits, L.M. (2009). *Seeking Safety:* An implementation guide. In A. Rubin & D.W. Springer (Eds.), *The clinician's guide to evidence-based practice.* Hoboken, NJ: Wiley.

National Institute of Corrections. (2004). *Implementing evidence-based practice in community corrections: The principles of effective intervention.* Washington, DC: Author.

Paul, G. (1967). Strategy of outcome research in psychotherapy. *Journal of Consulting Psychology, 31,* 109-118.

Parhar, K.K., Wormith, J.S., Derkzen, D.M., & Beauregard, A.M. (2008). Offender coercion in treatment: A meta-analysis of effectiveness. *Criminal Justice and Behavior, 35,* 1109-1135.

Prochaska, J.O., & DiClemente, C.C. (1982). Transtheoretical therapy: Toward a more integrative model of change. *Psychotherapy: Theory, Research, and Practice, 19,* 276-288.

Reese, L.E., & Vera, E.M. (2007). Culturally relevant prevention: The scientific and practical considerations of community-based programs. *The Counseling Psychologist, 35,* 763-778. doi: 10.1177/0011000007304588

Rogers, E.M. (1983). *Diffusion of innovations* (3rd ed.). New York: Free Press.

Samuelson, M., Carmody, J., Kabat-Zinn, J., & Bratt, M.A. (2007). Mindfulness-based stress reduction in Massachusetts correctional facilities. *The Prison Journal, 87,* 254-268.

SAMSHA. (2013). *SAMSHA's National Registry of Evidence-based Program and Practices.* Retrieved from nrepp.samsha.gov

Sexton, T.L., & Alexander, J.F. (2002). Family-based empirically supported interventions. *The Counseling Psychologist, 30,* 238-261. doi: 10.1177/0011000002302003

Sheidow, A.J., & Woodford, M.S. (2003). Multisystemic therapy: An empirically supported, home-based family therapy approach. *The Family Journal: Counseling and Therapy for Couples and Families, 11,* 257-263.

Schoenwald, S.K., Heiblum, N., Saldana, l., & Henggeler, S.W. (2008). The international implementation of multisystemic therapy. *Evaluation & the Health Professions, 31,* 211-225. doi: 10.1177/0163278708315925

Szapocznik, J., & Kurtines, W.M. (1989). *Breakthroughs in family therapy with drug abusing and problem youth.* New York: Springer.

Tashiro, T., & Mortensen, L. (2006). Translational research: How social psychology can improve psychotherapy. *American Psychologist, 61,* 959-966.

Tripodi, S.J., Bledsoe, S.E., Kim, J.S., & Bender, K. (2011). Effects of correctional-based programs for female inmates: A systematic reviews. *Research on Social Work Practice, 21,* 15-31. doi: 10.1177/1049731509352337

U.S. Department of Justice. (2006). *Criminal offenders statistics.* Washington, DC: Bureau of Justice Statistics. Retrieved from http://www.ojp.usdoj.gov.bjs.crimoff.htm

Van Voorhis, P., Wright, E.M., Salisbury, E.J., & Bauman, A. (2010). Women's risk factors and their contributions to existing risk/needs assessment: The current state of a gender-responsive supplement. *Criminal Justice and Behavior, 37,* 261-288.

Wallace, B.C., Conner, L.C., & Dass-Brailsford, P. (2011). Integrated trauma treatment in correctional health care and community-based treatment upon reentry. *Journal of Correctional Health Care, 17,* 329-343. doi: 10.1177/1078345811413091

Watson, D.W., Bisesi, L., Tanamly, S., & Mai, N. (2003). Comprehensive residential education, arts, and substance abuse treatment (CREASAT): A model treatment program for juvenile offenders. *Youth Violence and Juvenile Justice, 1,* 388-401. doi: 10.1177/1541204003256312

Wexler, H. K., Prendergast, M. L., & Melnick, G. (2004). Introduction to a special issue: Correctional drug treatment outcomes—focus on California. *The Prison Journal, 84,* 3-7.

Wilson, D.B., Bouffard, L.A., & Mackenzie, D.L. (2005). A quantitative review of structured, group-oriented, cognitive-behavioral programs for offenders. *Criminal Justice and Behavior, 32,* 172-204. doi: 10.1177/0093854804272889

Wilson, J.Q., & Herrnstein, R.J. (1985). *Crime and human nature.* New York: Simon & Schuster.

Wolf, N.L., & Shi, J. (2010). Trauma and incarcerated persons. In C.L. Scott (Ed.), *Handbook of correctional mental health* (2nd ed., pp. 277-320). Arlington, VA: American Psychiatric Association.

Wormith, J.S., Althouse, R., Simpson, M., Reitzel, L.R., Fagan, T.J., & Morgan, R.D. (2007). The rehabilitation and reintegration of offenders: The current landscape and some future directions for correctional psychology. *Criminal Justice and Behavior, 34,* 879-892. doi: 10.1177/0093854807301552

Wright, E.M., Van Voorhis, P., Salisbury, E.J., & Bauman, A. (2012). Gender-responsive lessons learned and policy implications for women in prison: A review. *Criminal Justice and Behavior, 39,* 1612-1632. doi: 10.1177/0093854812451088

Youth Villages. (2013). *Multisystemic therapy (MST): Proven help for children and their families.* Retrieved from www.youthvillages.org/what-we-do/intensive-in-home-treatment/mst.aspx

5

Codependency

A Critical Review and Proposed Feminist-Based Model for Assessment and Treatment

Virginia A. Kelly, Elizabeth S. Miceli, Leslie V. Hammer,
James M. McGinn, & Emily Keuper[1]

*Codependency has been used to characterize individuals in close re-
lationships with an addict. This article examines the empirical support of the construct as well as the criticisms. The use of a feminist
framework for conceptualizing codependency is explored and a potential model for assessing and treating codependency is presented.*

Many helping professionals have embraced the conceptualization of
addiction as a family disease and there is empirical evidence that
disorders associated with drug and alcohol dependence affect everyone
in an addicted family (Baird, 2012; Collins, Leonard, & Searles, 1990;
Copello, & Lorna Powell, 2010; Gruber & Taylor, 2006; Rotunda, Scherer,
& Imm, 1995). In fact, treatment for addicts often includes marital and
family therapy approaches (Epstein & McCrady, 1998; Erikson, 2011;

1. Virginia A. Kelly, Elizabeth S. Miceli, Leslie V. Hammer, and Emily Keuper,
Counselor Education Department, Fairfield University; James M. McGinn, Kids in
Crisis, Inc., Cos Cob, CT. Correspondence concerning this article should be directed
to Virginia A. Kelly, Counselor Education Department, Graduate School of Education
and Allied Professions, Fairfield University, 1073 North Benson Rd, Fairfield, CT 06824.
Email: VKelly@fairfield.edu

Liddle, 2009; Rotunda & O'Farrell, 1997). In the 1980's, when the conceptualization of addiction as a family disease began to take hold, a distinct construct was introduced to characterize family members of addicts. The dysfunctional process linked to these individuals became known as codependency (Cermak, 1986; Wegscheider-Cruse, 1985; Whitfield, 1987; Woititz, 1983). Initially, self-help books on this topic flooded bookstores, and eventually research and scholarly inquiry emerged. However, while the impact of addiction on those closest to the addict is undisputed, the acceptance of the codependency label remains controversial.

The literature on codependency has primarily focused on the investigation of the impact of addiction on children of alcoholics (COAs) (Hussong, Zucker, Wong, Fitzgerald, & Puttler, 2005; Johnson & Leff, 1999; Jones et al., 2007; Puttler, Zucker, Fitzgerald, & Bingham, 1998; Schuckit, Smith, Pierson, Trim, & Danko, 2008; West & Prinz, 1987). The findings of these studies suggested that this population was at greater risk of struggling with emotional, behavioral and relational issues than their peers who did not have alcoholic parents. This recognition of the characteristics and needs of children of alcoholics supported the identification of codependency as a disease process attributable to individuals in close relationships with alcoholics and addicts. Codependency emerged as the construct for conceptualizing a set of behaviors and issues associated with living with an alcoholic or addict, and researchers attempted to empirically substantiate and describe its features.

It is the purpose of this article to review the literature on codependency. Several definitions of codependency will be presented. The nature and level of empirical support for codependency as a construct with identifiable characteristics will be reviewed, and the criticisms of codependency will be explored. In light of the criticisms raised, a theoretical orientation for conceptualizing codependency will be presented in order to begin the process of solidifying a helping model that might benefit counselors in their work with this client population. Finally, a potential model for the assessment and treatment of codependency will be presented.

Definitions of Codependency

Initially, several definitions of codependency emerged, representing a variety of theoretical orientations (Table 1). Ultimately though, all of the definitions put forward include a description of codependency as an illness of relationship that has its roots in an individual's primary and persistent relationship with someone who struggles with the disease of addiction. Fundamentally, the criteria used to define codependency describe an inability to form and sustain relationships that are healthy and based on reciprocity and mutuality. The codependent individual has developed behavior patterns and perceptual disturbances that prohibit reality-based methods of evaluating relationships. It is suggested that these disturbances are the result of relationships (primarily familial) with substance abusing individuals, in which the codependent is forced to develop ways of relating that do not threaten this primary relationship with the addict (Beattie, 1992).

In one of the earliest definitions of codependency, Norwood (1985), utilizing an interpersonal framework, explained that the codependent is an individual who has developed an unhealthy pattern of relating to others as a result of having been closely involved with an addict. Wilson-Shaef (1986) proposed a more global definition of codependence as a systemic disease process that has its roots in the primary system where individuals reside and develop. As such, it is an illness that can be characterized as having origins in factors and relationships that reside outside of the codependent individual. While there is an interactional component between the individual and the environment, whereby the factors leading to the formation of codependency interact with the individual to formulate the precise nature of the codependence, the inception of this disease has its basis in external forces beyond the control of the codependent.

There are a number of explanations for the process through which this interaction between the individual and the environmental influences leading to codependency occurs. Black (2001) suggested that there are three rules consistent within addicted family systems that lay the groundwork for defining codependency: Don't talk. Don't trust. Don't feel. Within a family system where these rules underlie family relationships, honest expression of authentic feelings is prohibited. When relationship patterns based on such rules become embedded and extend beyond relationships with family members, a codependent pattern of relating to the world ensues. Essentially, these rules become central to the identity of the codependent and become an organizing structure for future relationships. According to this definition, the codependent will inadvertently utilize these rules in the formation of relationships beyond that with the addict or with members of their family of origin.

Johnson and Leff (1999) addressed the issue of denial as a central feature of codependency. This type of denial often involves a covert agreement between a substance-abusing individual and either a partner, family member, friend, or even a clinician, that encapsulates the relationship. Between the abuser and the codependent, there develops an implicit understanding that this denial is crucial to the maintenance of the relationship. Thus, honest, direct communication regarding the addiction or the substance abuse that dominates their relationship is prohibited.

Johnson and Leff (1999) went on to suggest that this kind of denial could lead to either projective identification or splitting. Projective identification describes a situation in which the substance abuser projects feelings that they are unable to access and process onto the codependent individual. What distinguishes projective identification from classic projection is that the codependent individual assumes the projected attributes. In this way the substance-abusing individual is successful at not only projecting the feelings "onto" the codependent individual, but actually "into" that person. Cermak (1986) has suggested that this internalizing of the other's projection is one of the clinical indications that a client is actually codependent, as they will accept or at least wonder at their own culpability. Because their own sense of self is devalued, their ability to discern reality is diminished. They are not able to develop a clear understanding of which attributes or characteristics truly belong to them, and which the addict has projected upon them.

Splitting involves the use of, and firm belief in, rigid black and white thinking. Applied to codependency, the codependent individual often has a tendency to see individuals as all bad or all good. The distortions inherent in this type of thinking prevent the development of healthy, mature relationships. Individuals will be categorized as all good or all bad and will be related to on the basis of which group they inhabit. This type of thinking is part of the normal developmental process and appropriate for children and even for adolescents. However, healthy development includes a leveling out of this rigidity to incorporate ambiguity and an understanding that others are rarely all good or all bad. The use of splitting indicates a developmental issue whereby the codependent individual is frozen within this particular developmental process. In an attempt to control and protect the ego, the codependent holds firmly to the notion that individuals can be rigidly categorized as all good or all bad.

This notion of arrested development is consistent with Friel and Friel's (2010) description of codependency. In addition, these authors suggest that codependency involves overreacting to external events, while ignoring internal cues and feelings. If untreated, these behavior patterns may develop into an addiction of sorts, with the codependent experiencing a deep sense of being unable to alter their unhealthy patterns. According to their definition, codependent individuals have tremendous difficulty using internal cues and feelings to assess relationships. Having cut themselves off from these internal signals, they will tend to exaggerate external events and thus maintain a sense of hypervigilance, as they are not able to access any sense of personal power. They are always at the mercy of the external world and feel ill equipped to bring an honest self-evaluation to situations and relationships.

Other definitions of codependence include expansions on the precise roles codependent individuals might assume as they attempt to navigate the world on the basis of relationship tactics that have been assumed in order to maintain a primary relationship with an addict. Larsen (1985) was perhaps the first to characterize the codependent on the basis of predictable roles he or she might fill in an addicted family. These roles were further developed and expanded by Woititz (1983) and others within the addictions field and include the enabler, the hero, the scapegoat, the lost child, and the mascot. The enabler is often the addict's partner and is usually another adult within the system whose primary function in the maintenance of the system is to assist the addict in continuing use. This can be done through making excuses for the addict or ignoring the negative consequences of the addiction. The hero, scapegoat, lost child, and mascot are often children within an addicted family. The primary task of the hero within the system is to be successful, not to obtain personal recognition, but to increase status for the family. The scapegoat is often the child who is the identified patient in an addicted family, while the lost child presents little or no need. Finally, the mascot's role is to distract the family, often through the use of humor.

Charles Whitfield (1987), a medical doctor, defined codependency using a behavioral framework. In the medical tradition, Whitfield suggested that codependency is a primary condition with identifiable symptoms and a chronic and progressive prognosis similar to that of addiction. Wegscheider-Cruse (1985) operationally defined these symptoms. She described codependence as a condition that is characterized by extreme dependence (emotionally, socially, and sometimes physically) upon another person or an object. According to Wegscheider-Cruse (1985) this dependence eventually becomes pathological and begins to infiltrate all of the codependent's relationships. The specific characteristics associated with the disease of codependency include low self-esteem, frozen feelings, and stress-related medical disorders.

Cermak (1986) put forward the most thorough and comprehensive description of codependence to date, by establishing diagnostic criteria for Co-Dependent Personality Disorder. Initially, Cermak defined codependency by stating that, "the salient feature of codependency is continued investment of self-esteem in the ability to control feelings and behaviors, whether in oneself or others, in the face of adverse consequences" (p. 11). He went on to describe the codependent individual as someone with boundary distortions that include enmeshed relationships and an exaggerated sense of one's own responsibility to meet the needs of others while neglecting the meeting of their own needs. In elaborating upon this definition, he went on to suggest that, because codependence is comprised of a recognizable pattern of personality traits predictably found within most members of chemically dependent families, specific diagnostic criteria are warranted. Thus, in 1986, Cermak presented a set of diagnostic criteria for codependence and proposed it for inclusion within the DSM-III. While it was not adopted for inclusion into the DSM-III, this framework is perhaps the most comprehensive and inclusive listing of characteristics associated with codependency. The characteristics that Cermak suggested are attributable to codependence span both emotional and relational issues and included depression, anxiety, low self-esteem, boundary disturbances, hypervigilance, and extreme caretaking.

Cermak (1991) additionally provided a distinction between what he referred to as primary codependence and secondary codependence. In primary codependence a child is subjected to a psychic wounding process throughout crucial developmental stages. In an unhealthy family system (e.g., one in which one or both parents are addicts or have some level of substance abuse disorder) the developing child receives a preponderance of conflicting, often destructive messages. This experience inhibits the development of an authentic self (Whitfield, 1987). In response, the child begins the process of negating and eventually destroying the true self, developing a codependent self to engage the world. This leaves the individual with a deep sense of emptiness and shame, and feeling that they would certainly be abandoned by anyone who knew their true or authentic self. Primary codependence is difficult to treat and has been characterized as a personality disorder. The dysfunction is deeply ingrained, as the individual develops unhealthy patterns of behavior beginning in early childhood.

Secondary codependence presents as a more reactionary pattern of unhealthy behaviors (Cermak, 1991). In this case, an otherwise healthy individual may begin to develop unhealthy behavior patterns in response to a relationship with an addicted or substance-abusing individual. Secondary codependence may be easier to treat, in that the individual is more likely to have a healthy and solid core. The unique features associated with secondary codependence reside in the fact that these individuals will likely describe a childhood that has not been dominated by adults with addiction or alcoholism issues. Instead, for individuals presenting with secondary codependence issues, the relationships that have created the codependent behaviors will have emerged later in life, perhaps in late adolescence, early adulthood or middle adulthood.

Finally, Cermak (1991) described the relationship between narcissism and codependency as a defining characteristic of codependency. He suggests is that codependents are naturally attracted to narcissists and that a symbiotic relationship of sorts often exists between codependent individuals and individuals with characteristics of narcissistic personality disorder. Because the narcissist possesses personality traits that encompass a sense of grandiosity and entitlement, the codependent is perhaps the perfect mate. While the codependent is generally in search of methods by which they can channel their sense of self into another, the narcissist is simultaneously in search of individuals who can support the grandiose self they have constructed. Interestingly, both personality types are grounded in shame, and it has been suggested that both disorders might best be characterized as having roots in a defense against shame (Whitfield, 1987). In addition, Gabbard (1993) proposed a type of narcissism that is hypervigilant. The hypervigilant narcissist is plagued by oversensitivity, also characteristic of the codependent.

Review of Empirical Findings

Isolating codependency for the purpose of ascertaining the cluster of behaviors related to living with an addict is challenging, in part because the number of potential confounding variables makes the precise attribution of specific characteristics difficult (Dear, Roberts, & Lange, 2005; Collins, et al., 1990). Accurately measuring codependency and the characteristics associated with it is perhaps even more difficult (Benshoff & Janikowski, 2000; Harkness, Swenson, Madsen-Hampton, & Hale, 2001). The potential consequences of living with an addict span depression, anxiety, low self-esteem, boundary disturbances, hypervigilance, and extreme caretaking (Douglass, 2010; Hoenigmann-Lion & Whitehead, 2007; Jones, et al., 2007). Very few assessments yield precise measures of these constructs. Nonetheless, a body of empirically-based literature emerged that sought to describe and define codependency.

Harkness (2001) conducted a study to investigate whether dissociation might be a mediating factor linking substance abuse in the family of origin with codependency in the offspring of substance abusers. In this study, substance abuse in the family of origin was found to be significantly associated with scores on the Dissociative Experience Scale (DES; Carlson & Putnam, 1986). Dissociation has been described as a loss of integration of an individual's psychological functioning (Carlson, Yates, & Sroufe, 2009). Clients experiencing dissociation often report a sense of detachment that has been colloquially described as feeling numb or shutting down. Individuals who experience dissociation often report losing their connection to their own feelings and needs, resulting in boundary disturbances. Their sense of self becomes diffuse as they shut down the internal mechanisms that keep them grounded in a secure identity (Carlson, et al., 2009).

More recent studies of codependency include the investigation of the causes, development, and maintaining factors associated with a close relationship with an addict. In one qualitative study, grounded theory analysis was used to investigate the thoughts, feelings, behaviors, and experiences that characterized participants' subjective experiences of codependency, and the internal dynamics that contributed to the development and maintenance of codependent ways of relating (Douglass, 2010). A number of themes emerged for this sample of self-identified codependent individuals, all of which have been described in the literature for several decades. These included other focus, insecure-preoccupied attachment, enmeshed self, confusion of identities, and difficulty negotiating emotions. The self-identified codependent individuals expressed feelings of intense focus on others' needs and insecurity that led them to be hypervigilant and preoccupied with meeting the needs of others. In addition, these individuals reported experiencing boundary difficulties such that they felt easily enmeshed with others and unable to maintain a strong sense of individual identity.

In another recent study, Reyome, Ward, and Witkiewitz (2010) found that codependent individuals were more likely to engage in self-silencing than their non-codependent peers. Codependent participants reported a loss of identity certainty in relationships, and felt unable to assertively express their needs and feelings. In addition, these participants tended to report having intimate relationships that were fraught with caretaking, self-sacrifice, and a focus on the other person's needs. The codependents' characterization of relationships also included utilizing hypervigilance as a coping strategy.

Hoenigmann-Lion and Whitehead (2007) examined the relationship between codependency and borderline and dependent personality traits. Findings of this investigation indicated that codependency is strongly related to borderline personality disorder, and related to a lesser degree to dependent personality traits. In another study moderators of psychological distress in adult offspring of substance abusers were assessed (Harkness, Manshire, Blanchard, & Darling, 2007). This study examined the relationship between codependency and anxiety, interpersonal sensitivity, and somatic distress. Findings indicated significant differences between codependent participants and non-codependent participants with the codependent group displaying higher levels of all three attributes.

Throughout the literature, empirical support for a unique cluster of behaviors that characterizes individuals who live with addicts is evident. Codependent individuals have been distinguished from non-codependents on the basis of identifiable and specific attributes. The investigations described support the development of treatment protocols that are responsive to the specific issues faced by individuals who live with addicts.

Criticisms of Codependency

Despite the evidence that has defined, described and empirically validated the construct of codependency, criticisms of this label have emerged. Some clients and helping professionals have resisted the acceptance of a label for individuals deemed ill by virtue of the illness of another (Dear & Roberts, 2002; Dias, 2003; Granello & Beamish, 1998; Rotunda

& Dorman, 2001). In particular, children of alcoholics and women in intimate relationships with addicts have raised concerns regarding the codependency label. In fact, within the literature, codependents have been described as highly resilient individuals with coping skills that are not significantly different than their non-codependent peers' (Granello & Beamish, 1998; Kelly & Myers, 1996).

A distinct body of literature emerged that challenged the codependency label on the basis of both the lack of empirical evidence to support the construct, and on the basis of its discriminatory nature, specifically with regard to its characterization of women (Dear & Roberts, 2002; Dias, 2003; Granello & Beamish, 1998; Rotunda and Dorman, 2001). While this topic has been primarily discussed conceptually, Dear and Roberts (2002) conducted a canonical correlation analysis to determine the relationship between codependence and femininity and masculinity. Findings indicated that there was in fact a moderate relationship between codependency and gender role identification. Specifically, external focus (approval seeking) was associated with high scores in femininity. While this study lends support for the feminist critique of codependency, the relationship between gender role identification and codependency appears to be highly complex.

Granello and Beamish (1998) explored the concept of codependency from political, economic and social perspectives. They reframed the construct as a coping strategy that could be conceptualized as resiliency-based, with roots in feminine self-in-relation theory. Rotunda and Dorman (2001) asserted that the codependency construct perpetuates the societal belief that men are dominant over women. This occurs when a woman in a relationship with a male addict is labeled sick by association with the addict. The responsibility for healing is then, on some level, shifted from the male addict to the female codependent, perpetuating a discriminatory stereotype. Peled and Sacks (2008) made the argument that in order to take on responsibility for healing, women must possess the strength to both support their partners' dependence and maintain responsibility for the relationship. Thus, they may in fact be a population that over-functions and possesses unique strengths.

A final criticism of codependence as a diagnostic construct is that many of the attributes and behaviors attributed to codependents are not unique to individuals who have lived with an addict or been raised in an addicted family (Dias, 2003). In fact, many of the criteria used to define codependency are applicable to a wide variety of individuals, suggesting that the common thread might be that this cluster of behaviors is frequently seen in individuals who grow up in dysfunctional families. As any counselor is aware, this phenomenon is widespread and may encompass the vast majority of clients seen in virtually any setting.

Ultimately, a critical review of the literature on codependency supports the identification of a construct to characterize clients who live with addicts. Studies consistently reveal distinctions between individuals who live with addicts and those who do not, and empirical evidence suggests that that there is a specific set of identifiable characteristics attributable to this lifestyle. To date, codependency provides the only available framework for describing this population of clients, suggesting that the utilization of this construct has merit. However, the body of literature that substantiates a set of valid criticisms of codependency creates a tension that presents challenges to counselors working with this population. The exploration of potential models that combine the empirical evidence supporting the construct of codependency and the criticisms raised is indicated.

Implications for Practice

Potential Theoretical Orientation

The implications for practice culled from this review include the adoption of a feminist theoretical orientation in work with codependent clients. Viewed through a feminist lens, codependence, as it has traditionally been studied, has ignored basic tenets of feminist theory. The adoption of feminist theory as a foundational basis from which to begin the counseling process provides a philosophical orientation, allowing for the use of a variety of approaches and techniques (Worrell & Remer, 2003).

Worrell and Remer (2003) suggest that traditional theories of counseling are inclined to use male-oriented processes and assumptions to guide clinical work. In addition, traditional theories tend to emphasize the differences between men and women, and this distinction has been criticized in the literature on codependency. Similarly, more traditional theoretical perspectives have a predominantly intrapsychic orientation, whereby struggles are attributable to internal causes. This orientation toward the conceptualization of psychological distress often results in blaming the victim, as the presenting issue is conceptualized as existing within the individual. In the case of codependency, this notion has been challenged and represents the criticism of this construct that is cited most often.

Feminist theorists believe that oppression and socialization affect identity development and emotional wellbeing (Gilligan, 1982; Turner & Werner-Wilson, 2008). An understanding of oppression and the incorporation of multicultural awareness are heavily emphasized within this theoretical perspective (Brown & Root, 1990; Enns & Byars-Winston, 2010), raising the possibility that the codependent label is experienced as oppressive or marginalizing for particular clients. Because the principles of feminist therapy include a valuing of women's perspectives, a mutual understanding that the client's experiences will be honored is implicit when working from this theoretical orientation. Finally, an intentional focus on strengths is fundamental to the use of a feminist theoretical orientation. This can assist clients and counselors in redefining psychological distress in a way that is not interpreted as blaming the victim. Instead, the focus can remain on resiliency and the overcoming of symptoms that exist as the result of a relationship with an addict, not as the result of the client's inherent weakness (Worrell & Remer, 2003).

There is no doubt that the disease of addiction affects numerous individuals and does not reside in the addict alone. However, care must be taken in conceptualizing a dysfunctional process that has its roots in the disease of another. The application of feminist theory, with an emphasis on how women typically respond in the context of relationships is critical. Despite the criticisms raised however, codependency remains the best organizing structure available for conceptualizing the pattern of behaviors and feelings that seem to emerge for individuals living with an addict.

Assessment and treatment

The above-mentioned definitions of codependency provide a basis for assessing and treating codependent clients. According to these definitions, the issues that characterize codependency cluster around a set of predictable intrapersonal issues (depression, anxiety, and low self-esteem) and interpersonal issues (boundary disturbances, caretaking, and hypervigilance) (see Figure 1). In addition, the literature suggests that denial and identity diffusion encapsulate these more specific characteristics of codependence. Viewed from this perspective, a counselor will want to proceed with an understanding that breaking through a client's denial system and assisting the client in establishing a strong and separate sense of identity certainty will serve as overarching goals throughout treatment. Using these as broad goals, the counselor will work toward assessing and treating the specific intrapersonal and interpersonal characteristics for individual clients.

Initially, counselors may emphasize work with intrapersonal issues (i.e., depression, anxiety, low self-esteem), as addressing these will result in an increase in ego strength and coping capabilities. A strengthening of reality-based ego has the potential of assisting with the identification of the denial systems that fostered the development of symptoms. Increasing coping skills will support identity certainty, as clients begin to experience their unique ability to cope and address issues in a proactive manner. The preliminary assessment of intrapersonal characteristics can be achieved early on in the counseling relationship, through interviewing or the use of inventories. As the work progresses, and again remaining aware of the client's denial mechanisms and sense of identity, the counselor may move on to assess the level of interpersonal struggle experienced by a codependent client. This will involve looking explicitly at boundary disturbances, hypervigilance, and extreme caretaking behavior within the context of the client's relationships. The assessment of these behaviors is reliant upon the client's descriptions of important relationships within their lives. As the client begins to reveal details pertaining to their relationships, the counselor can help them to discern patterns whereby the client engages in behaviors that are indicative of boundary disturbances, hypervigilance or extreme caretaking. This engagement can be conscious, and thus dealt with directly, or unconscious, feeling to the client like an instinctive reaction to relating to another. These patterns will assist in revealing the nature of the denial mechanisms that have maintained them over time and facilitate the assessment of identity formation. The counselor can then simultaneously work on these overarching issues as well as the specific intrapersonal and interpersonal issues presented by the client.

Overall, the implications for practice are directly linked to the symptomatology presented by codependent clients. The literature reveals that depression, anxiety, and low self-esteem are all related to codependency. These issues reside within the client. In terms of relationships with others, codependence has been shown to result in boundary disturbances, hypervigilance, and excessive caretaking. Work on these two sets of issues is the primary focus in treating codependency. Using a feminist theoretical orientation toward addressing the specific issues for each client allows for mutual understandings that support the client and do not imply blame. Within this framework, counselors can work on establishing rapport and forming a therapeutic alliance with the client. With these relationship attributes firmly in place, counselors can begin to use strategies and techniques from varying theoretical orientations.

Implications for Future Research

The study of codependency remains difficult. The uniqueness of each individual's situation, the abundance of confounding variables, and the difficulties involved in the measurement of codependency present challenges. However, the need for a more solid body of research related to the impact of living with an addict remains imperative. With rates of alcoholism and addiction remaining consistent, individuals collaterally impacted by this disease will continue to seek treatment.

A more precise and empirically validated picture of this population can enhance efforts to address the specific needs of these clients. The model presented here represents a structure for assessing and treating codependency that can be tested. The presence of the identified intrapersonal and interpersonal characteristics for individual clients can be measured to ascertain that issues related to these characteristics are typical for codependent clients. In addition, research addressing the use of a feminist framework and its impact on the counseling process can assist in supporting the use of this theoretical orientation. Finally, research that looks at treatment outcomes for clients treated using this model may assist in the further development of a cohesive model for addressing codependency.

Conclusion

Any professional counselor who has dealt with the issue of addiction knows that the impact of this disease is far reaching and extends well beyond the addict. In addition, most practicing counselors are intuitively aware that there exists a cluster of symptoms that seem to be associated with individuals in close relationships with addicts, and this is supported throughout the literature. The best efforts at describing this phenomenon to date reside in the literature on codependency. Despite the controversy surrounding this construct, it provides counselors with a structure and set of issues characteristic of this population of clients. Therefore, using what has already been discovered in the formulation of an assessment and treatment model may be effective. Using the model described here, with a heightened sensitivity to and understanding of the gender issues raised, may provide the practicing counselor with a structure from which to base work with a codependent client. In addition, the development of such a model provides a basis upon which future research into the treatment of this client population can be conducted.

References

Baird, C. (2012). Families and addiction. *Journal of Addictions Nursing, 22*(4), 229-231. doi: 10.3109/10884602.2011.625159

Beattie, M. (1992). *Codependent no more.* Center City, MN: Hazelden Foundation.

Benshoff, J. & Janikowski, T. (2000). *The rehabilitation model of substance abuse counseling.* Belmont, CA: Wadsworth.

Black, C. (2001). *It will never happen to me.* Bainbridge Island WA: MAC Publishing.

Brown, L. S., & Root, M. (1990). *Diversity and complexity in feminist therapy.* New York: Hayworth.

Carlson, E., & Putnam, F. (1986). Dissociative Experiences Scale.

Carlson, E. A.,Yates, T. M., & Sroufe, A. (2009). Dissociation and development of the self. In P. F. Dell & J. A. O'Neill (Eds.), *Dissociation and the dissociative disorders: DSM-V and beyond* (pp. 39–52). New York, NY: Routledge.

Cermak, T. L. (1986). Diagnostic criteria for codependency. *Journal of Psychoactive Drugs, 18*(1), 15-20.

Cermak, T. L. (1991). Co-addiction as a disease. *Psychiatric Annals,* 21 (5), 266-272.

Collins, R. L., Leonard, K. E., & Searles, J. S. (1990). *Alcohol and the family: Research and clinical perspectives.* New York, NY: Guilford Press.

Copello, A. T., & Lorna Powell, J. (2010). The impact of addiction on the family: Estimates of prevalence and costs. *Drugs: Education, Prevention and Policy, 17,* 63-74. doi: 10.3109/09687637.2010.514798

Dear,G. E.,&Roberts,C. M.(2002).The relationships between codependency and femininity and masculinity. *Sex Roles, 45* (5/6), 159–166. doi: 10.1023/A:1019661702408

Dear, G. E., Roberts, C. M., & Lange, L. (2005). Defining codependency: A thematic analysis of published definitions. In: Shohov, Serge P. (Ed.), *Advances in Psychology Research, Vol. 34 (pp. 189-205).* Hauppauge, NY: Nova Science Publishers.

Dias, M. (2003). Deconstructing codependency: The relationship of codependency to femininity and related psychopathological factors. *Dissertation Abstracts International: Section B. The Sciences and Engineering, 63* (9-B), 4365.

Douglass, M. D. (2010). Codependency: Relationship to self and other. *Dissertation Abstracts International: Section B. The Sciences and Engineering, 70* (9-B), 5815.

Enns, C. Z., & Byars-Winston, A. (2010). Multicultural feminist therapy. In H. Landrine & N. F. Russo (Eds.), *Handbook of diversity in feminist psychology* (pp. 367-388). New York: Springer.

Epstein E. E., & McCrady, B. S. (1998). Behavioral couples treatment of alcohol and drug use disorders: Current status and innovations. *Clinical Psychology Review, 18* (6), 689-711. doi: 10.1016/S0272-7358(98)00025-7

Erikson, C. K. (2011). *Addiction essentials: The go-to guide for clinicians and patients.* New York, NY: W W Norton & Company.

Friel J. C., & Friel, L. D. (2010). *Adult children: Secrets of dysfunctional families.* Deerfield Beach, FL: Health Communications, Inc.

Gabbard, G. O. (1993). On hate in love relationships: The narcissism of minor differences revisited. *The Psychoanalytic Quarterly, 62* (2). 229 – 238.

Gilligan, C. (1982). *In a different voice.* Cambridge, MA: Harvard University Press.

Granello D. H. & Beamish, P. M. (1998). Reconceptualizing codependency in women: A sense of connectedness, not pathology. *Journal of Mental Health Counseling, 20* (4), 344–358.

Gruber, K. J., & Taylor, M. F. (2006). A family perspective for substance abuse: Implications from the literature. *Journal of Social Work Practice in the Addictions, 6* (12), 1-29. doi: 10.1300/J16ov06no1_01

Harkness, D. (2001). Testing Cermak's hypothesis: Is dissociation the mediating variable that links substance abuse in the family of origin with offspring codependency? *Journal of Psychoactive Drugs, 22* (1), 75–82. doi: 10.1080/02791072.2001.10400471

Harkness, D., Manshire, H., Blanchard, J., & Darling, J. (2007). Codependent attitude and behavior: Moderators of psychological distress in adult offspring of families with alcohol and other drug (AOD) problems. *Alcoholism Treatment Quarterly, 25*(3), 39–53. doi: 10.1300/J020v25n03_04

Harkness, D., Swenson, M., Madsen-Hampton, K, & Hale, R. (2001). The development, reliability, and validity of a clinical rating scale for codependency. *Journal of Psychoactive Drugs, 33,* 159–171. doi: 10.1080/02791072.2001.10400481

Hoenigmann-Lion, N. & Whitehead, G. (2007). The relationship between codependency and borderline and dependency traits. *Alcoholism Treatment Quarterly, 24*(4), 55–77. doi: 10.1300/J020v24n04_05

Hussong, A. M., Zucker R. A., Wong, M. M., Fitzgerald, H.E., Puttler L.I. (2005). Social competence in children of alcoholic parents over time. *Developmental Psychology, 41*(5), 747–759. doi: 10.1037/0012-1649.41.5.747

Johnson, J. L., & Leff, M. (1999). Children of substance abusers: Overview of research findings. *Pediatrics, 103* (5), 1085–1099.

Jones, A. L., Perera-Diltz, D. M., Dilani, M., Salyers, K. M., Laux, J. M., & Cochrane, W. S. (2007). Testing hypothesized differences between adult children of alcoholics (ACOAs) and non-ACOAs in a college student sample. *Journal of College Counseling, 10* (1), 19 – 26. doi: 10.1002/j.2161-1882.2007.tb00003.x

Kelly, V. A. & Myers, J. E. (1996). Parental alcoholism and coping: A comparison of female children of alcoholics with female children of non-alcoholics. *Journal of Counseling and Development, 74* (5), 501–504. doi: 10.1002/j.1556-6676.1996.tb01900.x

Larsen, E. (1985). *Stage II recovery: Life beyond addiction.* Minneapolis, MN: Winston Press.

Liddle, A. (2009). Mulitdimensional family therapy: A science based treatment system for adolescent drug abuse. In Bray, J. H., & Stanton, M. (Eds.). *The Wiley-Blackwell handbook of family psychology (pp. 341-354).* Wiley-Blackwell.

Norwood, R. (1985). *Women who love too much.* New York, NY: Penguin Putnam, Inc.

Peled, E., & Sacks, I. (2008). The self-perception of women who live with an alcoholic partner: Dialoguing with deviance, strength, and self- fulfillment. *Family Relations, 57*(3), 390–403. doi: 10.1111/j.1741-3729.2008.00508.x

Puttler, L. I., Zucker, R. A., Fitzgerald, H. E., & Bingham, C. R. (1998). Behavioral outcomes of children of alcoholics during the early and middle childhood years: Familial subtype variations. *Alcoholism: Clinical and Experimental Research, 22* (9), 1962–1972. doi: 10.1097/00000374-199812000-00011

Reyome, N. D., Ward, K. S., & Witkiewitz, K. (2010). Psychosocial variables as mediators of the relationship between childhood history emotional maltreatment,codependency, and self-silencing. *Journal of Aggression, Maltreatment andTrauma, 19*(2), 159–179. doi: 10.1080/10926770903539375

Rotunda, R. J., & Dorman, K. (2001). Partner enabling of substance use disorders: Critical review and future directions. *American Journal of Family therapy, 29*(4), 257–270. doi: 10.1080/01926180152588680

Rotunda R. J., & O'Farrell, T. J. (1997). Marital and family therapy of alcohol use disorders: Bridging the gap between research and practice. *Professional Psychology: Research and Practice, 28*(3), 246–252. doi: 10.1037/0735-7028.28.3.246

Rotunda, R. J., Scherer, D. G., & Imm, P. S. (1995). Family systems and alcohol misuse: Research on the effects of alcoholism on family functioning and effective family interventions. *Professional Psychology: Research and Practice, 26*(1), 95–104. doi: 10.1037/0735-7028.26.1.95

Schuckit, M. A., Smith, T. L., Pierson, J., Trim, R., & Danko, G. P. (2008). Externalizing disorders in the offspring from the San Diego prospective study of alcoholism. *Journal of Psychiatric Research, 42*(8), 644 – 652. doi: 10.1111/j.1530-0277.2007.00465.x

Turner, L. C., & Werner-Wilson, R. J. (2008). Phenomenological experiences of girls in a single-sex day treatment group. *Journal of Feminist Family Therapy, 20*(3), 220-250. doi: 10.1080/08952830802264532

Wegscheider-Cruse, S. (1985). *Choicemaking.* Pompano Beach, FL: Health Communications, Inc.

West, M. O. & Prinz, R. J. (1987). Parental alcoholism and childhood psychopathology. *Psychological Bulletin, 102*(2), 204 – 218. doi: 10.1037/0033-2909.102.2.204

Whitfield, C. (1987). *Healing the child within.* Deerfield Beach, FL: Health Communications, Inc.

Wilson-Shaef, A. (1986). *Co-dependence: Misunderstood—mistreated.* Minneapolis, MN:Winston Press.

Woititz, J. G. (1983). *Adult children of alcoholics.* Deerfield Beach, FL: Health Communications, Inc.

Worrell, J., & Remer, P. (2003). *Feminist perspectives in therapy: Empowering diverse women* (2nd ed.). New York: Wiley.

Table 1: Definitions of Codependency

Source	Definition's Salient Features
Black, (2001)	Three rules of addicted families: Don't talk. Don't trust. Don't feel.
Friel & Friel, (2010)	Adherence to the dysfunctional rules of addicted families leads to identity disturbances within family members. Once this occurs, it no longer requires the presence of the dysfunctional family system in order to remain active.
Johnson & Leff, (1999)	Denial is the defining characteristic of codependence, leading to projective identification or splitting.
Larsen, (1985)	Defined codependence in terms of the specific roles family members will assume that will dominate behavior in all relationships.
Norwood, (1985)	Codependence is the result of a close relationship with an addict leading to the following intrapsychic symptoms: low self-esteem, a need to be needed, a strong urge to change and control others, and a willingness to suffer.
Wegscheider-Cruse, (1985)	A condition characterized by extreme dependence on a person or object, leading to denial, compulsions, frozen feelings, low self-esteem, and stress-related medical conditions.
Whitfield, (1987)	Codependence is a primary illness with a recognizable set of symptoms and a chronic progressive prognosis.
Wilson-Shaef, (1986)	Defined the addictive process, which includes any process we feel we have to lie about, including codependency.

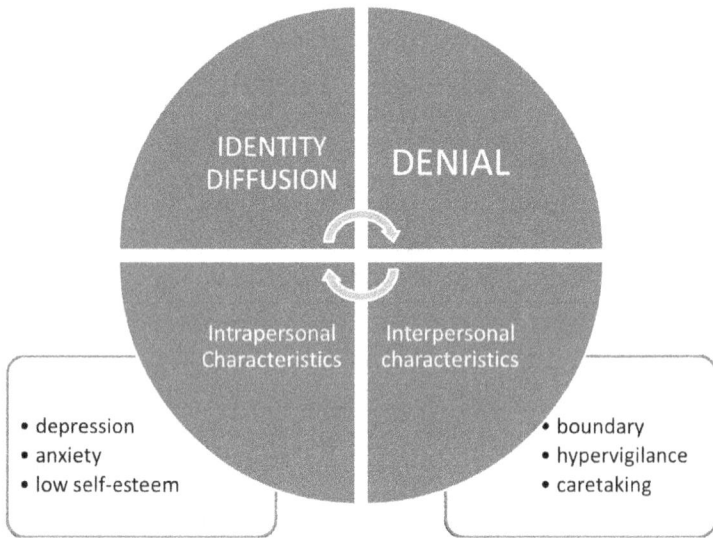

Figure 1: Codependency Assessment and Treatment Model

6

Forgiving Betrayals

A Treatment Model for Couples Affected by Addiction

Kaylee K. Vance, Andrew P. Daire, and Jennifer M. Johnson[1]

This paper examines the commonalities between extramarital affairs and chemical addiction, which are conceptualized as betrayals in a marital relationship that create discord and barriers. Gordon and Baucom's (1998) forgiveness model, a treatment model developed for extramarital affairs, is generalized to treating couples affected by the betrayal of chemical addiction. Causes of betrayals, couples treatment for betrayals, and clinical issues in treatment are addressed.

Counselors often treat families affected by betrayals, defined as acts of disloyalty that result in hurting individual members of a family and the relationships among them. Although betrayals frequently take the form of infidelity, many other betrayals exist within the context of relationships. This paper focuses on utilizing research about treating infidelity with the forgiveness model to help clinicians treat couples and families experiencing betrayals from the effects of chemical addiction.

---

1. Kaylee K. Vance, Andrew P. Daire, and Jennifer M. Johnson, Department of Clinical Psychology, University of Central Florida. Correspondence concerning this article should be addressed to Kaylee K. Vance, P.O. Box 10412, Daytona Beach, FL 32120. Email: kvance86@gmail.com

Forgiveness is a complex, multifaceted construct that has found its way into the clinical research and practice of working through infidelity in families (Sells & Hargraves, 1998). Pingleton (1989) defines forgiveness as "the antithesis of [an] individual's natural and predictable response to violation and victimization" (p. 27), which occurs over a period of time (Sells & Hargraves, 1998). In using forgiveness models (e.g., Gordon & Baucom, 1998; Gordon, Baucom, & Synder, 2004), extramarital affairs are conceptualized as betrayals within the marital relationship. For this reason, Lusterman (1998) describes infidelity as "the breaking of trust . . . [that] occurs when one person in a relationship continues to believe that the agreement to be faithful is still in force, while the other partner is secretly violating it" (p. 3).

There is a dearth of research into forgiving other types of betrayals, namely those resulting from alcohol and drug addiction. These types of betrayals may take the form of an individual emotionally separating from the family due to numbing with a chemical substance, stealing from the family in order to support the habit, lying to the family in order to protect the addiction and avoid shame, injuring the family through abuse while under the influence of a substance, or other substance-induced behaviors that may lead to a rupture of communication, complex relationship issues, or a partner's experience of anger, lack of trust, and deep hurt that may or may not be directly associated with the substance use (Doweiko, 2009; Worthington, Scherer, & Cooke, 2006). Few articles exist exploring this component of addiction treatment and how forgiveness models that include families and partners may be integral to the therapeutic process to overcome the damage from addictions. In order to contribute to the field of addictions, this paper investigates the commonalities between addictions and affairs that lead to betrayals within relationships, hypothesize a similar treatment trajectory, and address common clinical issues arising through the process of forgiveness and regaining trust.

Factors Contributing to Betrayals

Betrayals within a relationship often coincide with an existing problem, but this problem is not necessarily associated directly with the relationship. The form the betrayal takes as a response to the existing problem may vary across relationships, and may simply take the form of an existing pattern in an individual's life (i.e. a predisposition to chemical addiction).

It is imperative that a treatment provider understands both the existing problem and its relationship to the betrayal when establishing treatment goals for the couple. Gordon, Baucom, and Snyder (2004) suggest a few factors that contribute to an affair, including situational factors outside of the relationship (i.e., job stress) and internal factors within the relationship (i.e., characteristics of the participating and injured partners, like insecurities or emotional difficulties). Brown (2001) focuses on internal factors, suggesting that affairs tend to be about the avoidance of pain, the desire to feel alive, and betrayal, and he identifies five types of affairs— (a) *conflict avoidance* affairs, (b) *intimacy avoidance* affairs, (c) *exit* affairs, (d) *split self* affairs, and (e) *sexual addiction* affairs. These affairs possess unique blueprints in terms of their etiology and trajectory, and may also shed light on an individual's reasons for turning to a chemical addiction as opposed to an affair partner.

Conflict and Intimacy Avoidance Affairs

Conflict and intimacy avoiders use affairs to avoid discord or closeness (Brown, 2001; Gordon, Baucom, & Snyder, 2004). Conflict avoiders lack, or believe they lack, the skills necessary to successfully navigate conflict for fear of losing control or being abandoned (Brown, 2001). Therefore, the affair occurs when the relationship has sufficiently eroded due to an inability to face conflicts and provides an "out," so to speak, for both partners (Brown, 2001). Intimacy avoiders seek affairs in order to maintain the barriers that keep them from being too close to their partners (Brown, 2001).

In an individual with a chemical addiction, the use of drugs and alcohol may help the individual cope with or avoid stress or situations that produce stress (Carver, Weintrauf, & Scheier, 1989; Cooper, Russell, Skinner, & Windle, 1992), of which relationship discord or discomfort with intimacy could be examples. Cooper, et al. (1992) assert that individuals who use alcohol as a means to cope tend to have drinking problems that create social dysfunction, which may take the form of relationship problems and a sense of betrayal. Conflict and intimacy avoiders, therefore, may use drugs and alcohol to produce that barrier between them and their partners to avoid the conflicts or vulnerability inherent in a relationship.

Exit Affairs

The *exit* affair is an exacerbation of the conflict avoidance affair in that the decline in the relationship is rooted in the inability or refusal of the partners to deal with conflict directly (Brown, 2001). However, the distinguishing factor between *exit* and *conflict avoidance* affairs is the individual's decision that he/she wishes to end the relationship. In exit affairs, the affair simply becomes a convenient justification to end the relationship (Brown, 2001).

Instead of entering into an affair with another individual, an individual with an addiction may use his/her addiction as the justification to end the relationship. In addition, substance use may eliminate the inhibition of other behaviors providing a relationship exit, such as abuse.

Split Self Affairs

The *split self* affair occurs when both individuals in the relationship devote their entire lives—time, energy, resources—to the survival of the partner or the relationship, and in doing so, have neglected to meet their own needs independently (Brown, 2001). Eventually, the pressure is too much, and the affair becomes an escape and an excusable way to meet one's own needs, which have been sacrificed to the relationship up to that point.

For some individuals, an addiction is a way to take care of oneself, whether by providing the energy to cater to the needs of the spouse and family, enhancing positive emotions (Cooper et al., 1992), or by providing a coping mechanism (Cooper et al., 1992). In a co-dependent relationship, an individual may eventually fall into an addiction in order to take care of himself/herself, and may eventually use the addiction as an escape from the demands of a relationship that perhaps no longer meet the enhancement or coping needs that the individual perceives that he/she can get from the addiction.

Sexual Addiction Affairs

Sex addiction plays an interesting part with substance addiction, if present. In the extramarital affair, Brown (2001) asserts that individuals who are addicted to sex use it to numb pain and emptiness. Keane (2004) describes the powerful mood-altering effects of sex and how its ability to simultaneously stimulate and soothe makes it a highly addicting behavior. These mood-altering qualities are shared with alcohol and other drugs and are often-cited reasons that individuals use to explain their substance addiction (Cooper et al., 1992). In individuals with a pre-existing addiction to a substance, the addiction to sex may be a way to increase the numbing or used interchangeably with the substance when one or the other cannot be attained (Schneider, 1994; Turner, 2009). When an individual addicted to sex or chemicals is in a relationship, he/she may face much more discord in his/her relationship because the individual now has two distinctly different "objects" of his/her affair. Because of the deleterious effects of sex addiction on a relationship, Turner (2009) stresses the importance of involving the individuals in couples therapy along with adjunctive treatments for the individuals.

The theory of sex addiction stems from research on behavioral addictions, which may have implications in the topic of affairs. Keane (2004) describes addiction as a "disorder of desire," thereby broadening the scope of addiction to encompass both chemical addictions as well as behavioral addictions, with etiologies stemming from a desire for intimacy that is lacking elsewhere in an individual's life, or simply from an attraction to an indulgence that alters mood. Peele (1998) echoes this theory when he asserts that anyone can become addicted to anything as long as it powerfully modifies mood or has an inherent ability to fill a hole left empty in some other area of an individual's life. Affairs can produce modifiers in mood similar to those found in chemical addiction through the release of chemicals in the brain resulting in the feeling of new infatuation. Fisher, Aron, and Brown (2005) conducted a fMRI study investigating the neurochemical changes in the brain that occur when a participant looks at a picture of an individual whom he/she loves. They found that the same reward pathways active during infatuation and love are also active when an individual consumes his/her substance of choice in chemical addiction. Therefore, an individual may seek out a chemical or another partner in order to modify his/her mood or enhance a positive emotion.

Treating Betrayals

When treating couples affected by betrayals from affairs or addiction, it is important not only to look at the individual who has the affair or addiction, but also to look at the effects of the betrayal on the partner, the effects on the relationship, and the partner's subjective experience of the addiction or affair. Perhaps, most importantly, the counselor should also assess whether or not the injured partner possesses the desire to work through the betrayal. An individual suffering from an addiction or involved in an affair often incurs resentment from his/her partner related to changing family patterns (Rosenau, 1998; Worthington, Scherer, & Cooke, 2006). The injured partner perceives an unequal distribution of responsibility and energy towards the family or relationship because his/her partner devotes a portion of his/her time and energy to the affair or addiction. Worthington, Scherer, and Cooke (2006) suggest that family members often feel fear, anger, and blame towards the addicted family member. Similarly, the injured spouse may react to marital infidelity with anger, grief, shock, and depression (Olson, Russell, Higgins-Kessler, & Miller, 2002; Rosenau, 1998). Spouses of addicted individuals may also feel embarrassment or humiliation for the actions of their loved ones related to their substance (Worthington, Scherer, & Cooke, 2006), which parallels similar feelings in the injured spouse within the context of an extramarital affair. Some partners will feel "jealous" of the addictive substance because they feel that their partners are spending more time with the substance than with them. In these cases, the "relationship with drinking [or using] can feel like infidelity—but one in which the alcohol [or drug] cannot be confronted" (Worthington et al., 2006, p. 128). Here, the parallel between "the other woman (or man)" and the addictive substance is clear.

Despite similarities in the clinical issues for couples affected by addiction and extramarital affairs, the current focus of treatment is very different. The most important difference is that treatment for extramarital affairs is often conducted within the context of couples counseling, whereas treatment for addiction is generally individualized to the exclusion of the partner, despite research that suggests better treatment outcome when a cooperative and supportive partner or other family members are involved (Edwards & Steinglass, 1995; Joanning, Quinn, Thomas, & Mullen, 1992; Longabaugh, Beattie, Noel, Stout, & Mallow, 1993; McNabb & DerKarabetian, 1989). In most treatment that includes a partner, such as Motivational Enhancement Therapy or Behavioral Couples Therapy, the non-addicted partner is often utilized as an encouragement or support of the individual with an addiction, which neglects the needs of the injured partner (Fals-Stewart, Birchler, & O'Fallell, 1996; Miller, 1995; Winters, O'Farrell, Fals-Stewart, Birchler, & Kelley, 2002), the relationships between the partners, as well as the existing problem that may have contributed to the onset or relapse of the chemical addiction.

Treatment for addiction that includes a focus not only on the individual but also on those closest to that individual who are affected by the addiction may provide a longer-lasting effect because of the focus on changing the system as opposed to just one problem in one individual. In 2006, Worthington, Scherer, and Cooke proposed the use of forgiveness models to treat persons with alcohol problems within the family. They assert that although forgiveness models cannot treat the addiction itself, they may help mitigate the triggers of an unforgiving family and increase support of the family for the individual's recovery.

Forgiveness is an important component in extramarital affairs treatment and may benefit couples that have been affected by the betrayal of an addiction. Using research from treating extramarital affairs may help clinicians conceptualize the course of forgiveness and reconciliation in treating couples afflicted by addiction. Comparing what a couple affected by addiction is experiencing to the experiences from an infidelity could provide clinicians with a framework for treatment goals and expectations as well as provide the couple a framework, expectation, and even a language for the journey on which they are to embark, as well as what will be required of them and how long the journey might take. Exploring a forgiveness model effective in the use of couples counseling for affairs would benefit clinicians seeking a treatment modality for couples experiencing betrayals from addiction.

The Forgiveness Model

In 1998, Gordon and Baucom developed a treatment model for couples that focused on forgiveness as the primary vehicle for healing and repairing relationships affected by extramarital affairs. Their model for forgiving extramarital affairs includes three stages: (a) Impact Stage, (b) Definition Stage, and (c) Moving on Stage. Their model is based on a synthesis of forgiveness, trauma recovery, cognitive-behavioral therapy, family systems, and insight-oriented theories. It conceptualizes the betrayal of an affair as an interpersonal trauma and forgiveness as a process involving the forgiver, the forgiven, and the dyadic relationship between them (Gordon & Baucom, 1998). This model provides an excellent framework for addressing betrayals from chemical addiction.

Stage 1: Impact Stage

Stage Introduction—The first stage in Gordon and Baucom's (1998) model of forgiveness involves a cognitive awareness that a breach in the expected rules or standards of the interpersonal relationship have been violated (Gordon & Baucom, 1998), resulting in intense feelings of betrayal, confusion, hurt, lack of control, and sense of violation in the injured partner (Gordon & Baucom, 1999), as well as emotions vacillating between intense anger fueling the desire towards separation and feelings of guilt and inadequacy fueling the desire for reunification (Olson, Russell, Higgins-Kessler, and Miller's, 2002). Such a breach in the relationship may result in shattered assumptions, such that the injured partner comes to realize that the relationship they had believed was safe and predictable has suddenly become unsafe and unpredictable (Gordon & Baucom, 1998).

Similarly, for partners of individuals with a chemical addiction, the addiction is perceived as a transgression or violation of boundaries, which offends, hurts, or evokes resentment from the spouse (Worthington, Scherer, and Cooke, 2006). According to Halford, Bouma, Kelly, and Young (1999), female partners of alcoholics suffer from higher levels of depression, somatic complaints and anxiety; and both partners report lower relationship satisfaction (Jacob, Dunn, & Leonard, 1983; O'Farrell & Birchler, 1987). Like an affair, the addiction can uproot feelings of safety and stability within the family, leaving the injured partner with similar feelings of anxiety, fear, anger, and resentment (Orford et al., 1998). Gordon and Baucom (1998) assert that a victim's cognitive attributions about his/her partner's intent to harm plays a large part in evaluating the impact the betrayal has on the relationship, and thus, the desire to separate or remain together. In both extramarital affairs and addiction, the couple will often seek treatment only when the betrayal has caused disruption in the homeostasis of the relationship.

Treatment Goals—During this initial stage, treatment goals are concrete and cognitive-behavioral in nature, giving the couple a sense of balance, control, and direction after the disruption from the betrayal. Setting boundaries and limits is an important part of this stage (Gordon & Baucom, 1999), and partners are encouraged to set limits on their negative interactions and adjust boundaries related to expectations and trust (i.e., checking in more frequently in order to reduce levels of anxiety in the injured partner) (Gordon & Baucom, 1999).

In addition, couples focus on self-care, including social and spiritual support (Gordon & Baucom, 1999). In working with chemical dependency, self-care may involve referring the non-addicted spouse to Al-Anon, a 12-step support group for friends and families of individuals suffering from addiction, which focuses on caring for oneself, reducing enabling, and "working a program" independent of the addicted person. Dittrich (1993) asserts that Al-Anon increases self-esteem and decreases depression and anxiety in wives of alcoholics. This may serve to decrease some of the extreme negative emotions of this stage in order to prepare for the definition stage. During the impact stage, Gordon and Baucom (1998) suggest that partners agree to a moratorium, which may be beneficial in increasing self-esteem and independence (Rhodes, 1984). In chemical addiction, this moratorium may occur when the addicted individual enters into residential treatment.

Finally, this stage in the forgiveness model for affairs should include a discussion of the impact the affair has had on the relationship, which is not a time for blaming and shaming but rather a time for each partner to express emotional reactions to the affair and its disclosure, hopefully with the result of increasing empathy (Gordon & Baucom, 1998). This can be an important aspect of recovery for an individual with a chemical addiction. In 12-step models, which are the treatment of choice in many treatment centers, steps eight and nine are dedicated to "making amends" with the people who have been harmed by the addict's addiction (Alcoholics Anonymous World Services [AAWS], 2006, p. 59). In the 12-step tradition, these steps are seen as the beginning of a long process towards forgiveness.

Treatment Obstacles—A variety of problems can surface during the Impact Stage that can impede treatment if not addressed. These include defensiveness, lack of affect, crises (or relapses), and ambivalence, which are also cited in Schneider and Schneider's (1996) research in sex addiction. Other problems may result from differences in the partners' perception of their relationship's future and/or the purpose of couples counseling. Most of these treatment obstacles can be mitigated by a thorough assessment of each individual's needs, treatment expectations, and goals. Referrals to separate treatment groups, individual treatment, and support groups during the course of couples counseling would also be beneficial for increased coping and relapse prevention, which will improve the course of couples counseling.

Stage 2: Definition Stage

Stage Introduction—The second stage in Gordon and Baucom's (1998) forgiveness model is cognitive as well as insight-oriented in nature and focuses on the search for meaning (Olson, Russell, Higgins-Kessler, & Miller, 2002), involving an exploration of the context in which the affair took place in order to "re-contextualize" the offender and possibly change inaccurate attributions and re-establish predictability in the relationship (Enright et al., 1991; Gordon & Baucom, 1998, 1999). This is an important stage for both partners because it alleviates the effects of the trauma of the betrayal in the injured partner by providing a context (Horowitz, 1985; Horowitz et al., 1991, Janoff-Bulman, 1989; McCann et al., 1988), while simultaneously lessening the negative focus and blame on the other partner. Couples are ready to move into this stage when they are able to regain control of their emotions (Gordon and Baucom, 1998).

This stage allows for an exploration of any underlying problems that may have contributed to the affair or onset/relapse of the chemical addiction. Brown's (2001) five types of affairs, discussed earlier in this paper, may provide a starting point for this stage. Educating the couple on the disease model of addiction and other pertinent areas in addiction literature (i.e. the effect of addiction on the family system, enabling and co-dependency, and common relapse patterns) will also provide the couple with a context for the betrayal. Discussing external factors prompting the betrayal may also be helpful.

Treatment Goals—An important goal in the definition stage is the ability of the non-offending partner to experience and work through the negative emotions evoked by the betrayal (Gordon & Baucom, 1998; Olson, Russell, Higgins-Kessler, & Miller, 2002). Worthington, Scherer, and Cooke (2006) encourage family members of the individual with a substance use disorder to express their negative emotions and then learn to replace these with positive emotions in the forgiveness process. Along with emotional catharsis, cognitive restructuring may be employed to combat faulty assumptions and to re-establish a proper balance of power within the relationship to set the atmosphere for a safe apology and acceptance of apology (Gordon & Baucom, 1998; Schneider & Schneider, 1996).

Within the context of a couple affected by addiction, Worthington, Scherer, and Cooke (2006) term this process *meaning-focused coping strategies* and view it as a process aimed at putting an event into perspective and accepting the offense as it is. This stage, for a couple dealing with addiction, would most likely include an exploration of co-dependency and enabling as well as an exploration of the individual's addiction. A closer look into the meaning behind addiction, enabling, and the system created in the relationship can foster empathy in both partners as well as understanding, decreased guilt, and shared responsibility. The main goal here is to define the betrayal within its multi-faceted context and increase empathy in both partners in preparation for forgiveness and the moving on stage.

Treatment Obstacles—Difficulties encountered in the definition stage include resistance to exploration of the affair, lack of empathy, and reluctance to acknowledge progress. According to Worthington, Scherer, and Cooke (2006), these difficulties can also generalize to couples working through addiction and result in a stagnant state and inability to forgive. As these treatment obstacles arise, the individual struggling may benefit from referral to a separate treatment or support group to help him/her with coping skills. Struggles during this stage may also indicate that the progress from the Impact Stage to the Definition Stage happened too quickly, and the couple may benefit from readdressing some issues from the Impact Stage.

Stage 3: Moving On Stage

Stage Introduction—The third and final stage of Gordon and Baucom's (1998) forgiveness model occurs when the initial intensity of the impact has subsided and a couple is able to make the decision to forgive, acknowledging that earlier emotions may creep back into the relationship because forgiveness is a nonlinear process (Gordon & Baucom, 1998). It is important in this stage for the injured partner to relinquish the habit of looking for reasons to maintain distrust of his/her partner and instead look for reasons to trust the partner and ways in which the partner is exhibiting change. Injured partners should be encouraged to create new, healthier expectations for, standards of, and assumptions about their partners and their partners' behaviors (Gordon & Baucom, 1998). Worthington, Scherer, and Cooke (2006) emphasize committing to forgiveness and holding onto forgiveness "in the face of doubts" (p. 138). Often, in dealing with betrayals, especially in addiction when there are multiple instances of betrayal across a long span of time, it is easy to be mistrustful and forget the initial reasons for forgiveness. At times like these, it is only the commitment to holding onto forgiveness that maintains the repaired relationship.

Treatment Goals—During the Moving on Stage, a therapist should foster compassion in order to increase empathy and ease the transition to forgiveness, which may include the reintroduction of loving behaviors that may not have taken place since before the affair disclosure (Olson, Russell, Higgins-Kessler, & Miller, 2002). Worthington, Scherer, and Cooke (2006) term these loving behaviors "other-oriented emotions," in the context of forgiving a person with an alcohol problem, and include empathy, sympathy, compassion, and altruistic or romantic love. They assert that replacing negative emotions with these other-oriented emotions aids in the forgiveness process by attending to the person's positive attributes as opposed to the person's negative attributes. This is sometimes referred to as the emotional replacement model of forgiveness (Worthington, Scherer, & Cooke, 2006).

In this stage, the choice to forgive is encouraged. Worthington, Scherer, and Cooke (2006) insist that forgiveness is important not only to the transgressor but also for the forgiver because it reduces stress and increases the health of the individual. They term the former motive of forgiveness "altruistic forgiveness" because it considers the benefit to the individual forgiven. They term the latter "self-enhancement forgiveness" because it focuses on the benefits of forgiveness on the forgiver. Worthington, Scherer, and Cooke encourage altruistic over self-enhancement.

In addition, this stage marks a time for decision—will the partners choose to remain together after forgiveness or choose to separate? (Gordon & Baucom, 1998). In this decision, it is important to be mindful that forgiveness does not necessarily lead to reconciliation. In the former, the injured partner is making the decision to relinquish blame and negative feelings towards the offender that continue to produce separation between them. Reconciliation implies the commitment to stay together after forgiveness. This decision is important in working with both couples who face extramarital affairs as well as couples who face addiction. For couples that choose to remain together, Olson, Russell, Higgins-Kessler, and Miller (2002) assert that trust building must take place during this stage, which involves "reengagement, taking responsibility, reassurance of commitment, communication, and forgiveness" (p. 428). Trust building, especially in fostering healthy communication, may offer some protective factors against relapse as the couple utilizes better joint coping mechanisms to reduce triggers in the partner with a substance use disorder.

Treatment Obstacles—Problems encountered in this stage of the forgiveness model include resistance to forgive, difficulty rebuilding trust, and a decision to separate without forgiving (Gordon & Baucom, 1999). Inherent in this stage is also the fear of relapse, which in most couples with addiction has been a repeating pattern throughout their relationship. Encouraging the couple to focus on positive periods of the relationship, perhaps before the onset of the betrayal, may help individuals through this stage and foster hope for the future of the relationship. An emphasis on thoughts over feelings and the encouragement that changing behaviors and thoughts have the potential to change feelings may also be helpful during this time when negative feelings hinder the forgiveness process. Time is also an important factor, and allowing the individuals to take their time through this process and encouraging partners to be patient about this time may produce better outcomes.

Case Study

Joe, a white, middle-aged male with a diagnosis of Opioid Dependence, was admitted into a 16-week outpatient program. His wife, Mary, expressed a desire to be included in her husband's treatment, so the couple engaged in a mix of individual and couples therapy sessions throughout the course of his treatment. Individual treatment for Joe focused on relapse prevention and engagement in supportive recovery networks outside of treatment. Major themes in the couples counseling sessions revolved around trust and forgiveness. The therapist utilized the forgiveness model in conceptualizing the betrayal within the marriage and mapping a course for treatment. Mary and Joe agreed that they could conceptualize his substance abuse as a betrayal in their marriage and expressed a desire to reconcile their relationship.

Impact Stage

During the impact stage, which lasted about 10 weeks, Mary appeared consumed with the disruption in their marital relationship by Joe's dependence on oxycodone. At this stage in treatment, Mary would repeatedly bring up instances in which Joe's opioid use had rendered him incapable of contributing to his family as a father and husband, describing him as emotionally disconnected. The goals during this stage were to encourage Joe and Mary to process their feelings about the addiction and betrayals within their marriage, help them learn self-soothing techniques, and restructure unhealthy cognitive and behavioral patterns that were developed throughout the course of the addiction.

Before attempting cognitive restructuring in the impact stage, Mary was referred to Al-Anon meetings in order to learn coping skills and regain a sense of balance and stability after the betrayal. Joe worked on coping skills in individual and group therapy in the outpatient program. Once both had developed separate wellness plans, they were ready to move forward with cognitive and behavioral restructuring. During the course of the addiction, Mary lost trust in Joe and developed a checking-in pattern that Joe perceived as invasive and unnecessary. The goal for restructuring was to develop a compromise in which Mary could check-in on Joe in a way that reassured her that he was not using while allowing Joe to feel that he was not being judged or blamed. In order to accomplish this, Joe was encouraged to give Mary permission to share with him when she was worried that he was using again; and in order for Joe to feel that Mary was being loving and not blaming, she was encouraged to accept his answer to her questions, and if she had residual worries or mistrust, to channel these into her wellness plan to care for herself. Being a part of Joe's treatment and medical care also helped Mary to trust that he was going to his appointments and following through with treatment suggestions. With these measures in place, Joe and Mary were able to process their emotions surrounding the addiction in a more peaceful and loving way than they had at the beginning of treatment.

Definition Stage

The definition stage was very important for Joe and Mary, as both of them had a desire for the relationship to move past the addiction. The goal in this stage was to help the couple explore and define the context in which his addiction and betrayal occurred in order to make sense of it and to help them develop empathy for each other. Throughout treatment, Joe had a difficult time taking ownership of his addiction and making a meaningful apology to Mary. He believed that his addiction was justified and that Mary had mistrusted him for so long that apologizing to her would not change anything. When they entered treatment, their relationship had fallen into a pattern in which Mary's mistrust of Joe resulted in Joe's emotional detachment, which in turn increased Mary's mistrust because, she reported, Joe always pulled away from her when he was using. On a behavioral level, the couple was encouraged to change their routine. Joe was asked to reach out to Mary in an affectionate way whenever they were in contact. In turn, Mary was asked to continue to deal with her residual emotions through self-care. Once their routine had been established, treatment focused on how their pattern of mistrust and anger had been perpetuated through a lack of forgiveness. Mary was able to take responsibility for holding onto mistrust, and Joe was able to take responsibility for pulling away from Mary through drug use or through a lack of affection.

Once these new patterns were established, Joe and Mary were able to begin talking about the context of Joe's addiction. Joe's opioid addiction began with a pain medicine prescription following a back injury, and he eventually began abusing his prescription and getting pills from other addicted family members. Joe discussed his struggle with his addiction and his feelings that he was entitled to using pills because of the stress and strain of his job and the physical pain he underwent on a daily basis. In turn, Mary was given the opportunity to discuss her feelings of loss during his addiction and how she felt the he was emotionally detached from the family. This conversation was possible because the new patterns had broken down Joe's defensiveness and helped Mary find ways to cope outside of the relationship. In addition, Joe and Mary were able to empathize with each other within the context of the betrayal.

Moving On Stage

During the Moving on Stage, Joe and Mary decided to forgive each other, and Mary had to make the decision to stop looking for reasons to distrust Joe and question his sobriety. At this point, the couple was challenged to take the behavioral routine established in the previous stage to a new level, reincorporating spontaneity into their relationship in terms of sharing affections. Because the program was only 16 weeks, Joe and Mary were just beginning the moving on stage when Joe was discharged. Joe and Mary were referred to continued couples counseling as a part of Joe's aftercare plan, during which Joe and Mary were able to continue working through forgiveness and reconciliation. During this phase of their treatment, goals included Joe's commitment to continued sobriety, reengagement in the relationship, and trust building.

Significant treatment outcomes included Mary's self-reliance and ability to self-soothe, Joe's continued sobriety, Mary's ability to trust that her husband and recognize when she was allowing her emotions to inhibit her judgment, and a decrease in Joe's feelings of shame and an increase in his desire to show affection towards his wife without the fear of her rejection. These outcomes facilitated their forgiveness and reconciliation and will provide a healthier system to prevent falling back into old patterns that contributed to the betrayal.

Conclusion

Treatment Limitations

Because Gordon and Baucom's (1998) forgiveness model was developed specifically for treating couples suffering from an extramarital affair, there are limitations to using this model in the treatment of betrayals of chemical addiction. Some couples may be resistant to the language used in this model as it pertains to relational betrayals. In addition, this model may not be inclusive enough to address various problems besides the addiction, including domestic abuse, legal problems, and co-occurring mental illness. These issues would need to be addressed before this treatment could be implemented. The nature of chemical addiction may also present some problems, in particular, the presence of relapses, which can disrupt the process of regaining trust and developing forgiveness. It is important that the individual receive chemical addiction treatment as an adjunct to couples counseling and that the individual has a sufficient amount of clean time to enable him/her to focus on the relationship.

Implications for Future Research

The striking parallels in the experience of betrayal for couples dealing with extramarital affairs and couples dealing with chemical addiction lay a foundation for future clinical research in generalizing forgiveness models to the treatment of couples affected by the disease of addiction, and provides a framework for integrating the partners of individuals suffering from addiction in the process of recovery. It is imperative to increase the research focus to treating systems as opposed to just the individual, especially given that individuals suffering from addiction often cite marital problems as a common trigger for relapse (Epstein & McCrady, 2002; Stanton, 2005; Worthington, Scherer, & Cooke, 2006). Future research should focus on exploring similarities across betrayals in order to encourage the development of a treatment model that can be utilized in a variety of contexts for couples facing a variety of betrayals, including chemical addiction. Future research should also focus on the efficacy of the forgiveness model for treating couples presenting with relational difficulties related to chemical addiction.

Implications for Clinicians

This manuscript offers clinicians a direction in which to take couples on the journey of healing from an addiction. The need exists for more treatment models that include the non-addicted partner in the treatment process in order to heal the system as well as the individuals within the system. In treating the relationship as a vital component of addiction treatment, clinicians are also treating the individual and preventing relapse, which may also result in preventing the destruction of the relationship. When working with a couple suffering from the effects of chemical addiction, timing and knowledge of resources is very important. Beginning this work may cause an increase in stress for the couple, which may be detrimental to an individual in early recovery if he/she does not have a strong relapse prevention plan and support network. Ensuring that the individual has enough clean time and that both individuals are ready to engage in this work is pivotally important for the success of this treatment. Also, the clinician should be knowledgeable about community resources for both the individual with the addiction and his/her partner so that the clinician can refer them to support groups, twelve-step meetings, Al-Anon or co-dependency meetings, individual counseling, treatment centers, and any other resources that may be beneficial to the clients outside of couples counseling.

Hopefully, this manuscript will inspire further research into similarities across betrayals in order to encourage the development of a treatment model that can be utilized in a variety of contexts for couples facing a variety of betrayals. Of course, betrayals are vastly different, and a couple would probably not make the statement that working through an extra-marital affair is the same as working through an addiction in *content*. However, the *process* can be very much the same. Perhaps, then, there is hope for implementing a treatment across betrayals that will provide a roadmap for couples and therapists alike in traversing the journey towards forgiveness.

References

Alcoholics Anonymous World Services (2006). *Alcoholics Anonymous: The story of how many thousands of men and women have recovered from alcoholism* (4th ed.). United States of America: Alcoholics Anonymous World Services, Inc.

Brown, E. M. (2001). *Patterns of infidelity and their treatment* (2nd ed.). Ann Arbor, MI: Edwards Brothers.

Carver, C. S., Wintraub, J. K., & Scheier, M. F. (1989). Coping strategies: A theoretically based approach. *Journal of Personality and Social Psychology, 56*(2), 267-283.

Cooper, M. L., Russell, M, Skinner, J. B., & Windle, M. Development and validation of a three-dimensional measure of drinking motives. *Psychological Assessment, 4*(2), 123-132.

Dittrich J. (1993). Group programs for wives of alcoholics. In T. J. O'Farrell (ed.) *Treating Alcohol Problems: Marital and Family Interventions*. New York: Guilford Press, 1993: 78-114.

Doweiko, H. E. (2009). Addiction as a disease of the human spirit. In *Concepts of Chemical Dependency* (7th ed., pp. 36-45). Belmont, CA: Brooks/Cole, Cengage Learning.

Doweiko, H. E. (2009). Addiction and the family. In *Concepts of Chemical Dependency* (7th ed., pp. 300-308). Belmont, CA: Brooks/Cole, Cengage Learning.

Edwards, M. E., & Steinglass, P. (1995). Family therapy treatment outcomes for alcoholism. *Journal of Marital and Family Therapy, 21*, 475-509.

Enright, R. D., & The Human Development Study Group. (1991). The moral development of forgiveness. In W. Kurtines & J. Gewirtz (Eds.) *Handbook of Moral Behavior and Development*. Hillsdale, NJ: Lawrence Erlbaum Associates.

Epstein, E. E., & McCrady, B. S. (2002). Couple therapy in the treatment of alcohol problems. In A. S. Gurman & N. S. Jacobson (Eds.), *Clinical handbook of couple therapy* (3rd ed.), pp. 597–628. New York: Guilford Press.

Fals-Stewart, W., Birchler, G. R., & O'Farrell, T.J. (1996). Behavioral couples therapy for male substance-abusing patients: Effects on relationship adjustment and drug-using behavior. *Journal of Consulting and Clinical Psychology, 64*(5), 959-972.

Fisher, H., Aron, A., & Brown, L. L. (2005). Romantic love: An fMRI study of a neural mechanism for mate choice. *The Journal of Comparative Neurology, 493*, 58 62.

Gordon, K. C., & Baucom, D. H. (1998). Understanding betrayals in marriage: A synthesized model of forgiveness. *Family Process, 37*, 425-449.

Gordon, K. C., & Baucom, D. H. (1999). A multitheoretical intervention for promoting recovery from extramarital affairs. *Clinical Psychology: Science and Practice, 6*(4), 382-399.

Gordon, K. C., Baucom, D. H., & Snyder, D. K. (2004). An integrative intervention for promoting recovery from extramarital affairs. *Journal of Marital and Family Therapy, 30*(2), 213-231.

Halford, W. K., Bouma, R. O., Kelly, A., & Young, R. McD. (1999). The interaction of individual psychopathology and marital problems: Current findings and clinical implications. *Behavior Modification, 23*, 179-216.

Horowitz, M. J., (1985). Disasters and psychological responses to stress. *Psychiatric Annals, 15*(3), 161-167.

Horowitz, M. J., Stinson, C., and Field, N., (1991). Natural disasters and stress response syndromes. *Psychiatric Annals, 21*(9), 556-562.

Jacob, T., Dunn, N. J., & Leonard, K. (1983). Patterns of alcohol abuse and family stability. *Alcoholism: Clinical and Experimental Research, 7*, 382-385.

Janoff-Bulman, R., (1989). Assumptive worlds and the stress of traumatic events: Applications of the schema construct. *Social Cognition, 7*, 113-136.

Joanning, H., Quinn, T., Thomas, F., & Mullen, R. 1992. Treating adolescent drug abuse: A comparison of family systems therapy, group therapy, and family drug education. *Journal of Marital and Family Therapy, 18*, 345-356.

Keane, H. (2004). Disorders of desire: Addiction and problems of intimacy. *Journal of Medical Humanities, 25*(3), 189-204.

Longabaugh, R., Beattie, M., Noel, N., Stout, R., & Mallow, P. (1993). The effect of social investment on treatment outcome. *Journal of Studies on Alcohol, 54*(4), 465-478.

Lusterman, D. D. (1998). *Infidelity: A survival guide.* Oakland, CA: New Harbinger Publications.

McCann, I. L., Sakheim, D. K., and Abrahamson, D. J., (1988). Trauma and victimization: A model of psychological adaptation. *The Counseling Psychologist, 16*, 531-594.

McNabb, J., & DerKarabetian, A. (1989). Family involvement and outcome in treatment of alcoholism. *Psychological Reports, 65*, 1327-1330.

Miller, W. R. (1995). *Motivational enhancement therapy with drug abusers.* Albuquerque, NM: Department of Psychology and Alcoholism, Substance Abuse, and Addictions (CASAA).

O'Farrell, T. J., & Birchler, G. R. (1987). Marital relationships of alcoholic, conflicted, and non-conflicted couples. *Journal of Marital and Family Therapy, 13*, 259-274.

Olson, M. M., Russell, C. S., Higgins-Kessler, M., & Miller, R. B. (2002). Emotional processes following disclosure of an extramarital affair. *Journal of Marital and Family Therapy, 28*(4), 423-434.

Orford, J., Natera, G., Davies, J., Nava, A., Mora, J., Rigby, K., Bradbury, C., Copello, A., & Velleman, R. (1998). Stresses and strains for family members living with drinking or drug problems in England and Mexico. *Salud Mental (Mexico), 21*, 1-13.

Pascoe, W. (2001). Restoration of intimacy and connection in the treatment of couples with substance abuse issues. In B. D. Brothers (eds.) *Couples, Intimacy Issues, and Addiction.* Binghamton, NY: The Hawthorne Press, Inc.

Peele, S. (1998). *The meaning of addiction: An unconventional view.* San Francisco, CA: Jossey Bass Publishers.

Pingleton, J. P. (1989). The role and function of forgiveness in the psychotherapeutic process. *Journal of Psychology and Theology, 17*, 27-35.

Rhodes, S. (1984). Extramarital affairs: Clinical issues in therapy. *The Journal of Contemporary Social Work, 65*(9), 541-546.

Rosenau, D. E. (1998). Extramarital affairs: Therapeutic understanding and clinical interventions. *Marriage & Family: A Christian Journal, 1*(4), 355-368.

Sells, J. N., & Hargrave, T. D. (1998). Forgiveness: A review of the theoretical and empirical literature. *Journal of Family Therapy, 20*(1), 21-36.

Schneider, J. P. (1994). Sex addiction: Controversy within mainstream addiction medicine, diagnosis based on the DSM-III-R, and physician case histories. *Sexual Addiction & Compulsivity: The Journal of Treatment & Prevention, 1*(1), 19-44.

Schneider, J. P., & Schneider, B. H. (1996). Couple recovery from sexual addiction/co-addiction: Results of a survey of 88 marriages. *Sexual Addiction & Compulsivity, 3*, 111-126.

Stanton, M. (2005). Couples and addiction. In M. Harway (Ed.). *Handbook of Couples Therapy* (pp. 313-336). Hoboken, NJ: John Wiley & Sons, Inc.

Turner, M. (2009). Uncovering and treating sex addiction in couples therapy. *Journal of Family Psychotherapy, 20*(2/3), 283-302.

Winters, J., O'Farrell, T. J., Fals-Stewart, W., Birchler, G. R., & Kelley, M. L. (2002). Behavioral couples therapy for female substance-abusing patients: Effects on substance use and relationship adjustment. *Journal of Counseling and Clinical Psychology, 70*(2), 344-355.

Worthington, E. L., Jr., Scherer, M., & Cooke, K. L. (2006). Forgiveness in the treatment of persons with alcohol problems. *Alcohol Treatment Quarterly, 24*(1), 125-145.

7

Diminishing Relationship Discord While Practicing Motivational Interviewing and Cognitive Behavior Therapy

MELANIE M. IARUSSI[1]

Three case examples, derived from a phenomenological study, are presented to demonstrate how counselors might use motivational interviewing (MI) to diminish relationship discord while practicing a MI+CBT combination with clients who are experiencing substance-related problems. Specifically, these counselors' perceptions and responses to discord using MI are described.

Discord, or dissonance within the therapeutic relationship (Miller & Rollnick, 2013), is commonly encountered when working with clients who are required to seek counseling, which is often the case in addiction and offender counseling (Shearer & Ogan, 2002b). As Shearer and Ogan (2002a) noted, some clients are receptive to mandated counseling, but many are not, and counselors often pay little attention to identifying

1. Melanie M. Iarussi, Department of Special Education, Rehabilitation, and Counseling, Auburn University. Correspondence concerning this article should be addressed to Melanie M. Iarussi, Department of Special Education, Rehabilitation, and Counseling, 2084 Haley Center, Auburn University, Auburn, Alabama 36849. E-mail: miarussi@auburn.edu.

these differences. Motivational interviewing (MI), a guiding counseling style that seeks to elicit and strengthen individuals' intrinsic motivation to change, offers specific strategies to diminish discord within the therapeutic relationship and to enhance client engagement in treatment (Miller & Rollnick, 2009, 2013; Moyers & Rollnick, 2002; Westra, 2004). Specific to addiction counseling, using the MI approach to diminish discord can help improve the therapeutic relationship and clear the way for client ambivalence and motivation to be explored (Shaffer & Simoneau, 2001), as well as lead to improved client outcomes (see Miller, Benefield, & Tonigan, 1993). In regard to offender counseling, using MI has led to enhanced treatment retention, increased motivation to change, and reduced recidivism (McMurran, 2009).

Counselors who practice MI may use it in combination with other counseling therapies (Miller & Rollnick, 2004, 2009), such as cognitive behavior therapy (CBT). It has been suggested that these two approaches can produce a synergistic effect in that MI aims to establish a sound therapeutic alliance and enhance client motivation and commitment to change and CBT focuses on skills that may be necessary for clients to successfully implement and maintain change (Arkowitz & Westra, 2004; Burke, Dunn, Atkins, & Phelps, 2004). Given their complimentary foci, recent studies have suggested that the MI+CBT combination may improve client outcomes, including when treating anxiety (Kertes, Westra, Angus, & Marcus, 2011; Westra, Arkowitz, & Dozois, 2009) and co-occurring disorders (Cleary, Hunt, Matheson, & Walter, 2009). However, currently little is known about how counselors implement the MI+CBT combination. The purpose of this manuscript is to describe how relationship discord is perceived and addressed through the MI framework and to present three case examples of counselors' accounts of diminishing discord while practicing MI and CBT with clients who presented with substance-related problems.

Discord from an MI Perspective

Prior to exploring discord specifically, it is important to understand the underlying spirit with which MI is practiced. The MI spirit is described by its four components: (a) a collaborative client-counselor partnership, (b) unconditional acceptance of the client, (c) compassion for the client, and (d) a focus on client evocation (for a full description of the MI spirit see Miller & Rollnick, 2013). The MI spirit is retained throughout the therapeutic process, regardless if discord is present within the therapeutic relationship.

Due to negative connotations commonly associated with the term "resistance," Miller and Rollnick (2013) replaced this term with "discord" in the third edition of *Motivational Interviewing: Helping People Change*. They contended that the term "resistance" often places responsibility with or even blames the client for "being difficult" and it seems to mischaracterize interpersonal dynamics of the therapeutic relationship as client pathology (p. 197). Instead, in MI discord is perceived as a product of the interaction between two people, and the responsibility to recognize and respond to this relationship dissonance is placed on the counselor. MI emphasizes that counselor responses impact the presence of relationship discord, and the MI approach contains specific clinical skills to diminish discord (Miller & Moyers, 2006; Miller & Rollnick, 2013). As such, MI encourages counselors to avoid confrontation and argumentation and instead to seek understanding about the presence of discord (Arkowitz, 2002; Miller & Rollnick, 2013). Arkowitz (2002) further characterized discord as a source of information for clinicians. He suggested that discord may serve a function for clients, and the reasons for discord should be respected and explored in order to facilitate understanding about what is preventing the client from engaging in the therapeutic relationship. Miller and Rollnick (2013) suggested responding to discord with strategic reflective statements, apologizing when appropriate, affirming the client, and shifting focus in order to improve the client-counselor alliance in a manner that is consistent with the spirit of MI.

Differentiating Sustain Talk and Relationship Discord

Within the MI literature, "sustain talk," or client speech that favors the status quo and suggests ambivalence when heard with change talk, has been distinguished from "resistance" or discord (Miller, Moyers, Amrhein, & Rollnick, 2006; Miller & Rollnick, 2013). The term "sustain talk" is used to describe client speech that supports the status quo or is against change. It represents one side of ambivalence (i.e., feeling two ways about change), which is considered a natural component of the change process. On the other hand, counselors become aware of relationship discord through client behaviors such as defending, interrupting, attempting to engage in a power struggle, or disengaging from the conversation (Miller et al., 2006; Miller & Rollnick, 2013). Therefore, qualitative differences exist between client speech that suggests discord and that which characterizes ambivalence, and both may be present when working with clients. The manner in which counselors respond to sustain talk and discord is important. By reducing interpersonal dissonance and developing an effective therapeutic alliance, the counselor may provide an opportunity for the client to explore and resolve his or her ambivalence and then move in the direction of change (Shaffer & Simoneau, 2001). During this exploration of ambivalence, MI counselors intentionally and purposefully elicit and reinforce clients' reasons, needs, desires, and abilities to change to help strengthen their motivation to change. Diminishing discord, however, is oftentimes a necessary precedent to enhancing motivation to change.

Approaches to Diminishing Discord

Recognizing and responding to relationship discord is an integral component of MI, so much so that the fifth of the eight stages of learning MI is dedicated to this skill (Miller & Moyers, 2006). One strategy historically used in MI to diminish discord was described as "coming alongside" clients. This strategy was based on the belief that arguing with clients to change will lead to clients reinforcing and strengthening their counter-change arguments, resulting in clients moving further away from change and potentially damaging the therapeutic relationship (Arkowitz & Westra, 2004; Miller & Moyers, 2006; Miller & Rollnick, 2002). Therefore, counselors practicing MI refrain from arguing *for* change in order to circumvent opportunities for clients to argue *against* change. The practice of coming alongside employed empathic reflective statements to convey an understanding of the client's perspective and it is intended to diminish discord within the relationship (Miller & Rollnick, 2002). More recently, Miller and Rollnick (2013) suggested using various types of reflective statements (e.g., simple, amplified, and double-sided) in order to enhance and express understanding and to establish a working alliance. Other strategies used to diminish discord include agreeing with a twist, emphasizing autonomy, apologizing, shifting focus, reframing, and affirming the client (see Miller & Rollnick, 2013, for full descriptions). By using these MI-consistent skills, the counselor assumes a role that might be unanticipated by the client, as he or she may be accustomed to engaging in argumentation and power struggles. Thus, such responses to discord may begin the process of diminishing discord, establishing a working alliance, and setting the stage to begin exploring and strengthening the client's motivations to change.

In regard to the MI+CBT combination, Arkowitz and Miller (2008) discussed the potential for MI's approach to discord to conflict with some CBT conceptualizations of resistance, potentially causing a dissention for clinicians. Resistance is frequently considered synonymous with noncompliance in CBT, which may include not completing homework assignments, not following through on behaviors discussed in session, interrupting the clinician, and placing unreasonable demands on the clinician (Newman, 2002). CBT practitioners may attribute resistance to the client's cognitions that are creating a resistant response to the therapy process (Arkowitz & Westra, 2004; Beck, 2011; Ellis, 2005; Leahy, 2008). Therefore, in order to manage resistance, CBT counselors may help clients identify and restructure their cognitions that are interfering with the therapeutic relationship and change process. Depending on the type of CBT practiced, counselors will have varying strategies to approach resistance. For example, Ellis (1985) suggested several cognitive methods to help manage resistance (e.g., show clients "that they usually are battling you . . . because they believe that they must win, even in therapy, or will rate themselves as worthless individuals" p. 36), and other methods for specific types of clients, such as persuading involuntary clients that they can use help and "pushing and encouraging" (p. 36) depressed clients. CBT counselors who perceive clients to be reactant may implement paradoxical interventions (Brehm & Brehm, 1981; Dowd & Sanders, 1994). Other CBT practices encourage counselors to normalize reluctance to change, use reflective listening to express empathy, and provide education about what the client may expect from the CBT process (Beck, 2005; Leahy, 2003).

It becomes evident that across the scope of CBT practices, some approaches appear to be more consistent with MI than others with respect to addressing and managing discord within the therapeutic relationship. Although there is some discussion in the literature about resistance in the practice of CBT, resistance is typically not of any special focus (Arkowitz & Miller, 2008) as it is commonly assumed that clients presenting for treatment are ready to change (Arkowitz & Westra, 2004). This presents a sharp contrast to MI in which meeting clients where they are in the process of change and aiding clients in their exploration and strengthening of their personal motivations to change are defining characteristics.

As MI and CBT focus on varying aspects of the change process (Burke et al., 2004), there has been considerable discussion about the benefits of integrating MI and CBT (Arkowitz & Westra, 2004; Burke et al., 2004; Westra, 2004; Westra, et al., 2009). MI targets the "why" of change and seeks to cultivate and elicit clients' intrinsic motivation to change, whereas CBT focuses on the "how" of change and attempts to identify and alter clients' dysfunctional cognitions and behaviors and provide clients with what the therapist perceives to be lacking (e.g., coping skills, education; Burke et al., 2004; Miller & Rollnick, 2009). However, such discussions have been based primarily on speculation and reason, and little is known about how counselors actually experience this integration. The current study thus sought to investigate counselors' use of MI and CBT in their work with actual clients.

Method

The following case examples are a portion of the findings derived from a hermeneutic phenomenological study that investigated counselors' experiences of client-counselor speech, or verbal behaviors, while using MI and CBT with a select client (see Iarussi, 2011). The research question posed in this study was, "What are counselors' experiences of client and counselor language while using MI and CBT to facilitate client change?" Criterion sampling (Patton, 2002) was used to ensure participants would be able to speak in depth about the phenomenon under investigation. Participants in the study were six licensed professional counselors, three of whom described perceiving and conceptualizing discord as well as using specific strategies to diminish discord (as presented below). Two of these three participants were recruited using the snowball strategy (Polkinghorne, 2005) and one was recruited by an invitation through the Motivational Interviewing Network of Trainers professional listserv. Each participant reported being licensed as a professional counselor in his or her respective state of practice in the United States, having been trained in MI and CBT (at least 20 hours of training in each approach), using MI and CBT in his or her customary practice with clients, and conducting at least five counseling sessions in a typical week. Participants whose case examples are presented below ranged in age from early 30s to 50s and all were

Caucasian. Years of experience as a professional counselor ranged from 2–30 years, and participants ranged from 4–30 years practicing CBT and from 6 to 8 years practicing MI.

Each participant completed two individual interviews during which they discussed their experiences of using MI and CBT with a client of their choosing, and each interview was transcribed in full. Following the suggestions of van Manen (1990) for data analysis in hermeneutic phenomenological studies, wholistic, selective, and detailed analysis procedures were conducted with each transcribed interview. The researcher engaged in reflexivity, memo writing collected in an audit trail, and two sessions with a peer reviewer. Five main themes, each with at least two subthemes, resulted from this process. "Diminishing resistance" was a sub-theme housed beneath the main theme, "Counselors identify what is needed in the therapeutic relationship and then respond to meet those needs." A full description of data collection and analysis, credibility procedures, findings, and considerations can be found elsewhere (see Iarussi, 2011).

Results

The following case examples present participants' descriptions of the presence of discord within the therapeutic relationship with the clients they chose to discuss for this study. These participants then described how they interacted with their clients to diminish discord and to establish a working therapeutic relationship. Here, brief synopses of the work each participant described with a single client of his or her choosing are presented, including how each participant perceived and diminished discord and integrated MI and CBT in their work with these clients.

Case Example One

Participant 1 (P1) described his work with an adult male who was in his 50s and who had immigrated to the United States. P1 was licensed as a professional counselor and as a chemical dependency counselor, and he was working with this client at a community agency in an urban area. Per P1's description, this client had several psychiatric diagnoses including Bipolar Disorder with Psychotic features, Posttraumatic Stress Disorder, and alcohol dependence. P1 described his work with this client to address these issues along with medication compliance, poverty, homelessness, and acculturation concerns in that the client mistrusted Americans. When he was assigned to P1's caseload, the client was living in temporary housing of poor condition located in an area known for drug activity. Their work together lasted eight months, and P1 saw the client three or four times per week.

Perceiving Discord—From the client's speech, P1 interpreted that the client lacked trust in the housing and mental health systems, and he credited this mistrust to hindering the client's engagement in therapeutic work. As P1 stated:

> I realized that the system had pretty much forced him to [a major metropolitan city] against his will to begin with, so we had to begin with the premise of trust. . . . The mistrust that [he had] . . . isn't in the mistrust of the counselor, it's mistrust in the system. The system has put the recipes for their success together and says you have to do it this way or you'll never succeed but it has very little insight into what a person goes through.
>
> He had given me a play by play, blow by blow of absolutely everybody that had wronged him. . . . He had given me the names, dates, specifically what other case managers had tried to do with him, what he felt they were trying to do, and . . . it was going into his delusional complex where he thought that they were after . . . his demise.

In addition to mistrusting the systems and people who were providing the client services, P1 also described that the client mistrusted Americans in general due to difficulties with acculturation:

> There was a lot of mistrust because we [Americans] were so into material things. There was a complete utter mistrust because we ran free. Just as much as you would think that that would give him more autonomy, it actually decreased his autonomy . . . In a sense there were so many choices, he had none.

Diminishing discord—P1 reported that, when addressing the client's alcohol use, he intentionally approached the client differently than previous counselors to avoid intensifying discord: "No more reprimands. No assessment of his character, nothing like that." He also described how he approached the therapeutic relationship as a team and empathized with the client:

> I used the motivational interviewing to kind of give him an op-
> portunity to build trust. . . . I had to go in there as an open ear to
> understand and just to kind of get into his world. . . . He began to
> disclose more thinking again that I fully understood where he was
> coming from and can empathize with him. . . . So he was kind of
> more apt to listen to me, more conversationally, and it would kind
> of change his impression of me . . . [as] kind of a comrade. Which
> was the only way [I was] going to garner his trust. . . . I often call
> the client and I, when I'm working with motivational interview-
> ing, "a team."

In order to foster trust within their relationship and address the cross-cultural issues, P1 elicited information from the client about his culture and took the position of a learner to gain an understanding of the client's mistrust of Americans. P1 perceived that, "It bred tons of trust when he saw I was actually curious." P1 was also intentional about being genuine with the client on the issues of homelessness and the culture of poverty. As he described, "I can pretend like I know a culture of poverty, but that's going to come across as rather insincere. If motivational inter-viewing is ever effective it's when that counselor is sincere and trying to understand their clients."

Finally, P1 affirmed the client (an MI-consistent behavior) and ac-knowledged his strengths. As he described:

> I trumpet a lot of what I think it takes to survive homelessness.
> There's a fabric in a human being of survival that a lot of people
> who have never had to live without never have to have, and when
> you compliment their wherewithal, their ability to survive the
> worst environments man has to offer . . . you use that to empower
> them.

Affirming the client and acknowledging the strength required to survive homelessness served as another way P1 honored the client in or-der to enhance their therapeutic relationship and engage the client in the counseling process.

Integrating MI and CBT—P1 conveyed that he used MI to guide his interactions with the client in order to establish a working therapeutic relationship and enhance the client's intrinsic motivations for change. He described incorporating MI strategies including using reflections to communicate understanding and to express empathy, developing discrepancies, exploring the clients' ambivalence about change, and affirming the client. P1 described using CBT to help the client learn coping skills, further develop his social skills, and modify his problematic behaviors (e.g., alcohol use). Throughout their work together, P1 used MI+CBT in combination in that he used MI to enhance the client's engagement in treatment and to help the client prepare to make changes and then CBT when he perceived the client to be ready for implement changes. For example, P1 described developing discrepancies (a strategy commonly used in MI; Miller & Rollnick, 2002) between the client's alcohol use and his desire for employment. Upon perceiving that the client was ready to change his alcohol use behaviors, P1 discussed behavioral strategies with the client, including starting to drink later in the evening and substituting coffee for alcohol, to help the client reduce his alcohol use and enhance the likelihood of gaining employment. To address the number of issues facing this client and the client's varying degrees of readiness to change each of the target behaviors (i.e., alcohol use reduction, medication compliance), P1 described using MI and CBT in tandem, choosing strategies that matched the client's current place in the change process while maintaining the spirit of MI throughout. Overall, P1 reported witnessing significant progress with this client before their work together ended after about eight months of intensive treatment.

Case Example Two

Participant 2 (P2) was a licensed professional counselor and a licensed addictions specialist. He described his work with an adolescent Hispanic male who was referred to counseling at a substance abuse community agency after being suspended from school for using cannabis at school and for anger outbursts. Over the course of four weeks, P2 met with this client twice individually and then three times in group counseling sessions.

Perceiving Discord—Based on the client's initial presentation (e.g., closed posture) and speech (e.g., using profanity to describe referral sources), P2 interpreted the client to be "precontemplative" and "resistant" to the idea that he had a problem with cannabis and that he would benefit from counseling. P2 described his perception:

> Very closed posture. And, you know, the answer to the question, "So you've been referred by this person . . . How do you feel about this referral?" He'd [respond] in his dictionary of curse words. . . . Very, "You're not going to break me" kind of mentality. . . . So there was a good amount of resistance up front. . . . He was very precontemplative, very resistant to the fact that . . . he even had a problem let alone needing to change anything.

P2 identified threats to the client's autonomy and discrepancies between what the client and other people considered to be "the problem" as preceding factors that likely lead to the presence of discord:

> The reason for the referral stemmed from the fact that people were kind of forcing him to do stuff that he didn't want to or telling him that he had problems where he didn't believe that he did. . . . He, of course, did not believe any of it was a problem. [He] really didn't see any point to . . . talking about marijuana use or learning anything about it.

Diminishing Discord—P2 explained that he responded to his perception of discord by using reflective statements to empathize with the client's initial skepticism of the counseling process. From P2's perspective, this helped to "break the ice or allow him to then say, 'Yeah, I feel like you're getting it.'" P2 further described how he conducted the MI sessions to mitigate discord by expressing empathy and eliciting from the client what he saw as potential problems with his cannabis use:

> Just talking to him and kind of processing the fact that he was angry at everybody, you know. One, reflecting just how it was normal and validating that it was normal to be very upset about . . . people forcing him to be somewhere that's uncomfortable. . . . And using motivational interviewing and the skills of motivational interviewing were very helpful and having a different approach with him and actually having someone ask him . . . "What do you enjoy about smoking marijuana?" but also validating that yes, it is enjoyable and it's normal to like that kind of stuff. . . . [I said] "Help me understand better . . . What works with the marijuana and what are some issues you're having?"

P2 described the client's response to his use of MI as, "Then he opened up. . . . He didn't need to defend himself. He was just kind of free to talk, and [I was] there to support him regardless of what he was doing." P2 interpreted the client's response to indicate that the client "felt like he was being heard as opposed to being told what to do or why he needed to do something." P2 noted his perception that the initial discord was a product of the client's previous interactions with other people, and his goal was to invite the client "to take that space to discuss it and to explore it without being told that this is right or wrong." By being given the opportunity to explore the issues for himself, the client was able to identify what he believed were some negative aspects of using cannabis. As P2 described, "He was resistant to what other people were saying, but the [problems] that were his, he had it. But he didn't really connect it due to being told so often what the problems were with marijuana." In taking this approach, the client began to discuss problems in his relationship with his girlfriend and with school that were related to his cannabis use. P2 described that eventually, the client began "to get the insight of maybe the fact that I smoke marijuana and that I'm different when I do, that's what's causing the problem."

P2 also described how he focused on eliciting the client's goals for treatment, as opposed to adopting the goal of abstinence from the referral source:

> Instead of telling him what the risks were, what issues he was having, [I was] using again the skills of asking him what he thought were some of the things. . . . Honing in on the goals [the client] had in mind as opposed to imposing the more abstinence-based goal on [him]. . . . Abstinence is not our ultimate goal, although that may be the goal that [referral sources] may have or that the school may have. . . . So abstinence by no means was the goal. It was, "What is this person, where are they at, what are they willing to change, how will they get the skills to do it?"

Integrating MI and CBT—P2 reported using the Cannabis Youth Treatment (CYT; Sampl & Kadden, 2001) protocol to guide his work with this client. The CYT protocol included two individual MI sessions that focused on enhancing motivation to change followed by three CBT group sessions in which the spirit of MI was retained. The two MI sessions took place within the same week and were each 30 to 40 minutes long. The three CBT group sessions began the week following the MI sessions, occurred on a weekly basis, and were each 75 minutes long. A face-to-face follow-up assessment was conducted 90 days following the final CBT group session.

P2 reported that by the close of two MI sessions, the client was engaged in the counseling process, he had identified problems with his cannabis use as he saw them (e.g., conflicts with his girlfriend, school suspensions), he developed his own goals for counseling including abstaining from using while at school and reducing overall use, and he committed to participating in the three CBT group sessions to attain refusal and assertiveness skills to help him reach his goals. P2 described his belief that learning refusal and assertiveness skills in CBT group counseling sessions would assist this client meet his goal of abstaining from cannabis use while at school. At the 90-day follow-up assessment, the client reported sustained behavior changes including not having been suspended from school for using cannabis and overall reductions in use.

Case Example Three

Participant 3 (P3) was a licensed professional counselor and a certified alcohol and drug counselor. P3 described her use of MI and CBT with an adolescent White male who was referred to counseling by school officials after the client consumed alcohol at a school function. In addition to alcohol use, P3 described this client's issues to include depression, anger, family conflicts, and having bigoted beliefs which he described using offensive language. P3 reported she worked with this client for approximately two years in a private practice setting where she saw this client on a weekly basis except during the summers when they met every other week.

Perceiving Discord—Upon their first meeting, P3 interpreted the client to be "guarded" after hearing the negative language he used to describe his previous therapists and his feelings about counseling. She decided to use "straight MI" to engage the client in the counseling process and build a therapeutic relationship. P3 described her interpretation of discord in the relationship and her intended response to diminish it:

> When he first came he was very guarded, very angry, frustrated it was a mandated assessment from the school. He had other experiences with therapists and he related them to me saying all therapists were idiots, and he used a different term, and I'm not going to say that term, but he was very negative about the counseling experience. And so I just thought I had to do straight engagement. MI is the most effective because I'm just going to honor where he

is at and not push anything else on him. . . . Because I knew that if I did anything that was in any way confrontative or me leading the conversation, he would've run away.

Diminishing Discord—Given her interpretation of discord within the therapeutic relationship, P3 decided to use MI in an attempt to reduce dissonance and engage the client in the counseling process. P3 described her use of MI-consistent language and the client's response to her efforts:

Every time that I put it back in his lap, he physically would relax. . . . Every time I would reflect back his statements or even ask him open-ended questions about what he just talked about, it was "She hears me," "She gets me," "She hears me," and he would come in tightly wound and sitting very straight and by the end of the session he would always be a little bit loungy, more like an adolescent draping himself on furniture. . . . He would always give me a little bit more every session. A little bit more about the full story. And so it was almost like unwrapping an onion with him in that he gave me the rough terrible outside, that prickly paper that was really caustic, and I unwrapped it with him and he gave me little pieces here and there.

Integrating MI and CBT—After approximately four months of practicing MI with this client, P3 heard the client verbalize his own, intrinsic reasons to change which included no longer wanting to feel depressed and expressing his discontent with the lack of diversity among his friends. P3 interpreted the client's speech to suggest that he was ready to begin challenging and modifying his beliefs that were leading to problematic behaviors. P3 used CBT to assist the client in making these changes, but she retained the MI style and emphasized the client's personal choice and control to ensure they were moving at the client's pace and that he remained engaged in the counseling process. By the time she terminated treatment with this client, P3 reported he had made significant changes, including modified beliefs about diverse persons, improved relationships with his parents, and abstaining from substance use. P3 also conveyed that he appeared to transform into a "relaxed" and "comfortable" young man.

Discussion

These case examples were extracted from a hermeneutic phenomenological study that investigated counselors' experiences of client-counselor verbal behavior while practicing MI and CBT. All three of these participants explicitly described using MI alone to diminish discord and develop a working therapeutic relationship. With their adolescent male clients, P2 and P3 described their use of MI to diminish discord and enhance client engagement in the counseling process. They both described using reflective statements to express empathy and then they elicited the clients' perspectives about their situations. Although their clients presented with different issues and participated in different treatment, discord was diminished in both relationships and the clients reportedly became engaged in the counseling process. In addition, according to the narrative accounts of P2 and P3, both clients made significant progress on their presenting issues and completed treatment. Similarly, P1 described using MI to express empathy and to develop trust with his client. P1 also reported promoting his client's autonomy, affirming the client, and truly attempting to get a sense of what it might be like to be in this client's shoes. P1 indicated that he was able to establish trust and develop a therapeutic relationship with his client. These participants' accounts of using MI are consistent with previous literature that has recommended using MI to manage discord (Arkowitz, 2002; Moyers & Rollnick, 2002; Westra, 2004) and to enhance client engagement in the counseling process (Moyers, Miller, & Hendrickson, 2005). As P3 stated, "MI is so incredible for engagement and honoring the client."

Differentiating Sustain Talk and Discord

These three participants' descriptions supported the distinction between sustain talk and discord (Miller et al., 2006; Miller & Rollnick, 2013). P2 and P3, who both described their work with adolescent males who were referred to counseling by their schools for substance–related infractions, described discord that was communicated verbally and nonverbally. These participants interpreted closed posture, guardedness, and use of profanity to describe their referral sources and previous therapists as discord as well as their clients' expressions of anger due to having to attend counseling sessions. On the other hand, sustain talk was described by participants as client statements that were the opposite of change talk (e.g., speaking against change or promoting the status quo) and were spoken when the clients were giving voice to their ambivalence. For example, P2's client demonstrated sustain talk when he discussed the benefits he experienced from cannabis use and when he described the reasons he used which were related to the drug-promoting culture of his peers. In general, participants interpreted the presence of sustain talk along with change talk as evidence of the client's ambivalence or internal conflict of feeling two ways about change. Overall, participants interpreted discord as clients saying, "I don't want to be here," whereas sustain talk was interpreted as the opposing side of ambivalence and a natural aspect of the change process.

MI and CBT: Complementary Approaches

Kertes et al. (2011) investigated client experiences of MI and CBT and found that four of the five clients who experienced MI and CBT described the two approaches as complementary and to have worked well together to facilitate change. Participants in Kertes et al.'s study described how MI helped them prepare for change and CBT provided assistance in implementing change. Although the case examples presented here describe the counselors' experiences and not those of the clients, they are consistent with the findings of Kertes et al. in that these counselors described using MI to diminish discord, establish a therapeutic relationship, and enhance client readiness and commitment to change and then they used CBT to help clients implement change.

Even after using MI and clients possess a sufficient amount of motivation to change, in many cases another treatment is needed in order for clients to understand how to change (Miller & Rollnick, 2009). These three case examples portrayed several examples of Burke et al.'s (2004) explanation that MI and CBT may be used together to help facilitate change in that MI can help clients answer the question, "Why might I change?" whereas CBT targets clients' question, "How do I change?" For example, P2 explained that he believed in MI's usefulness to enhance client motivation to change, but noted that his client would have been "left hanging" if treatment had been terminated after the two MI sessions without giving the client an opportunity to learn and practice refusal and assertiveness skills through the course of three CBT group sessions. P2 also noted his belief that his client would not have been engaged in the CBT sessions had MI not been used first to diminish discord, foster client engagement in counseling, and enhance the client's intrinsic motivation and commitment to change. In another example, P1 helped his client realize the conflict between his heavy alcohol use and his desire for employment. By discussing these discrepancies with the client, the client developed his own reasons and motivation for wanting to change his drinking. This enhanced motivation in-of-itself, however, would be insufficient for successful behavior change. Thus, P1 then helped the client develop plans for how, specifically, to change his drinking behaviors using CBT methods. These examples illustrate how a combination of MI+CBT can be useful to clients, as had one approach or the other not been implements, client outcomes may have suffered.

Implications, Considerations, and Future Directions

Diminishing discord and enhancing client engagement are common challenges for counselors, especially those who work with involuntary clients in addiction and offender counseling. MI is an approach that can help counselors accomplish these tasks to increase the likelihood of positive client outcomes. In addition, many counselors currently practice CBT when working with these populations and adding MI may be a valuable addition to their repertoire of skills, especially considering the preliminary evidence that a synergistic effect may occur when MI and CBT are paired. As noted by the participants of this study and by previous literature, clients may not reach their full potential in counseling if they are not given the opportunity to explore their own, personal motivations for change in a dissonance-free environment prior to being taught cognitive and behavioral skills with the expectation of implementing changes. Further, these case examples demonstrate the use of MI+CBT with ethnically diverse clients and clients of various ages (e.g., adolescents and adults).

These case examples provide a sample of how counselors might implement MI upon their perception of discord and subsequently incorporate CBT when practicing an MI+CBT combination in a variety of settings (community agencies, private practice). A specific type of psychotherapy integration for this combination has yet to be defined; however, consistent with these participants' accounts, recent literature has described implementing MI to address client readiness to change prior to incorporating CBT (often retaining the spirit of MI) to help clients implement change (Arkowitz & Westra, 2004; Burke et al., 2004). Counselors may also use MI during therapy when client motivation appears to wane. As such, a strength of MI may be its versatility for use with CBT and other approaches in various ways. Constantino, DeGeorge, Dadlani, and Overtree (2009) proposed that MI may be "a bellwether for context-responsive psychotherapy integration" (p. 1246), a type of psychotherapy integration wherein counselors shift between MI and other therapies as they see fit based on client needs and the limitations of other therapies. More research is needed to understand the counselor process of practicing an MI+CBT combination, including understanding how and when counselors make decisions to transition between or to integrate the two approaches.

A consideration of the study from which these case examples were derived includes that participants chose a client case that they wished to describe. It may be anticipated that participants chose to discuss their work with a client that was meaningful to them or that they believed illustrated their best work using MI and CBT. Participants' accounts of client success and progress are presented from the participants' subjective perspectives. Future research might compare counselor and client perspectives of the MI+CBT combination.

Another area of research lies in identifying effective pedagogical practices to teach counselors the MI+CBT combination. As noted by Arkowitz and Miller (2008), counselors currently practicing CBT might struggle with adopting some of the MI practices. Such learning may include not only learning MI-consistent behaviors, but also diminishing behaviors that conflict with MI (e.g., confrontation, providing unsolicited advice without client permission). Research is need to delineate effective ways to help counselors who currently practice CBT retain this practice, yet modify their behaviors as needed to incorporate the MI approach when appropriate. Further, research is needed to inform pedagogical practices of the MI+CBT combinations for counselors-in-training.

Overall, using MI to diminish relationship discord and practicing the MI+CBT combination with substance abusing clientele appears to have promising results. The current manuscript presented three case examples from a qualitative study to demonstrate how this might be accomplished. More attention is needed to further understand how counselors might learn and practice an integration of these two therapies.

References

Arkowitz, H. (2002). Toward on integrative perspective on resistance to change. *Journal of Clinical Psychology/In Session, 58,* 219–227.

Arkowitz, H., & Miller, W. R. (2008). Learning, applying, and extending motivational interviewing. In H. Arkowitz, H. A. Westra, W. R. Miller, & S. Rollnick (Eds.), *Motivational interviewing in the treatment of psychological problems* (pp. 1–25). New York: Guilford Press.

Arkowitz, H., & Westra, H. A. (2004). Integrating motivational interviewing and cognitive behavioral therapy in the treatment of depression and anxiety. *Journal of Cognitive Psychotherapy, 18,* 337–350.

Beck, J. S. (2005). *Cognitive therapy for challenging problems: What to do when the basics don't work.* New York: Guilford Press.

Beck, J. S. (2011). *Cognitive therapy: Basics and beyond* (2nd ed.). New York, NY: Guilford Press.

Brehm, S. S., & Brehm, J. W. (1981). *Psychological reactance: A theory of freedom and control.* Orlando, FL: Academic Press.

Burke, B. L., Dunn, C. W., Atkins, D. C., & Phelps, J. S. (2004). The emerging evidence base of motivational interviewing: A meta-analytic and qualitative inquiry. *Journal of Cognitive Psychotherapy: An International Quarterly, 18,* 309-322.

Cleary, M., Hunt, G. E., Matheson, S., & Walter, G. (2009). Psychosocial treatments for people with co-occurring severe mental illness and substance misuse: systematic review. *Journal of Advanced Nursing, 65,* 238-258.

Constantino, M. J., DeGeorge, J., Dadlani, M. B., & Overtree, C. E. (2009). Motivational interviewing: A bellwether for context-responsive psychotherapy integration. *Journal of Clinical Psychology, 65,* 1246-1253.

Dowd, E. T., & Sanders, D. (1994). Resistance, reactance, and the difficult client. *Canadian Journal of Counseling, 28,* 13–24.

Ellis, A. (1985). Approaches to overcoming resistance: IV. Handling special kinds of clients. *British Journal of Cognitive Psychotherapy, 3,* 26-42.

Ellis, A. (2005). Rational emotive behavior therapy. In R. J. Corsini & D. Wedding (Eds.), *Current psychotherapies* (7th ed., pp. 166–201). Belmont, CA: Brooks/Cole.

Iarussi, M. (2011). *Counselors' experiences of client and counselor language while using motivational interviewing and cognitive behavior therapy to facilitate client change* (Doctoral dissertation). Retrieved from http://etd.ohiolink.edu

Kertes, A., Westra, H. A., Angus, L., & Marcus, M. (2011). The impact of motivational interviewing on client experiences of cognitive behavioral therapy for generalized anxiety disorder. *Cognitive and Behavioral Practice, 18,* 55-69.

Leahy, R. L. (2003). *Cognitive therapy techniques: A practitioner's guide.* New York: Guilford.

Leahy, R. L. (2008). The therapeutic relationship in cognitive-behavioral therapy. *Behavioural and Cognitive Psychotherapy, 36,* 769–777.

McMurran, M. (2009). Motivational interviewing with offenders: A systemic review. *Legal and Criminological Psychology, 14,* 83-100.

Miller, W. R., Benefield, R. G., & Tonigan, J. S. (1993). Enhancing motivation for change in problem drinking: A controlled comparison of two therapist styles. *Journal of Consulting and Clinical Psychology, 61,* 455-461.

Miller, W. R., & Moyers, T. B. (2006). Eight stages in learning motivational interviewing. *Journal of Teaching in the Addictions, 5*, 3–17.

Miller, W. R., Moyers, T. B., Amrhein, P., & Rollnick, S. (2006). A consensus statement on defining change talk. *MINT Bulletin, 13*(2), 6–7. Retrieved from http://motivationalinterview.net/mint/MINT13.2.pdf

Miller, W. R., & Rollnick, S. (2002). *Motivational interviewing: Preparing people to change* (2nd ed.). New York, NY: Guilford Press.

Miller, W. R., & Rollnick, S. (2004). Talking oneself into change: Motivational interviewing, stages of change, and therapeutic process. *Journal of Cognitive Psychotherapy: An international quarterly, 18*, 299–308.

Miller, W. R., & Rollnick, S. (2009). Ten things that motivational interviewing is not. *Behavioural and Cognitive Psychotherapy, 37*, 129-140.

Miller, W. R., & Rollnick, S. (2013). *Motivational interviewing: Helping people change* (3rd ed.). New York, NY: Guilford Press.

Moyers, T. B., Miller, W. R., & Hendrickson, S. M. L. (2005). How does motivational interviewing work? Therapist interpersonal skill predicts client involvement within motivational interviewing sessions. *Journal of Consulting and Clinical Psychology, 73*, 590-598.

Moyers, T. B., & Rollnick, S. (2002). A motivational interviewing perspective on resistance in psychotherapy. *Journal of Clinical Psychology/In Session: Psychotherapy in Practice, 58*, 185–193.

Newman, C. F. (2002). A cognitive perspective on resistance in psychotherapy. *Journal of Clinical Psychology, 58*, 165–174.

Patton, M. Q. (2002). *Qualitative research & evaluation methods* (3rd ed.). Thousand Oaks, CA: Sage.

Polkinghorne, D. E. (2005). Language and meaning: Data collection in qualitative research. *Journal of Counseling Psychology, 52*, 137-145.

Sampl, S., & Kadden, R. (2001). *Motivational enhancement therapy and cognitive behavioral therapy for adolescent cannabis users: 5 sessions, Cannabis Youth Treatment (CYT) Series, Volume 1*. Rockville, MD: Center for Substance Abuse Treatment, Substance Abuse and Mental Health services Administration.

Shaffer, H. J., & Simoneau, G. (2001). Reducing resistance and denial by exercising ambivalence during the treatment of addiction. *Journal of Substance Abuse Treatment, 20*(1), 99-105.

Shearer, R. A., & Ogan, G. D. (2002a). Measuring treatment resistance in offender counseling. *Journal of Addictions & Offender Counseling, 22*, 72-82.

Shearer, R. A., & Ogan, G. D. (2002b). Voluntary participation and treatment resistance in substance abuse treatment programs. *Journal of Offender Rehabilitation, 34*(3), 31-45.

Van Manen, M. (1990). *Researching lived experience: Human science for an action sensitive pedagogy*. Ontario, Canada: University of Western Ontario.

Westra, H. A. (2004). Managing resistance in cognitive behavioural therapy: The application of motivational interviewing in mixed anxiety and depression. *Cognitive Behaviour Therapy, 33*(4), 161–175.

Westra, H. A., Arkowitz, H., & Dozois, D. J. A. (2009). Adding a motivational interviewing pretreatment to cognitive behavioral therapy for generalized anxiety disorder: A preliminary randomized controlled trial. *Journal of Anxiety Disorders, 23*(8), 1106-1117.

8

Treatment of Alcohol Abuse among College Students

A New Look at REBT

EDWARD WAHESH AND JANE E. MYERS[1]

College student drinking interventions often fail due to psychosocial factors (e.g., identity development factors and social norms compliance) that contribute to irrational thinking. REBT offers methods for addressing irrational beliefs that can help prevent and treat alcohol abuse on college campuses.

The abuse of alcohol and other drugs on college campuses continues to be a problem for counselors, administrators, and health educators, and has been defined as a critical public health issue (National Institute on Alcohol Abuse and Alcoholism, 2007). According to the Core Institute (2008), over 46% of college students reported binge drinking in the previous two weeks. This alcohol abuse has resulted in a myriad of problems such as impaired driving, injury (Wechsler et al., 2002) and death (Hingson, Heeren, Winter, & Wechsler, 2005). The Substance Abuse and Mental Health Services Administration's National Survey on Drug Use

1. Edward Wahesh and Jane E. Myers, Department of Counseling and Educational Development, The University of North Carolina at Greensboro. Correspondence concerning this manuscript should be addressed to Edward Wahesh, Department of Counseling and Educational Development, The University of North Carolina at Greensboro, P.O. Box 26170 Greensboro, NC 27402. Email: e_wahesh@uncg.edu.

and Health (SAMHSA, 2010) found that the rates of alcohol abuse and dependence were highest among the traditional college age population (e.g., 18–25). Additionally, the rates of alcohol abuse among the next generation of college students strongly suggest that this will be a continuing challenge for counselors. Among the 1.8 million youths (age 12–17) who needed treatment for an alcohol or drug problem, only 150,000 received treatment (SAMHSA, 2010).

Commonly used approaches to prevent and treat alcohol abuse, such as Brief Alcohol Screening Intervention with College Students (Dimeff, Baer, Kivlahan, & Marlatt, 1999) and other multi-component brief motivational interventions (Carey, Henson, Carey, & Maisto, 2009), hold promise but have limited effectiveness (White, Mun, Pugh, & Morgan, 2007). In a meta-analytic review of brief interventions to reduce student drinking, Carey, Scott-Sheldon, Carey, and DeMartini (2007) found that these interventions were less effective with high-risk populations and recommended the development of interventions that addressed the core beliefs and values associated with substance use. Among college students, these core beliefs are understood in the context of social norms theory (Berkowitz, 2004), alcohol outcome expectancies (Sher, Wood, Wood, & Raskin, 1996), and psychosocial (i.e., identity) development. These factors may contribute to the development of inflexible and irrational beliefs related to alcohol abuse by college students.

Rational-Emotive Behavioral Therapy (REBT; Ellis, 1994), a model of cognitive-behavioral psychotherapy rooted in irrational thinking, has been shown to be effective with a variety of populations and diagnoses (David, Szentagotai, Eva, & Macavei, 2005; Gonzalez et al., 2004), and has been demonstrated by some REBT researchers to be more efficacious than other cognitive behavioral approaches (David et al., 2005). The scope of REBT research and replications of findings across cultures (e.g., Lega & Ellis, 2001) suggest that this approach has strong potential for applications with any disorders for which cognitive distortions may play a role in the development or perpetuation of the condition. Despite a paucity of research with college student alcohol abusers, the core theoretical principles of REBT present a compelling understanding of how to treat substance abuse disorders. Counselors working from a REBT framework can assist clients in exploring and challenging their underlying irrational beliefs that contribute to abuse.

In this paper, we discuss the dynamics and challenges of alcohol abuse among college students, including trends, psychosocial factors that contribute to abuse, and preferred interventions. REBT is briefly explained as a potentially effective paradigm for interventions with this population, and research related to REBT and alcohol abuse is explored. A case study demonstrating the application of REBT with a college student struggling with alcohol abuse is presented. Implications for counselors and for further research are discussed.

College Student Alcohol Abuse

Trends in College Student Drinking

The rates of alcohol abuse on college campuses in the United States remain relatively unchanged despite increased efforts in prevention and treatment (NIAAA, 2007). Wechsler et al. (2002) found no difference in the rate of binge drinking (consuming five drinks in a row for men, four drinks in a row for women) among college students compared to surveys conducted in 1993, 1997 and 1999. Factors such as race and gender are related to alcohol abuse among young adults entering college (Borsari, Murphy, & Barnett, 2007; Dowdall & Wechsler, 2002). For example, O'Malley and Johnston (2002) found that male Caucasian students drink the most. Hispanic students follow Caucasian students with African American students drinking the least (O'Malley & Johnston). Rates of alcohol-related negative consequences have been found to correspond with patterns of consumption by race (e.g., Caucasian students experience the most negative consequences, African American students experience the fewest; O'Malley & Johnston).

The rates of alcohol-related negative consequences experienced by college student drinkers are alarming. Hinsgon (2010) reported that 1,825 college students died from alcohol related unintentional injuries in 2005. According to the Core Institute (2008), over 22% of college students reported that they had driven a car while under the influence and 31% reported that they had a fight or argument while impaired. The frequency of reported negative consequences appears to be associated with increased consumption of alcohol. In a national sample of college students, Presley and Pimentel (2006) found that students who engaged in heavy and frequent binge drinking, defined as consuming five or more drinks on three or more days per week, made up a small percentage of total drinkers (15.4%) but experienced nearly half of all reported negative consequences (45.2%).

Although male college students reported greater use of alcohol (O'Malley & Johnston, 2002), the rates of alcohol-related consequences differ by gender. Howard, Griffin, and Boekeloo (2008) found that women reported higher prevalence of alcohol-related sexual assault than men did in a sample of 551 undergraduate students. Differences in body size, physiological composition, and metabolism place women at greater risk for alcohol-induced blackouts (White, Jamieson-Drake, & Swartzweider, 2002) and other physical consequences. In a study of alcohol-related negative consequences and gender with a sample of 1,331 college students, Sugarman, DeMartini, and Carey (2009) found that female students compared to their male counterparts were more likely to have reported alcohol-related problems such as developing tolerance, passing out, and injury. The differences in alcohol use and associated negative consequences among college students are influenced by psychosocial, environmental, and developmental factors.

Psychosocial Factors that Contribute to College Student Drinking

The psychosocial development of college students also sheds light on why alcohol abuse is a persistent problem on college campuses. A variety of theories have been proposed to explain the dynamics of this developmental period. These include theories of individual and cognitive-emotional development (e.g., Chickering & Reisser, 1993), alcohol outcome expectancies (Sher, Wood, Wood, & Raskin, 1996), and social norms theory (Berkowitz, 2004). Common to all of these theories is an emphasis on information processing, belief systems, and the strong influence of relationship factors.

Chickering and Reisser (1993) proposed that the major developmental tasks of the college years are developing competence, managing emotions, moving through autonomy toward interdependence, developing mature interpersonal relationships, establishing identity, developing purpose, and developing integrity. Substance use can be viewed within the context of testing limits and experimentation with one's self and self-management abilities. As students develop these skills, they may use alcohol to cope with negative moods and emotions and establish a sense of autonomy (Armeli, Todd, Conner, & Tennen, 2008; Borsari, Murphy, & Barnett, 2007) which may lead to long-term patterns of abuse. Students also may use alcohol to assist in developing relationships with peers (Stewart, Morris, Mellings, & Komar, 2006). In a study of 4,428 alumni from a large, Midwestern, public university, Demb and Campbell (2009) found that students who continued to abuse alcohol after college were more likely than those whose use decreased into adulthood to report that they used alcohol for developmental needs such as increasing self-confidence and coping with personal problems.

Theories of alcohol outcome expectancies help explain the etiology of these alcohol abuse patterns (Sher, Wood, Wood, & Raskin, 1996). Beliefs that alcohol will reduce tension, enhance activities, decrease shyness, and enhance performance, have been shown to predict college student alcohol use (Sher et al., 1996). Further, Kassel, Bornovalova, and Mehta (2007) found that negative mood regulation expectancies significantly predicted problem drinking.

College student beliefs about the intensity of drinking by their peers (Berkowitz, 2004) have also been shown to predict use among this population. According to social norms theory, college students overestimate the norms of alcohol use by their peers, thereby influencing their own personal use (Berkowitz, 2004). Students overestimate the use of others because behavior associated with excessive alcohol use is highly visible and often discussed among the student body (Berkowitz, 2004). As students misjudge the amount of alcohol use by their peers, they increase their own use so it adheres to the perceived norms.

Neighbors, Lee, Lewis, Fossos, and Larimer (2007) described two categories of normative beliefs held by college students. Injunctive norms refer to the perception of acceptability of excessive alcohol consumption of others and descriptive norms refer to the perception of the quantity and frequency of alcohol use of others. In a meta-analysis of 23 studies of social norms, Borsari and Carey (2003) found that injunctive normative beliefs were more likely than descriptive norms to predict drinking behavior and alcohol-related negative consequences. Injunctive beliefs are a powerful motivator because of the anticipated consequences associated with conforming or not conforming to the norms. Students may believe that their use must be consistent with the misperceived expectations of their peer group or they will be ostracized.

The level of influence due to the misperception of alcohol use becomes progressively greater as proximity (e.g., from all college students to close friends or teammates) of the reference group increases (Borsari & Carey, 2003). Labrie, Hummer, Neighbors, and Larimer (2010) found that among 3753 students surveyed on two different west coast colleges, perceived injunctive norms of close friends significantly predicted alcohol-related negative consequences. The influence of these misperceptions also is stronger among same sex groups (Neighbors, Lee, Lewis, Fossos, & Larimer, 2007).

Consistent with the tenets of social norms theory, the environment college students reside in may be a key contributor to the prevalence of alcohol abuse. In a study of alcohol use at eight universities, Weitzman, Folkman, Lemieux Folkman, and Wechsler (2003) found that alcohol retail outlet density and proximity was correlated with heavy drinking, frequent drinking, and drinking-related problems. Johnson, O'Malley, Bachman, and Schulenberg (2009) found that college students had higher rates of alcohol use compared to their peers not enrolled in college. Young adults enrolled in college may consume substances at higher rates because they view college as a break from the "real world" characterized by having less responsibility and more freedom (Colby, Colby, & Raymond, 2009). By perceiving college as a time to enjoy life before entering traditional adult roles, rigid beliefs held by students concerning the need to engage in high-risk behaviors for short-term benefits are reinforced and normalized. These beliefs affect participation in as well as the potential success of programs designed to prevent and treat college student drinking.

Prevention and Treatment of College Student Drinking

Promising treatment interventions developed to address the alcohol epidemic on college campuses have incorporated elements of cognitive-behavioral therapy with some but limited success (Larimer & Cronce, 2007). The Brief Alcohol Screening Intervention for College Students (BASICS) combines elements of cognitive-behavioral therapy (Marlatt, 2005), Motivational Interviewing (Miller & Rollnick, 2002), and personalized normative feedback into a brief program (Dimeff, Baer, Kivlahan, & Marlatt, 1999). In a meta-analytic review of 62 empirical studies on individual-focused college drinking interventions, Carey, Scott-Sheldon, Carey, and DeMartini (2007) found that risk reduction interventions that employ a cognitive-behavioral approach to treatment succeed in reducing high-risk drinking and alcohol-related negative consequences. However, these authors also reported that the magnitude of the effect size diminished over time and that these interventions were less successful with heavy drinkers or other high-risk groups, such as Greeks and student-athletes, due to "core beliefs, values, and norms" (p. 2488) held by these students. These limitations indicate the need for new treatment approaches that address the core beliefs held by high-risk users. Rational Emotive Behavior Therapy (REBT) is a promising evidence-based approach which is widely taught in counselor training programs, yet has had limited application to date with the problem of college student alcohol abuse.

Rational Emotive Behavioral Therapy

Rational Emotive Behavior Therapy (REBT), a form of cognitive behavioral counseling, was created by Albert Ellis in the 1950s (Ellis, 1997). Consistent with other cognitive behavioral approaches, REBT is a brief therapeutic intervention (Ellis, 1995). REBT is grounded in humanism in that it helps people maximize their individuality, freedom, and self-control by disputing and changing irrational beliefs (Dryden & David, 2008). Ellis (1976) believed that all humans have the tendency to think irrationally by holding rigid evaluative beliefs about oneself, others, and the world. Multiple studies across populations have established the validity of the model and the concept of irrational thoughts (David, Szentagotai, Eva, & Macavei, 2005).

The REBT "ABCDE" Model

The cornerstone of REBT is the "ABCDE" model developed by Ellis to explain how faulty thinking drives emotional disturbances (Ellis, 1994). According to this model, when an activating event or experience (A) occurs, a person will have either a rational or an irrational belief (B) about it. If the belief about the event is irrational, the person will experience dysfunctional behavioral and emotional consequences (C). These consequences can then result in new activating (A) events producing secondary disturbances. For example, a client is dumped by his girlfriend (A) and decides to cope with his intense feelings of hopelessness by abusing alcohol (C). The irrational beliefs (B) that the client holds (e.g., I am unlovable, I am a complete loser) produces the unproductive behavior and emotional response, not the activating event itself. REBT counselors encourage clients to dispute (D) and challenge the irrational beliefs (e.g., I am not worthless) in order to replace them with more efficient (E) or adaptive beliefs (e.g., there are plenty of fish in the sea) that result in more productive emotional, cognitive and behavioral responses (Ellis, 1994).

Irrational Beliefs

The concept of irrational beliefs and how they lead to disturbance has evolved since the initial development and practice of REBT. Irrational beliefs are understood now as falling in four categories of cognitive processes: demandingness, awfulizing/catastrophizing, global evaluation/self-downing, and low frustration tolerance (DiGiuseppe, 1996). Demandingness refers to rigid absolutistic thinking that is expressed by "musts," "shoulds," and "oughts." Ellis argued that all processes of irrational thinking are derived from demandingness (Ellis, 1997). Awfulizing or catastrophizing refers to evaluating an experience as more than 100% bad or worse (Lega & Ellis, 2001). Global evaluation/self-downing is the tendency to be overly self-critical or critical of others. Low frustration tolerance overemphasizes discomfort and maintains that frustration is impossible to bear (DiGiuseppe, 1996). Through the disputing process, individuals can be helped to replace dysfunctional irrational beliefs with functional rational beliefs. This more realistic and flexible way of thinking produces greater acceptance of self, others and life (Dryden & David, 2008).

Empirical Support for REBT

The REBT core belief that irrational thinking contributes to psychological distress has been supported in multiple studies. For example, Harris, Davies and Dryden (2006) conducted experiments that placed participants in real life stressful situations holding either a rational, irrational or a neutral belief. They found that those holding an irrational belief reported the greatest increase in anxiety and showed an increase in systolic blood pressure (Harris et al., 2006). Davies (2008) found that participants who were asked to study rational beliefs in an experimental setting reported an increase in unconditional self-acceptance when surveyed. Participants who were primed using irrational beliefs reported a decrease in unconditional self-acceptance (Davies, 2008). Investigations of irrational beliefs in Spanish-speaking countries have found support for their impact on medical conditions such as menopause (Lega & Ellis, 2001). In a study of college students, DiLorenzo, David, and Montgomery (2007) found that irrational beliefs were directly related to distress levels. Additionally, they determined that demandingness was mediated by awfulizing, low frustration tolerance, and global evaluation/self-downing, supporting the claim by Ellis that musts, shoulds, and oughts drive all styles of irrational thinking (DiLorenzo et al., 2007).

Since Ellis first developed REBT, hundreds of studies have been published on the general application of his theory of counseling. David, Szentagotai, Eva, and Macavei (2005) reviewed the research related to REBT since its inception and found that REBT was a more effective form of treatment when compared to other psychotherapies (e.g., psychodynamic). REBT has also been found to be equally effective for clients in clinical and nonclinical populations of children, adolescents and adults (David, Szentagotai, Eva, & Macavei; Gonzalez et al., 2004). These findings are tempered by several methodological concerns with the research, such as adherence of clinical protocols and the grouping of REBT with other forms of CBT in treatment outcome studies (Dryden & David, 2008). Recent clinical research, however, has demonstrated the efficacy of REBT when compared to other forms of psychotherapy. In a randomized clinical trial comparing Cognitive Therapy, REBT and pharmacotherapy in the treatment of Major Depressive Disorder, David, Szentagotai, Lupu, and Cosman (2008) found REBT to be significantly more effective than other cognitive methods at the 6-month follow up. Given the relative effectiveness of REBT to treat a range of psychological disorders, this approach holds promise for use with substance abuse.

REBT and Treatment of Substance Abuse

According to Ellis (1982), irrational beliefs are the cause of substance abuse and addiction. DiGiuseppe and McInerney (1990) described this relationship by presenting four patterns of irrational thinking and addictive behaviors. The "abstinence and Low Frustration Tolerance (LFT) pattern" (p.122) explains that drinking occurs after experiencing discomfort anxiety caused by LFT irrational beliefs. When clients abuse alcohol to avoid problems, they follow the "Intoxication coping pattern" (p.126). The "Intoxication equals worthlessness pattern" (p.130) predicts that irrational beliefs of self-downing (e.g., I am worthless) and dichotomous thinking (e.g., I cannot stop) will result in substance abuse. Finally, DiGiuseppe and McInerney (1990) believed that sensation seeking coupled with irrational thinking (e.g., I must never be bored) can result in a pattern of substance abuse.

The relationship between irrational beliefs and substance abuse is evident in college students who abuse alcohol. Given the developmental tasks of establishing autonomy and forming mature relationships, beliefs about peer expectations play a critical role in the decision to use substances. College student substance abusers may hold irrational beliefs regarding the need to adhere to the misperceived norms of their peer group (e.g., I must fit in with my peers by drinking to their standards or I am no good). Beliefs that alcohol will relieve affective distress may also influence the decision to use by students who experience low frustration tolerance or abuse substances to cope with problems. Addressing irrational beliefs with college students can be an efficacious approach to counseling because of the influence that social norms, alcohol outcome expectancies, and psychosocial development play in alcohol use.

A variety of cognitive, emotive and behavioral techniques are incorporated in the REBT approach to alcohol abuse. Prior to conducting these interventions, is it critical for REBT counselors to develop a strong therapeutic alliance with the client in order to develop goals and achieve tasks in counseling (Dryden & David, 2008). Ellis (1982) recommended teaching the ABC framework and using techniques such as disputing, shame-attacking, incorporating humor into counseling and skills training with clients who abuse alcohol. When working with clients who do not admit that they have a problem with alcohol, or who are in the Precontemplation Stage of Change (Prochaska, DiClemente, & Norcross, 1992), Bishop (2000) suggested that counselors use the ABC framework on a different client problem or for another person's problem in order to increase client awareness of irrational beliefs and how they influence emotions. With clients motivated to change their substance abuse, or who are in the Preparation or Action Stages of Change (Prochaska et al., 1992), Bishop (2000) recommended that counselors focus on the "Pre-AB's" (p.136). For example, if a client reports feeling depressed (C) after a night of heavy drinking (A), rather than explore the beliefs that resulted in feelings of depression, the counselor focus on the irrational beliefs that led to the activating event (A).

REBT techniques can be utilized in counseling to identify, dispute, and change irrational beliefs held by college students. Feedback regarding privately held descriptive and injunctive norms can be incorporated into disputing irrational beliefs pertaining to the need to abuse alcohol in order to fit in. Exploring the ABCs can increase awareness of the role that alcohol expectancies and discomfort anxiety play in the pattern of alcohol abuse. Shame-attacking exercises can be used by counselors to challenge clients to reevaluate beliefs of their peers. For example, a counselor can encourage a college student to give an overly dramatic and humorous refusal when offered an alcoholic beverage by a peer to challenge the rigid belief in the need for peer approval that creates shame and anxiety. Although these approaches can be applied to college student alcohol abuse, there is limited research to support their effectiveness with this population.

Considering the support in the literature for the use of REBT with a variety of psychological problems (e.g., depression), it is surprising that there is a paucity of empirical studies regarding its application with alcohol abuse. Terjesen, DiGiuseppe, and Gruner (2000) found only five studies and reported serious methodological limitations; however, support was found for change in irrational thinking and some behavior change using REBT. We were able to find only one additional study of alcohol use and REBT since 2000, and the focus was on spouses rather than abusers. De Los Angeles Cruz-Almanza, Gaona-Márquez, and Sánchez-Sosa (2006) observed increases in coping responses, assertiveness, and self-esteem among 35 Hispanic women whose husbands drank excessively, following a cognitive-behavioral intervention.

Research supporting the relationship between irrational beliefs and substance abuse is slightly more promising. Irrational beliefs have been found to partially mediate the relationship between stress and alcohol abuse among college students (Hutchinson, Patock-Peckham, Cheong, and Nagoshi, 1998). Denoff (1987) found that self-downing and catastrophizing predicted the frequency of drug use among adolescents residing in a residential drug program and shelter for runaways. This gap in the literature may be a factor in counselor selection of REBT in substance abuse treatment. According to the SAMHSA (2010), less than 50% of substance abuse treatment facilities in the United States report using REBT.

Despite this lack of empirical support, the application of REBT for substance abuse treatment is intriguing. In a meta-analysis of 53 randomized controlled trials of Cognitive Behavioral Therapy (CBT) with adult alcohol and other drug users, Magill and Ray (2009) found that across studies CBT produced a small but significant treatment effect that gradually diminished over time. These findings are consistent with those of Carey, Scott-Sheldon, Carey, and DeMartini (2007), who conducted a meta-analysis of cognitive behavioral interventions to reduce college student drinking.

Although there are many similarities between REBT and CBT, such as its short-term nature (Ellis, 1995), Dryden and David (2008) stated that a major difference between the theories was the REBT focus on belief change. When belief or philosophic change could not occur, the focus is then placed on creating other forms of client change (i.e., changes to behavior or cognitive inferences) using "inelegant REBT" or CBT (Dryden, 2008). Given this emphasis on changing core irrational beliefs and the range of cognitive, behavioral and emotive techniques available in counseling, REBT may produce longer lasting treatment outcomes and address the limitations of other cognitive behavioral approaches for substance abuse described by Magill and Ray (2009) and Carey, Scott-Sheldon, Carey, and DeMartini (2007).

Case Study

The following case illustration demonstrates the use of REBT in the treatment of alcohol abuse with a college student client. The case represents a composite of previous clients seen by the first author. The author selected a composite because it has been argued that it allows for a broader presentation of an approach and provides greater protection of client privacy compared to a disguised case study (Sperry & Pies, 2010).

Background

The client, Ryan, was a 20-year-old single White male who attended college in the northeastern part of the United States. Ryan sought counseling services at the strong urging of his parents after he was cited for a public intoxication violation in the neighborhood adjacent to campus. He had moved to an off campus residence not affiliated with the university two years earlier after he received several alcohol violations while in on-campus student housing. An average student not in jeopardy of failing academically, he reported regular alcohol consumption, on average 3 or more times per week, with consumption of 4–5 drinks in a sitting. His use increased to 9–10 drinks when he attended large parties and other social functions. Reported negative consequences related to his use of alcohol included infrequent blackouts, hangovers and arguments with friends.

Initial Concerns

At the start of the first session, the counselor learned that Ryan had no prior experience with counseling and worked to establish rapport by exploring his current situation. Ryan believed that he did not have a significant problem with alcohol because his use was consistent, if not less than, the use of his friends. He stated that his public intoxication violation was caused by "bad luck and a grumpy police officer."

After exploring the disadvantages of Ryan's use, the counselor engaged him in identifying target problems to explore in counseling. Though he did not experience blackouts on a regular basis, Ryan stated that he would like to avoid them in the future because he is ashamed of his behavior when blacked out. The counselor responded by asking Ryan if avoiding blackouts would mean a change to his drinking. Ryan responded that he is "somewhat fine" drinking less in certain situations, if it prevents dangerous or embarrassing experiences. However, he was not sure how he could reduce his quantity of use because past strategies, such as drink counting and eating beforehand, have been ineffective.

Introducing the Client to REBT

I introduced the client to REBT by sharing a handout describing the theory and containing an overview of the ABCDE model. After reviewing the ABC steps using a hypothetical example with a rational belief, I explored Ryan's response to the model. He seemed interested and was able to describe a past experience using the framework. Ryan's homework was to read the remainder of the handout and record an experience using the ABC framework to share during the second session.

During the second session, I continued to explain the ABCDE model and the REBT process of disputing irrational beliefs. Ryan shared that he drank excessively at crowded parties because he felt uncomfortable being sober in these situations. His behavior also was related to his belief that he needed to drink excessively in order to fit in with his friends. Throughout this process, I assisted Ryan in identifying the demandingness and low frustration tolerance inherent in these statements, and prompted him to consider other expressions of these beliefs in his life.

Goal Setting

Goals for counseling were formulated during the second session. Ryan hoped to leave counseling with more functional and realistic beliefs about himself, others and life. We developed a plan for four sessions in order to (a) further explore the underlying core irrational beliefs that influence his behaviors and emotions, (b) dispute his irrational beliefs and replace them with rational beliefs, and (c) practice behavioral strategies that are consistent with his new beliefs. Ryan expressed confidence that disputing and replacing his irrational beliefs will provide him with the ability to control his drinking.

Ryan returned for session 3 appearing sad and dejected. During the past weekend, he had attended a party and drank more than planned. Ryan had tried disputing his irrational beliefs, but was unsuccessful. He remembered leaving the party but was not sure how he got home. I commended Ryan for disputing and explained that changing irrational beliefs takes practice, hard work and a willingness to deal with temporary setbacks. Moreover, it would be irrational to assume that any plan will work out 100% of the time. I used this experience as an opportunity to explore the discomfort anxiety that led to his excessive use of alcohol and the secondary disturbance caused by his behavior. Ryan decided not to enter situations where he would drink excessively until he was more confident in his ability to challenge his irrational thinking and manage the emotions caused by these beliefs.

Cognitive, Emotive, and Behavioral Interventions

Throughout counseling, I incorporated several cognitive, emotive and behavioral techniques to uncover and change Ryan's irrational beliefs.

Once he understood the ABCDE model, I focused on working with him to identify the core irrational beliefs that shaped the thinking that caused his problems. For example, Ryan acknowledged that his belief "I must be cool and relaxed with my peers" leads to discomfort anxiety and excessive drinking. I challenged him to identify the irrational belief that fuels all examples of low frustration tolerance in his life (e.g., I must be comfortable, I must be liked or I am no good).

As Ryan began to reflect on his core irrational beliefs, we began to explore his emotions. I used this approach because Ryan had initially struggled to explain the emotional consequences of his irrational beliefs. Over time, his description of his emotional consequences evolved from "I felt awkward" to "I felt angry and frustrated that I wasn't in my comfort zone." Using imagery, Ryan was able to experience the health and functional emotional consequences of new rational beliefs. Clarifying Ryan's emotions also enabled him to more accurately track his progress during counseling.

A major focus of our sessions was on disputing his irrational beliefs related to alcohol use. Ryan was challenged to reflect on his belief that all of his peers drank in the same manner and approved of his behavior. After speaking to several of his close friends, Ryan recognized that he had misperceived their acceptance of his behavior. Rather than rationalizing his drinking as acceptable college student behavior, his closest friends said that he "goes way overboard." This surprised Ryan and provided incentive for him to make changes.

In addition to disputing, we developed a list of forceful rational statements that he could use to replace his present irrational beliefs. These preferences, rather than demands, were developed primarily by Ryan with my input to ensure that they reflected flexibility and self-acceptance. They also incorporated humor and included swear words as emphasizers chosen by the client. I also incorporated behavioral strategies, with homework including intentionally and incrementally exposing Ryan to situations that created discomfort. He found that with practice, he experienced less discomfort anxiety.

Ending the Counseling Relationship

By the fourth session, Ryan reported fewer negative consequences related to his alcohol use. His frequency of alcohol use had not changed, but he was no longer experiencing heavy nights of use that would result in a blackout or other problem. Ryan reported changes in other parts of his life including his interactions with family and friends. He believed that these changes were due to the rational beliefs and new strategies he learned in counseling. I reflected that he seemed more confident in his ability to challenge his irrational beliefs. He agreed to practice the behavioral (slowly exposing himself to these situations), cognitive (disputing and using rational self-statements), and emotive (identifying and spending time with his emotions) techniques used during counseling and to contact the counselor if he needed support in the future.

Discussion

This case study illustrated an REBT approach for addressing alcohol abuse with college students. By placing the emphasis of counseling on the beliefs that create the problems, rather than on reducing the quantity of alcohol use, the client was empowered to make widespread and deep change in his life. This change also may be long lasting because the client has developed skills to identify and dispute irrational thinking in the future.

Although this case study demonstrates the potential of REBT as a promising approach to college student alcohol abuse, several limitations should be noted. In this illustration, the client is willing to explore his beliefs. If the client were unable or unwilling to engage in this conversation, the use of "inelegant REBT" or cognitive-behavioral therapy would be a more appropriate treatment option. Utilizing Motivational Interviewing (Miller & Rollnick, 2002) to increase engagement in treatment and readiness to change may also be a fitting intervention with under-motivated clients. Furthermore, little is known regarding the effectiveness of REBT with diverse populations, given that most clinical research has been done with participants who tended to be the YAVIS (Young, Attractive, Verbal, Intelligent, and Sensitive) type (David, Szentagotai, Eva, & Macavei, 2005). Finally, the use of REBT to treat alcohol abuse has not undergone rigorous evaluation (Terjesen, DiGiuseppe, & Gruner, 2000). The use of REBT as a stand-alone intervention, or as an integrated intervention combining elements of Motivational Interviewing (Miller & Rollnick) as proposed by Bishop (2000), can be studied to determine efficacy.

Despite these limitations, REBT holds promise as an effective intervention for college student alcohol abuse. REBT can be utilized by counselors to challenge the underlying core beliefs held by high-risk drinkers. The short-term approach of REBT makes it a viable treatment approach in lieu of common risk-reduction interventions.

References

Armeli, S., Todd, M., Conner, T. S., & Tennen, H. (2008). Drinking to cope with negative moods and the immediacy of drinking within the weekly cycle among college students. *Journal of Studies on Alcohol and Drugs, 69*(2), 313-322.

Barnett, N. P., & Read, J. P. (2005). Mandatory alcohol intervention for alcohol-abusing college students: A systematic review. *Journal of Substance Abuse Treatment, 29*(2), 147-158. doi:10.1016/j.jsat.2005.05.007

Berkowitz, A. D. (2004). The social norms approach: Theory, research, and annotated bibliography. Retrieved from http://www.alanberkowitz.com/articles/social_norms .pdf

Bishop, F. M. (2000). Helping clients manage addictions with REBT. *Journal of Rational-Emotive & Cognitive Behavior Therapy, 18*(3), 127-151. doi:10.1023/A:1007874820119

Borsari, B., & Carey, K. B. (2003). Descriptive and injunctive norms in college drinking: A meta-analytic integration. *Journal of Studies on Alcohol, 64*, 331-341. Retrieved from http://libproxy.uncg.edu

Borsari, B., Murphy, J. G., & Barnett, N. P. (2007). Predictors of alcohol use during the first year of college: Implications for prevention. *Addictive Behaviors, 32*, 2062-2086. doi:10.1016/j.addbeh.2007.01.017

Carey, K. B., Scott-Sheldon, L. A. J., Carey, M. P., & DeMartini, K. S. (2007). Individual-level interventions to reduce college student drinking: A meta-analytic review. *Addictive Behaviors, 32*, 2469-2494. doi:10.1016/j.addbeh.2007.05.004

Carey, K. B., Henson, J. M., Carey, M. P., & Maisto, S. A. (2009). Computer versus in-person intervention for students violating campus alcohol policy. *Journal of Consulting and Clinical Psychology, 77*, 74-87. doi:10.1037/a0014281

Chickering, A.W. and Reisser, L. (1993). *Education and identity.* 2nd Ed. San Francisco: Jossey-Bass.

Colby, S. M., Colby, J. J., & Raymond, G. A. (2009). College versus the real world: Student perceptions and implications for understanding heavy drinking among college students. *Addictive Behaviors, 34*(1), 17-27. doi:10.1016/j.addbeh.2008.07.023

Core Institute. (2008). Statistics on alcohol and other drug use on American campuses. Carbondale, IL: Author. Retrieved from http://www.core.siuc.edu/pdfs/report0608 .pdf

David, D., Szentagotai, A., Eva, K., & Macavei, B. (2005). A synopsis of rational-emotive behavior therapy (REBT); Fundamental and applied research. *Journal of Rational-Emotive & Cognitive Behavior Therapy, 23*(3), 175-221. doi:10.1007/s10942-005-0011-0

David, D., Szentagotai, A., Lupu, V., & Cosman, D. (2008). Rational emotive behavior therapy, cognitive therapy, and medication in the treatment of major depressive disorder: A randomized clinical trial, posttreatment outcomes, and six-month follow-up. *Journal of Clinical Psychology, 64*, 728-746. doi:10.1002/jclp.20487

Davies, M. F. (2008). Irrational beliefs and unconditional self-acceptance. II. Experimental evidence for a causal link between two key features of REBT. *Journal of Rational-Emotive & Cognitive Behavior Therapy, 26*(2), 89-101. doi:10.1007/s10942-007-0060-7

De Los Angeles Cruz-Almanza, M., Gaona-Márquez, L., & Sánchez-Sosa, J. J. (2006). Empowering women abused by their problem drinker spouses: Effects of a cognitive-behavioral intervention. *Salud Mental, 29*, 25-31.

Demb, A., & Campbell, C. M. (2009). A new lens for identifying potential adult persistent problem drinkers during college. *Journal of College Student Development, 50*(1), 1-18. doi:10.1353/csd.0.0048

Denoff, M. S. (1987). Irrational beliefs as predictors of adolescent drug abuse and running away. *Journal of Clinical Psychology, 43*, 412-423. doi:10.1002/1097-4679(198705)43:3<412::AID-JCLP2270430316>3.0.CO;2-6

DiGiuseppe, R. (1996). The nature of irrational and rational beliefs: Progress in Rational Emotive Behavior theory. *Journal of Rational-Emotive & Cognitive Behavior Therapy, 14*(1), 5-28. doi:10.1007/BF02238091

DiGiuseppe, R., & McInerney, J. (1990). Patterns of addiction: A rational-emotive perspective. *Journal of Cognitive Psychotherapy, 4*(2), 121-134.

DiLorenzo, T. A., David, D., & Montgomery, G. H. (2007). The interrelations between irrational cognitive processes and distress in stressful academic settings. *Personality and Individual Differences, 42*, 765-776. doi:10.1016/j.paid.2006.08.022

Dimeff, L.A., Baer, J.S., Kivlahan, D.R., & Marlatt, G.A. (1999). *Brief alcohol screening and intervention for college students (BASICS): A harm reduction approach.* New York: The Guilford Press.

Dowdall, G. W., & Wechsler, H. (2002). Studying college alcohol use: Widening the lens, sharpening the focus. *Journal of Studies on Alcohol, SUPPL14*, 14-22.

Dryden, W. (2008). *Rational Emotive Behaviour Therapy: Distinctive features.* London: Taylor & Francis.

Dryden, W., & David, D. (2008). Rational emotive behavior therapy: Current status. *Journal of Cognitive Psychotherapy, 22*(3), 195-209. doi:10.1891/0889-8391.22.3.195

Ellis, A. (1976). The biological basis of human irrationality. *Journal of Individual Psychology, 32*(2), 145-168.

Ellis, A. (1982). The treatment of alcohol and drug abuse: A rational-emotive approach. *Rational Living, 17*(2), 15-24.

Ellis, A. (1994). *Reason and emotion in psychotherapy: A comprehensive method of treating human disturbances: Revised and updated (Rev Sub.).* New York: Citadel.

Ellis, A. (1995). *Better, deeper and more enduring brief therapy: The rational emotive behavior therapy approach* (1st ed.). New York: Routledge.

Ellis, A. (1997). Must musturbation and demandingness lead to emotional disorders? *Psychotherapy: Theory, Research, Practice, Training, 34*(1), 95-98. doi:10.1037/h0087779

Gonzalez, J. E., Nelson, J. R., Gutkin, T. B., Saunders, A., Galloway, A., & Shwery, C. S. (2004). Rational Emotive Therapy With Children and Adolescents: A Meta-Analysis. *Journal of Emotional and Behavioral Disorders, 12*(4), 222-235. doi:10.1177/10634266040120040301

Harris, S., Davies, M. F., & Dryden, W. (2006). An experimental test of a core REBT hypothesis: Evidence that irrational beliefs lead to physiological as well as psychological arousal. *Journal of Rational-Emotive & Cognitive Behavior Therapy, 24*(2), 101-110. doi:10.1007/s10942-005-0019-5

Hingson, R. W. (2010). Magnitude and prevention of college drinking and related problems. *Alcohol Research & Health, 33*(1-2), 45-54. Retrieved from http://pubs.niaaa.nih.gov/publications/arh40/45-54.pdf

Hingson, R., Heeren, T., Winter, M., & Wechsler, H. (2005). Magnitude of alcohol-related mortality and morbidity among U.S. college students ages 18-24: Changes from

1998 to 2001. *Annual Review of Public Health, 26*, 259-279. doi:10.1146/annurev.publhealth.26.021304.144652

Howard, D. E., Griffin, M. A., & Boekeloo, B. O. (2008). Prevalence and psychosocial correlates of alcohol-related sexual assault among university students. *Adolescence, 43*, 733-750. Retrieved from http://libproxy.uncg.edu

Hutchinson, G. T., Patock-Peckham, J. A., Cheong, J., & Nagoshi, C. T. (1998). Irrational beliefs and behavioral misregulation in the role of alcohol abuse among college students. *Journal of Rational-Emotive & Cognitive Behavior Therapy, 16*(1), 61-74. doi:10.1023/A:1024950407778

Johnston, L. D., O'Malley, P. M., Bachman, J. G., & Schulenberg, J. E. (2009). Monitoring the future national survey results on drug use, 1975–2008: Volume II, College students and adults ages 19–50. NIH Publication No. 09-7403. Bethesda, MD: National Institute on Drug Abuse. Retrieved from http://monitoringthefuture.org/pubs/monographs/vol2_2008.pdf

Kassel, J. D., Bornovalova, M., & Mehta, N. (2007). Generalized expectancies for negative mood regulation predict change in anxiety and depression among college students. *Behaviour Research and Therapy, 45*, 939-950. doi:10.1016/j.brat.2006.07.014

LaBrie, J. W., Hummer, J. F., Neighbors, C., & Larimer, M. E. (2010). Whose opinion matters? The relationship between injunctive norms and alcohol consequences in college students. *Addictive Behaviors, 35*, 343-349. doi:10.1016/j.addbeh.2009.12.003

Larimer, M. E., & Cronce, J. M. (2007). Identification, prevention, and treatment revisited: Individual-focused college drinking prevention strategies 1999-2006. *Addictive Behaviors, 32*, 2439-2468. doi:10.1016/j.addbeh.2007.05.006

Lega, L. I., & Ellis, A. (2001). Rational Emotive Behavior Therapy (REBT) in the new millennium: A cross-cultural approach. *Journal of Rational-Emotive & Cognitive Behavior Therapy, 19*(4), 201-222. doi:10.1023/A:1012537814117

Magill, M., & Ray, L. A. (2009). Cognitive-behavioral treatment with adult alcohol and illicit drug users: A meta-analysis of randomized controlled trials. *Journal of Studies on Alcohol and Drugs, 70*, 516-527.

Marlatt, G. A. (2005). *Relapse prevention: maintenance strategies in the treatment of addictive behaviors.* New York: Guilford Press.

Miller, W. R., & Rollnick, S. (2002). *Motivational interviewing: Preparing people for change* (2nd ed.). New York, NY: Guilford Press.

National Institute on Alcohol Abuse and Alcoholism (2007). *What colleges need to know now: An update on college drinking research.* NIH Publication, No. 07-5010. Retrieved from http://www.collegedrinkingprevention.gov/1College_Bulletin-508_361C4E.pdf

Neighbors, C., Lee, C. M., Lewis, M. A., Fossos, N., & Larimer, M. E. (2007). Are social norms the best predictor of outcomes among heavy-drinking college students? *Journal of Studies on Alcohol and Drugs, 68*, 556-565.

O'Malley, P. M., & Johnston, L. D. (2002). Epidemiology of alcohol and other drug use among American college students. *Journal of Studies on Alcohol, SUPPL14*, 23-39.

Presley, C. A., & Pimentel, E. R. (2006). The Introduction of the Heavy and Frequent Drinker: A Proposed Classification to Increase Accuracy of Alcohol Assessments in Postsecondary Educational Settings. *Journal of Studies on Alcohol, 67*, 324-331.

Prochaska, J. O., DiClemente, C. C., & Norcross, J. C. (1992). In search of how people change: Applications to addictive behaviors. *American Psychologist, 47*, 1102-1114. doi:10.1037/0003-066X.47.9.1102

Sher, K. J., Wood, M. D., Wood, P. K., & Raskin, G. (1996). Alcohol outcome expectancies and alcohol use: A latent variable cross-lagged panel study. *Journal of Abnormal Psychology, 105*, 561-574. doi:10.1037/0021-843X.105.4.561

Sperry, L., & Pies, R. (2010). Writing about clients: Ethical considerations and options. *Counseling and Values, 54*(2), 88-102.

Stewart, S. H., Morris, E., Mellings, T., & Komar, J. (2006). Relations of social anxiety variables to drinking motives, drinking quantity and frequency, and alcohol-related problems in undergraduates. *Journal of Mental Health, 15*, 671-682. doi:10.1080/09638230600998904

Substance Abuse and Mental Health Services Administration. (2010). *Results from the 2009.*

national survey on drug use and health: Volume I. Summary of national findings (Office of Applied Studies, NSDUH Series H-38A, HHS Publication No. SMA 10-4586 Findings). Rockville, MD. Retrieved from http://www.oas.samhsa.gov

Substance Abuse and Mental Health Services Administration. (2010). *The N-SSATS report: Clinical or therapeutic approaches used by substance abuse treatment facilities.* Rockville, MD. Retrieved from http://www.oas.samhsa.gov/2k10/238/238ClinicalAp2k10.htm

Sugarman, D. E., DeMartini, K. S., & Carey, K. B. (2009). Are women at greater risk? An examination of alcohol-related consequences and gender. *The American Journal on Addictions, 18*, 194-197. doi:10.1080/10550490902786991

Terjesen, M. D., DiGiuseppe, R., & Gruner, P. (2000). A review of REBT research in alcohol abuse treatment. *Journal of Rational-Emotive & Cognitive Behavior Therapy, 18*(3), 165-179. doi:10.1023/A:1007878921028

Wechsler, H., Lee, J. E., Kuo, M., Seibring, M., Nelson, T. F., & Lee, H. (2002). Trends in college binge drinking during a period of increased prevention efforts. *Journal of American College Health, Drinking on the college campus, 50*(5), 203-217. doi:10.1080/07448480209595713

Weitzman, E. R., Folkman, A., Lemieux Folkman, K., & Wechsler, H. (2003). The relationship of alcohol outlet density to heavy and frequent drinking and drinking-related problems among college students at eight universities. *Health & Place, 9*, 1-6. doi: 10.1016/S1353-8292(02)00014-X

White, A. M., Jamieson-Drake, D. W., & Swartzwelder, H. S. (2002). Prevalence and correlates of alcohol-induced blackouts among college students: Results of an e-mail survey. *Journal of American College Health, 51*(3), 117-119, 122-131. doi:10.1080/07448480209596339

White, H. R., & Jackson, K. (2004). Social and psychological influences on emerging adult drinking behavior. *Alcohol Research & Health, 28*(4), 182-190.

White, H. R., Mun, E. Y., Pugh, L., & Morgan, T. J. (2007). Long-term effects of brief substance use interventions for mandated college students: Sleeper effects of an in-person personal feedback intervention. *Alcoholism: Clinical and Experimental Research, 3*, 1380-1391. doi:10.1111/j.1530-0277.2007.00435.x

9

Voices of Substance Abuse Professionals

Hurricane Katrina and Post-disaster Experiences

TIM S. VANDERGAST AND PAMELA S. LASSITER[1]

This qualitative study examined experiences of 11 substance abuse professionals from hurricane-affected regions in the southeastern U.S. 12–18 months post-disaster. Findings revealed themes of challenges and responses post disaster. A discussion of results and implications is included.

Hurricane Katrina has been described as unprecedented (Pond, 2006), the deadliest and the most expensive disaster in American history (Kesler, Galea, Jones, & Parker, 2006), and the largest relocation in American history (North et al., 2008). Katrina's initial strike hit Gulf Port, Mississippi on August 31, 2005. A month later, Hurricane Rita followed devastating coastal regions in Louisiana and Texas. The aftermath and subsequent breech in the levees and floods demolished the city of

1. Tim S. VanderGast, Department of Special Education and Counseling, William Paterson University; Pamela S. Lassiter, Department of Counseling, University of North Carolina at Charlotte. Correspondence concerning this article should be addressed to Tim S. VanderGast, Department of Special Education and Counseling, William Paterson University, 1600 Valley Road, 3013, Wayne, NJ 07470-2103. E-mail: vandergastt@wpunj.edu

New Orleans, Louisiana. A year post-disaster, 1,000,000 people were displaced, 350,000 houses destroyed, and over 200,000 people were moved to evacuation centers spread over 18 states (Rodriguez & Aguirre, 2006). Between 1500 and 1800 people died as a result of the storm, and $100 billion in damages occurred, causing Katrina to be estimated as the most costly natural disaster in U.S. history (Bacon, 2005). Several years later and despite more than $100 billion in federal money to rebuild, the recovery process in the region continues.

Mental Health in Affected Areas

Prior to Hurricane Katrina striking the gulf coast region, mental health systems in the region were already strained. Louisiana and Mississippi's healthcare systems and service infrastructures were ranked 49th and 50th in the United States (Andrews, 2006). Houston, one of the major evacuation points for residents of the Gulf Coast region, experienced similar obstacles. The public mental health network in Houston was described as "in crisis" and "dire" prior to the arrival of more than 150,000 hurricane evacuees (Feldman, 2006). Houston's system was composed of hospitals, a county health association, and a university psychiatric center. Feldman identified these as operating beyond capacity prior to the arrival of evacuees. A year post-disaster, the complex system in the city of New Orleans and its healthcare structure remained devastated and was identified as being even more compromised than prior to Katrina (Rudowitz et al., 2006).

Research over a multiple state area found statistically significant higher estimated prevalence of serious mental illness than a previous survey from 2003 (Kessler et al., 2006). These authors estimated that mental illness doubled post-Katrina. Similar research revealed that post-disaster, PTSD, depression, anxiety, suicide, and substance abuse were expected to increase in residents, first responders, and health care workers (Weisler, Barbee, & Townsend, 2006). First responders reported increases in marital conflict and interest in mental health (Post-disaster response, 2006). Mental health assessments seven weeks post-Katrina yielded client concerns related to feeling isolated, crowded, overwhelmed as parents, family conflict, and a need for counseling services (Norris et al., 2006).

Substance Abuse Systems

When coupled with mental health stressors and diagnoses, addiction to alcohol and other drugs yields an "exponential impact" resulting in a significant challenge for individuals with pre-existing disabilities and medical conditions (Post-disaster response, 2006). These challenges extend to the substance abuse professionals who provide treatment for clients. Scenarios emerged for service providers including loss of facilities and resources for treating clients, the relocation of evacuees (i.e., loss of clients), providing services for clients who remained after the storms, and concerns related to their own needs for coping post disaster. Of the 1,000,000 homeless from Katrina, thousands were addicts and alcoholics ranging from those in treatment, to those who had never sought services (Keilman, 2005). Substance abuse treatment professionals faced the complex charge of caring for this population post-Katrina.

Evidence of the loss of facilities occurred in New Orleans where Charity Hospital which served as the dominant provider for the substance abuse population (Rudowitz et al., 2006). The State of Louisiana provided a total of 32 medical detoxification beds for four million residents, 20 beds being in Charity Hospital, which was decimated. In other post-hurricane scenarios, clients waited at treatment centers in need of methadone and faced challenges of drug withdrawal. A substantial disruption and reduction of substance abuse services was identified as a significant concern for treatment professionals (Druss, Henderson, & Rosenheck, 2007).

The association between disaster and trauma with changes in substance use has been documented from past disaster scenarios. Research demonstrates increased alcohol use for survivors after the 1995 Oklahoma City bombing (Pfefferbaum et al., 2002), and adults exposed to the September 11th, 2001 terrorist attacks in New York City (Adams, Boscarino, & Galea, 2006; Boscarino, Adams, & Galea, 2005). Similar research in New York post-9/11 identified increased cigarette consumption for individuals directly affected (e.g., job loss) and increased consumption for alcohol and marijuana for individuals who were part of the rescue effort (Vlahov et al., 2004). Vlahov et al., (2004) identified a public health concern for increased substance use/abuse long-term post disaster. Related research found an increased likelihood for relapse for those in recovery from alcohol dependence (Zywiak et al., 2003). North et al. (2008) cited gross underestimates for psychopathology and substance abuse in particular, in a study focused on Katrina evacuees. Although research documents a lack of change and instances of decreases in substance use post disaster (Simons, Gaher, Jacobs, Meyer, & Johnson-Jimenez 2005; US Department of Health and Human Services, 2008), findings support general increases in use/abuse of alcohol and other drugs. Increases in use/abuse and relapse are indicators of the demand for treatment professionals to provide services for a population with complex needs post-disaster.

The effects of disaster on substance abuse treatment programs and professional staff has also been examined. Similar to the aforementioned loss of facilities, Toriello et al., (2007) reported a reduction in staff from 80 to 3 in "the largest residential, addiction treatment program in New Orleans" six weeks post-Katrina (p.44). The personal impact on treatment professionals has been documented. A study of the September 11 attacks on a random sample of 15 treatment programs facilities in the five surrounding boroughs in New York was conducted (Frank, Dewart, Schmeidler, & Demirjian, 2006). Administrators reported concerns for professional staff related to depression, anxiety, and fear. The authors identified specific challenges for methadone programs, failed telephone communication systems, and the critical need for improved disaster planning future scenarios. In addition to improved disaster preparedness, Toriello et al., (2007) framed post-Katrina recovery as an opportunity for treatment programs to demonstrate resilience and implement changes for improvements in service provision.

Need and Purpose of the Study

To our knowledge, this article is the first qualitative study that focuses on substance abuse service provision from hurricane Katrina and affected regions from 2005. Despite a call for research related to the assessment of substance abuse agencies recovery from Katrina (Toriello et al., 2007), literature is sparse. Due to the expanse of the hurricanes' destruction, displacement, and extensive relocations as indicated by Voelker (2005), a qualitative investigation of substance abuse service providers over a wide geographic region is warranted. In order to investigate these areas of interest, this qualitative study aimed to reach service providers by investigating their experiences and perceptions through two primary research questions: (a) How did substance abuse counseling professionals perceive the effects of Hurricane Katrina on service provision to clients, and

(b) what were the needs of substance abuse treatment professionals in disaster affected areas 12-18 months post-disaster?

Methods

Participants

In order to understand perspectives from varying regions affected by Hurricanes Katrina and Rita, purposive sampling (Patton, 1990) was employed. Researchers recruited 11 participants through the use of verbal invitation via convenience and snowball solicitation by contacting program managers in substance abuse treatment agencies listed on public service websites in Mississippi, Louisiana and Houston, Texas. Whether agency personnel accepted or declined participation, they were asked for referrals to others in their area that might be willing to speak to the purposes of the research. The sample was somewhat diverse with respect to age (M = 52 years; R = 37-59 years), gender (n = 7 males; n = 4 females), ethnicity (n = 9 Caucasian, n = 1 African American, n = 1 Asian), and education (n = 1 Doctoral degree, n = 8 Master's degrees, n = 1 Nursing diploma, n = 1 Bachelor's degree). Seven of the 11 participants hold administrative positions in substance abuse treatment agencies and four hold positions as front-line clinicians. Six participants work in residential settings (including one from a correctional setting) and five work in outpatient settings. Participants reported years of professional work experience ranging from 3 to 30 years with an average of 18.8 years. Six participants were from Louisiana, three were from Mississippi, and two were from Houston.

Research Team

Because researchers are considered research instruments that affect data collection and analysis (Strauss & Corbin, 1990), they are an integral component of the study's design. The research team was made up of one Caucasian male and one Caucasian female, both with professional work experience as substance abuse counselors. Neither researcher lived in any of the hurricane-affected areas. Each had experience with qualitative research design.

Two training sessions were held in which instruction in semi-structured interviewing was provided by the researcher with more experience in qualitative methods. The sessions were designed to address challenges such as establishing rapport with participants over the telephone, minimizing interviewer influence on participant responses, completion of demographic and consent forms, and coding procedures. After the training sessions, the researchers created the initial interview protocol and proceeded with data collection.

Data Collection/Interview Protocol

Initial interview questions were developed to reflect the research questions and the existing substance abuse and post-disaster literature. These questions were then piloted to assess the clarity of questions and approximate length of an interview. The piloted sample provided feedback on the initial research questions, and the questions were further revised through discussions with the research team so that they more closely represented the research questions. For example, some questions were removed from the interview protocol due to redundancy and some were added (e.g., "What skills did you find you lacked as you faced challenges?"). Both researchers coded the pilot interview using open coding procedures (Miles & Huberman, 1994) and reached consensus independently for the purpose of triangulation (Lincoln & Guba, 1985), as well as consistency of coding among researchers. The interview protocol was developed from this process. Each participant completed a demographic sheet containing questions regarding cultural identity, education, work experience, work setting, and position. Participants responded to approximately 10 questions (See appendix) via telephone over a period of four months. The questions examined their experiences and perceptions of substance abuse counseling post-Hurricanes Katrina and Rita.

The primary researcher conducted 11 audiotaped telephone interviews, ranging from 45 to 90 minutes in length. The interviews were transcribed and transcripts were reviewed for accuracy with a majority of participants contacted for the purposes of member checking (Lincoln & Guba, 1985). This process included reactions to the interview content and process, confirmation that responses were accurate, and any further elaboration through use of examples as needed.

Data Analysis

Each researcher independently used open and axial coding (Miles & Huberman, 1994) to develop preliminary themes for the first five interviews. The codes were reviewed and consensus was reached through a series of meetings. Based on the codes from the first five interviews, an initial coding manual was developed. Six more interviews were conducted and analyzed using the same methodology and those codes were added to the coding manual.

After each round of interviews, researchers met to discuss the interview process for clarification and training purposes. Through constant comparative methods (Strauss & Corbin, 1990), the researchers compared codes across interviews to existing analyzed interviews, which resulted in further restructuring of the code list, including pattern coding (Miles & Huberman, 1994). Using inductive analysis (Lecompte & Schensul, 1999), codes were collapsed and grouped into categories. The researchers collaboratively assessed the codes for accuracy and concluded that the themes represented the data in the least complex way (Lincoln & Guba, 1985). This resulted in a final list of codes (i.e., coding manual) addressing the research questions. The researchers independently reviewed the coding manual as well as patterns among codes to ensure saturation of the data (i.e., data were fully represented by the themes and there was no new data to refute the findings).

Results

Participants reported a variety of perceptions concerning the effects of the hurricanes on service provision to substance abuse clients post-disaster. These responses can be conceptualized as challenges, responses, and lessons learned for future preparedness.

Challenges

Challenges represent those factors presented to substance abuse treatment facilities and counselors immediately following and 18 months after the devastation of the hurricanes. Responses from the 11 interviews resulted in four major themes related to challenges: client population, staff-related issues, service delivery, and facilities management.

Client Population

Participants described vastly shifting populations immediately following the hurricanes and continuing for many months as people who were displaced struggled to find new living arrangements. Some substance abuse service agencies were overloaded with requests for services while others were left with no populations to serve. Transportation was often a major issue, so that attending counseling services often required extra motivation on the part of clients. Often clients who lived a great distance from functioning agencies were unable to attend. Substance abuse counselors who participated in the study perceived many clients citing the storms as reasons for their relapses. Some participants viewed this as excuse making, but others perceived relapse as being tied to despair and hopelessness.

Participants described an increase in addiction to prescription drugs and overall numbers of clients with substance use disorders. Many participants attributed the increase in prescription drug addiction to reports that physicians were giving prescriptions for sedatives to people reporting stress symptoms in an effort to assist, not knowing which of those patients were drug-seeking, active addicts. Participants reported Federal Emergency Management Agency (FEMA) trailers often became drug havens and that federal stipends to victims were frequently used them to buy drugs. Some described an increase in mixing drugs and an increase in use of methadone, both legally and illegally. Participants also reported changes in client presenting issues including an increase in Post Traumatic Stress Disorder (PTSD), suicidal ideation, and medical acuity.

Regarding the increase in medical acuity, participants specifically described clients as more hostile, violent and suicidal. Participants described having to call on extensive crisis management skills and were often lacking vital resources needed to deal with volatile clients. A clinician in southern Louisiana described the experience this way "It was not something that was acute and faded away. It was more acute the first six months. It's become something more of almost a chronic acuity."

Participants also described client populations as less trusting of "the system" related to an overall mistrust that the government seemed not to care about the victims in the regions affected by the storms. Many perceived shifts in drug dealing and crime from urban to more rural areas post disaster as a result of displacement and the destruction of the offender system in urban areas. In many cases computers, court offices and the entire legal infrastructures were destroyed. This meant that records of criminals on probation and still under court sanction were irrevocably lost. Many criminals were essentially set free. One participant reported a major increase in crack cocaine use, estimating that three of four patients were presenting with addiction to this substance.

Staff-Related Issues

Participants reported many challenges to staff. Counselors were forced to go out into the field to work with clients when under normal circumstances all services would have been provided in the agency. Personnel were asked repeatedly and for long stretches of time to work beyond their normal boundaries and job requirements. Participants described staff as chronically overworked and overwhelmed, in many instances working up to 60 hours per week or more. This resulted in confused loyalties between one's own needs and professional responsibilities.

Personal loss and trauma for staff were seen as crucial challenges to service provision. One participant reported that one fourth of his/her staff died as a result of Hurricane Katrina. A participant from Louisiana reported "Many of our staff lost everything they owned." When describing an aid group sent to train agency staff on working with trauma, he stated "They said it was the first time they had been some place where the people they were there to teach, or reinforce teaching with, were themselves as much victims as the clients walking in the door." And nearly two years after the storm, "we still have staff living in FEMA trailers, trying to get their own housing restored." Another participant in New Orleans articulated the devastation to his agency, "we had four staff who died in the first four months after or during Katrina." Despite the trauma for both clients and staff, administrators viewed staff loyalty as very important and valued knowing that certain staff still cared about clients' welfare.

Finding personnel to provide services remained a challenge for more than a year post disaster. Participants reported difficulty finding people to fill job vacancies, lack of living spaces for those who were hired, and lack of transportation to work as major obstacles to service provision. In Southern Louisiana a participant estimated a loss of 60% of the psychiatrists. Essentially there were more clients and fewer services in nearly all the affected areas. More than a year and a half post-disaster, nothing appeared normal to participants and many were not sure what normal was anymore.

Service Delivery

Participants described entire regions as having lost all services. New Orleans for example had no services for substance abuse clients for many months post-disaster. Detoxification needs went unmet in many areas for long periods of time. Staff had difficulty connecting clients to needed services. Many private providers did not return. Service catchment areas had to be expanded beyond the normal parameters. Mobile treatment teams were developed and in some instances averted suicides related to trauma. Counseling personnel were forced to shift to crisis intervention and short-term intervention methods as emergency rooms were overwhelmed with mental health patients. Residential clients needed particular care in that they were wards of the agency, needing food, clothing, water, and other essential needs. Many participants stated that they were still not meeting client needs 18 months after the storms. Twelve step fellowships became smaller and were not as healthy as they were prior to the disaster.

Facilities

In terms of the challenges that facilities faced, space for treatment within surviving facilities was much more limited due to a need to shift services from areas that were completely without facilities. These facility challenges varied depending on location. Some participants reported complete deletion of services. A participant from a rural area reported there were no detoxification services, methadone clinics, or crisis beds available in the catchment area. In fact, the closest medical detoxification was 200 miles away. Inpatient services continued to be unavailable more than two years post disaster in many areas that had those resources prior to the disaster. Participants reported feeling frustrated with federal agencies that provided some services immediately after the storms, but pulled those services away just before the one-year anniversary. Other participants described their goal as a facility to "just get back to normal." Nearly two years post-Katrina, a participant described the state of his facility this way:

We haven't even been able to get post (trauma) . . . it is (still) really trauma. We aren't post anything. We still have many people waiting for a trailer to live in, living in cars. We have much more of a homeless population than we did prior to Katrina. Many of our staff lost everything they own and have to commute from further distances wherever they could find a place to rent. Our day to day living issues impact both our staff and our clients.

Responses

Responses to the challenges faced by the substance abuse providers post disaster were categorized into three areas: external support, administrative responses, and staff responses. Staff responses included those reactions from a personal perspective and from a professional perspective.

External Support

Participants reported experiencing positive support from the Substance Abuse and Mental Health Services Administration (SAMSHA) counselors and other entities sent to provide assistance, but that support came with built-in limitations. Some agencies were able to provide free services from federal grant money, but the financial support came with frustrating time limits and conditions. Because of this, agencies helped each other in unique and creative ways to extend resources to those most in need. External support resulted in new possibilities for some agencies in the form of new buildings with larger spaces to provide services. Help came from local churches, and some participants believed that individuals from the local community helped more than federal agencies sent to assist. One participant noticed how meaningful it was for volunteers who gave of their own time to assist substance abuse clients: "Lots of students from universities volunteered during their breaks and holidays. They came and said what can we do? Can we fold clothes for your clients? Anything. So it really was a huge outpouring. I have to say the quickest responses and the most meaningful came from people who volunteered their own time."

Administrative Responses

Participants described ways in which administrators in substance abuse treatment facilities had to be flexible in the provision of services. Administrators had to expand the boundaries of catchment areas, had to hire contract workers from outside of the area, and had to cross train available staff to provide services they were not originally trained or hired to do. Some participants who were administrators during the recovery phase described helping to meet staff basic needs, including food, shelter, and clothing before even attempting to serve clients. Administrators valued staff that were dedicated and loyal to the facility and reported firing some staff for lack of loyalty.

Staff Responses

Staff responses to the aftermath of the tragedy emerged in two categories: personal and professional. Personal responses included emotional and physical reactions to the trauma, as well as adaptations used to cope. Professional responses involved adaptation in terms of skills, knowledge and behavior in order to meet the needs of clients.

Personal Responses—Immediately following the disaster, participants reported feeling uncertain, confused, helpless, fearful, and angry. Anger increased as staff perceived the lack of local and national response to the emergency and at the slow pace of regaining resources. Tremendous grief and loss issues affected staff personally and some described physical effects such as increased hypertension, suppressed immunity, and other stress-related health problems. Most participants emphasized a need for staff to practice self-care by having a place to vent frustrations and to get support from supervisors. One administrator shared:

> A lot of staff are going through exactly the same thing that the clients are going through. Being very flexible with them to take time off, to go do things for themselves, and get away from here.

Another participant noted the connection between self care and counseling skills and stated:

> Be ready to meet the client where he is, and it may not be a pretty place, physically and emotionally, but be willing to do that if you

are going to work here. And take care of yourself because the amount of trauma that you are going to be dealing with is more than you think.

Some participants expressed resentment that evacuees coming to their areas received higher priority status for services than local clients. Adaptation came for some in the form of assisting others by carrying food and water. Rising above one's own needs gave some a sense of responsibility and felt rewarding in a time of great chaos and helplessness. It is important to note that there were regional differences in the experience of trauma. Those closest to the devastation seemed to feel the consequences more intensely and experience more loss.

Professional Responses. Participants described having to adapt in terms of stretching their abilities, cross-training (especially related to dually diagnosed clients), wider thinking in terms of client issues and resources, sharing treatment paradigms with other mental health workers and increasing collaboration with other disciplines. One participant stated:

> If you could imagine a half a million people suffering PTSD. To one degree or another, everybody in a single weekend their lives changed and will never change back in the same way.

Similarly, another professional explained:

> We are dealing with a totally different person now. We are dealing with people that have been traumatized, along with substance abuse. So its completely different, not just you come for AA or NA and that's it. You are dealing more so with a dual diagnosis, than we ever have before.

One participant reported an increase in dually diagnosed client populations by 80%. Knowledge of prescription medications and methadone treatment was essential in some areas due to the increase in prescriptions being given to combat stress related to trauma as well as helping to maintain clients who were under methadone treatment prior to the tragedy.

In terms of skills needed, prevention skills, assessment skills, knowledge of PTSD, trauma skills, empathy, and grief skills were all very important and useful in assisting clients. Participants described the ability to normalize the experience of trauma as essential and to practice with the awareness that the storm story is still "alive" in clients. Assessments for services had to include close listening to each storm story, which ultimately helped connect counselors with their clients.

Professionally it was important for participants to fight for clients needs and to go out on the street to help meet their basic needs and to do what needed to be done. Priorities shifted, counselors went beyond the call of duty, connected people to resources, and showed a high amount of flexibility in their approach to work. One participant described his most valuable professional counseling resource as "the patience and optimism" he has gained with age.

Lessons Learned

Participants expressed learning in the aftermath of the disasters in terms of pleasant and unpleasant surprises and lessons for preparedness in the future.

Surprises

Positive outcomes included new opportunities for agency growth that allowed previously underfunded visions for expansions to come to fruition. Federal funding allowed many agencies to boost services such as new drug education schools and to expand services to families and children. One participant was stunned that a celebrity donated money to rebuild an A.A. clubhouse destroyed in the storm. The disaster also forced agencies to create emergency preparedness plans where none existed previously. These emergency plans also forced more collaboration and communication between agencies that previously provided services in separate systems. Others were pleasantly surprised about how successful their agency was at meeting client needs despite initial struggles. This success was often related to staff pulling together, as well as the resilience of the system, clients and staff. As one participant stated, "I was surprised by the resilience of people. I'm amazed at the determination of people to rebuild, to regroup, to have a life." Another participant observed that the discomfort following the disaster caused more people to seek services for addiction who would not have done so before.

Unpleasant Surprises

Unpleasant surprises included the fact that many communities still exist in Third World conditions several years post-disaster. The perceived lack of national empathy was surprising to one participant from New Orleans who described it this way:

> The negative, I guess, was the fact unless you're here and you see it everyday, you do not realize how very far we have to go 18 months after the fact. People who don't live here don't see the abandoned cars where families are living. They don't see the destroyed, abandoned houses that have not been demolished. They don't see that in my own personal neighborhood I have no grocery store still. I live in Orleans Parrish, in an area where some of the greater devastation occurred. So I think that is very surprising to me that this whole situation from the beginning, when people were on roofs for five to six days begging to be saved in the United States of America, to today. Unless you're here, I know people get tired of hearing it, but we are living in Third World conditions . . . none of us who are U.S. citizens for life would've ever expected for this to occur in our town or country. And the fact that we are struggling to provide any level of health care to people in this area, from medical to psychiatric and addictive disorders, this far after the fact . . . that we're still struggling to find the resources.

Future Preparedness

Participants emphasized the need for staff and agency flexibility. They view clear communication and expectations set for staff and clients as important factors for future preparedness. The provisions of emergency transportation for staff, as well as having alternate forms of communication available were also expressed by them as important factors to enhance readiness. In addition, participants perceived compassion balanced with objectivity as an important component of preparedness for future disaster response as was being able to provide clients with education about how to connect with resources. Participants recommended counselors utilize excellent listening skills, observation and reflecting skills, empathy skills and recognize that their presence alone created reassurance for clients following Hurricane Katrina. It is crucial that counselors be prepared to meet clients where they are and to address the most immediate needs as they are presented. Many participants reported that they expect to be learning from these disasters for many years to come.

Discussion

This study was conducted to examine substance abuse professionals' experiences following Hurricane Katrina in the fall of 2005. Qualitative analyses revealed that professionals face a variety of challenges and responses 12-18 months post disaster. The results of this study indicate that post disaster shifts in population result in both an increased demand for services in some areas and loss of clients in others. Results indicated disruption, and in some instances a complete loss, in services. Findings also studies (Kessler et al., 2006; Weisler, et al., 2006) which concluded that professionals who provide substance abuse services have to consider other mental health concerns. Post-disaster, clients demonstrated increases in presenting problems with PTSD and suicidal ideation. In line with previous outcome research (Frank et al., 2006), the need for new and improved emergency preparedness plans for mental health and substance abuse agencies is warranted. In the current study, communication systems emerged as a specific concern for substance abuse treatment administrators post-hurricane. Finally, findings support (Zywiack et al., 2003) who concluded that individuals in recovery might experience an increased likelihood for relapse.

The finding of personal impact on treatment professionals is noteworthy. Participant experiences affected them on a variety of levels including personal loss, grief, and trauma while remaining in the role of service provider. This finding of mental health needs of professional staff is supported in previous research (Frank et al., 2006). Surprisingly, this finding manifested during the first author's telephone interviews for the study. Despite being 12-18 months post- Katrina, several research participants became noticeably emotional recounting their experiences. This indicated not only the personal impact of the hurricanes, but the nature of the long term recovery process for treatment professionals. The current study was initiated with a focus on service provision of treatment providers. Qualitative interviews yielded data that were more personal in nature.

Implications for Counselors and Future Research

Findings of the present study result yielded implications for substance abuse professionals and educators. First, the learning curve post-disaster continues. The current study suggests that emergency plans need to be reviewed in order to prepare agencies for disaster scenarios. Preparation exists on a personal level as treatment professionals are not immune from the impact of disaster. The importance of self-care, both post-disaster and long-term emerged from the current study. Staff needs should be addressed and managed for more effective service provision to clients. This may entail individuals recognizing their own needs and limitations for treating clients and seeking appropriate support. Results demonstrate implications for counselor education programs. Core skills including attending, reflecting, active listening, empathy, and demonstrating genuine care for client appear to be imperative when working with populations who have experienced disaster. In addition, training programs that offer coursework preparing substance abuse professionals should emphasize specialty areas such as grief, trauma, psychopharmacology, PTSD and other mental health disorders.

Future research of the personal and professional impact of disaster for substance abuse professionals is suggested. In-depth research focused on the personal experiences of treatment providers would add to disaster research. The current study could be replicated as a longitudinal study to examine the long-term impact of hurricane-affected areas five years post-disaster. Finally, quantitative studies focused on treatment providers would support, confirm the current study on factors such as co-morbidity of mental health and substance abuse diagnoses, agency needs, client needs, relapse, and others.

Limitations and Conclusion

The authors recognize limitations of the current study. While a limited number of participants is generic to qualitative research (Creswell, 1998), generalizability of the results of this study should be tempered with caution as 11 participants were included. Nevertheless, the data analysis revealed consistency within and between the participants' experience that supports the themes that resulted from the data analysis.

Weisler, et al. (2006) indicated when rebuilding a healthcare infrastructure, a primary focus of attention must include health care workers and consider the patients they serve. One goal of the present study was to provide a voice for substance abuse treatment professionals who experienced professional and personal challenges while serving clients during this turbulent moment in U.S. history. Findings indicated that 12–18 months after Hurricanes Katrina and Rita, participants remained in the thick of a long term, complex, professional and personal recovery process.

References

Adams, R. E., Boscarino, J. A., & Galea, S. (2006). Alcohol use, mental health status and psychological well being 2 years after the world trade center attacks in New York city. *The American Journal of Drug and Alcohol Abuse, 32,* 202-224.

Andrews, J. L. (2006, November/December). In Katrina's wake: Healthcare crisis in New Orleans. *The Humanist.*

Bacon, P., Jr. (2005, September 19). Paying for Katrina. *Time, 166,* 22.

Boscarino, J. A., Adams, R. E., & Galea, S. (2005). Alcohol use in New York after the terrorist attacks: A study of the effects of psychological trauma on drinking behavior. *Addictive Behaviors, Vol 31*(4), 606-621.

Creswell, J. (1998). *Qualitative Inquiry and Research Design; Choosing Among Five Traditions.* London, Thousand Oaks, Sage Publications.

Druss, B. G., Henderson, K. L., & Rosenheck, R. A. (2007). Swept away: Use of general medical and mental health services among veterans displaced by hurricane Katrina. *American Journal of Psychiatry 164*(1), 154-156.

Feldman, C. (2006, August 20). Overburdened long before Katrina, the public mental health network here is finding it impossible to meet need. *Houston Chronicle.* Retrieved from http://www.chron.com/cs/CDA/printstory.mpl/chronicle/4128667.

Frank, B., Dewart, T., Schmeidler, J., & Demirjian, A., (2006). The impact of 9/11 on New York City's substance abuse treatment programs. *Journal of Addictive Diseases, 25,* 5-14.

Keilman, J. (2005, September 09). Storm chaos cuts help for addicts. *Chicago Tribune,* Retrieved from http://www.chicagotribune.com

Kessler, R. C., Galea, S., Jones, R. T., & Parker, H A. (2006). Mental illness and suicidality after hurricane Katrina. *Bulletin of the World Health Organization,* article ID 06-033019.

Lecompte, M. D., & Schensul, J.J. (1999). Analyzing and Interpreting Ethnographic Data. In: Schensul, J.J. & Lecompton, M.D., eds. *Ethnographer's Toolkit,* Vol. 5. Walnut Creek, CA: Altamira Press.

Lincoln, Y. S., & Guba, E. G. (1985). *Naturalistic inquiry.* Newbury Park, CA Sage.

Miles, M. B., & Huberman, A. M. (1994). *Qualitative data analysis: A sourcebook of new methods* (2nd Ed.). Newbury Park, CA: Sage.

North, C. S., King, R. V., Fowler, R. L., Polatin, P., Smith, R. P., LaGrone, A., Tyler, D., Larkin, G. L., Pepe, P. E. (2008). Psychiatric disorders among transported hurricane evacuees: Acute-phase findings in a large receiving shelter site. *Psychiatric Annals, 38*(2), 104-113.

Norris, F. H., Speier, A., Henderson, A. K., Davis, S. I., Purcell, D. W., Stratford, B. D., Baker, C. K., Reissman, D. B., & Daley, W. R. (2006). Assessment of health-related needs after hurricane Katrina and Rita – Orleans and Jefferson Parishes, New Orleans Area, Louisiana, October 17-22, 2005. *Morbidity & Mortality Weekly Report,* January 20, 2006, 38-41.

North, C. S., Tivis, L., McMillen, J. C., Pfefferbaum, B., Spitznagel, E. L., Cox, J., . . . Smith, E. M. (2002). Psychiatric disorders in rescue workers after the Oklahoma City bombing. *American Journal of Psychiatry, 159*(5), 857-859.

Patton, M. Q. (1990). *Qualitative evaluation and research methods.* Newbury Park, CA: Sage Publications.

Post-disaster response. (2006) Post-disaster response: Learning from research (Part 2). SAMHSA News, 14(4) Retrieved from http://www.samhsa_News/VolumeXIV_4/text_only/article1txt.htm

Pfefferbaum, B., Shreekumar S. V., Trautman, R. P., Lensgraf, S. J., Reddy, C., Patel, N., & Ford, A. L. (2002). The effect of loss and trauma on substance use behavior in individuals seeking support services after the 1995 Oklahoma City bombing. *Annals of Clinical Psychiatry, 14*(2), 89-95.

Pond, M. H., (2006). Hurricane recovery guides preparedness planning (Part 1). SAMHSA News,14(4). Retrieved from http://www.samhsa.gov/SAMHSA_News/VolumeXIV_4/index.htm

Rodriguez, H. & Aguirre, B. E. (2006) Hurricane Katrina and the healthcare infrastructure: A focus on disaster preparedness, response, and resiliency. *Frontier of Health Services Management, 23*, 13-24.

Rudowitz, R., Rowland, D., and Shartzer, A. (2006). Health care in New Orleans before and after Hurricane Katrina. *Medical Benefits or Health Affairs Web Exclusives, August 29*, 2006.

Simons, J. S., Gaher, R. H., Jacobs, G. A., Meyer, D., & Johnson-Jimenez, E. (2005). Association between alcohol use and PTSD symptoms among American Red Cross disaster relief workers responding to the 9/11/2001 attacks. *The American Journal of Drug and Alcohol Abuse, 31*, 285-304.

Strauss, A. & Corbin, J. (1990). *Basics of qualitative research: Grounded theory procedures and techniques.* Newbury Park, CA: Sage.

Toriello, P. J., Pedersen-Wasson, E., Crisham, E. M., Ellis, R., Morse, P., & Morse, E. V. (2007). Surviving Hurricane Katrina: Winds of change transform a New Orleans treatment agency. *Journal of Addictions and Offender Counseling, 28*, 44-59.

US Department of Health and Human Services. (2008). Impact of hurricanes Katrina and Rita on substance use and mental health national survey on drug use and health: The NSDUH report. Retrieved from http://www.oas.samhsa.gov/2k8/katrina/katrina.pdf

Vlahov, D., Galea, S., Ahern, J., Resnick, H., Boscarino, J. A., Gold, J., Bucuvalas, M., & Kilpatrick, D. (2004). Consumption of cigarettes, alcohol, and marijuana among New York City residents six months after the September 11 terrorist attacks. *The American Journal of Drug and Alcohol Abuse, 30*(2), 385-487.

Voelker, R. (2005). Katrina's impact on mental health. *The Journal of the American Medical Association, 294*(13), 1599-1600.

Weisler, R .H., Barbee IV, J. G., & Townsend, M. H. (2006). Mental health and recovery in the Gulf Coast region after Hurricanes Katrina and Rita. *The Journal of the American Medical Association, 296*(5), 585-588.

Zywiak, W. H., Stout, R. L., Trefry, W. B., LaGrutta, J. E., Lawson, C. C., Khan, Nazia, Swift, R. M. & Schneider, R. J. (2003). Alcohol relapses associated with September 11, 2001: A case report. Substance Abuse, 24(2), 123-128.

Appendix

Semi-Structured
Interview Questions

1. Please describe substance abuse counseling practice in your area prior to hurricanes Katrina and Rita? Months after the disaster? One year post disaster?

2. Describe any obstacles or challenges you and your agency have faced over the past year in service provision to substance abusers and their families?

3. Have there been any positive effects for your agency as a result of the crisis?

4. Describe your work or interface with other agencies post disaster. (ex. FEMA, Red Cross)

5. How have presenting problems of clients changed?

6. In terms of your counseling skills, what areas have you drawn on the most?

7. What skill areas or competencies have been challenged the most?

8. What skills have you found lacking in your training that could have prepared you better to deal with the effects of the disaster?

9. Describe any changes in your agency to help deal with the needs of substance abuse clients post disaster.

10. Describe the needs for staff members who were personally affected socially or emotionally by the disaster.

11. What has surprised you most from this experience?

12. What message or advice would you have for substance abuse professionals related to disaster response?

13. What would you like to add from either the client's perspective or from your point of view?

10

Voices of Recovery

An Investigative Study of the Effectiveness of Gender-Sensitive Substance Abuse Treatment

TELSIE A. DAVIS AND CATHERINE Y. CHANG[1]

National treatment protocols recommend women be provided gender-sensitive substance abuse treatment (GSSAT). Although the benefit of such treatment appears obvious, little empirical data exists to support its efficacy. This study investigated the effectiveness of GSSAT from the female clients' perspective.

Approximately 1 in 10 Americans have a substance use disorder (Substance Abuse and Mental Health Services Administration [SAMHSA], 2003b). Substance abuse, an umbrella term for substance use disorders and substance misuse, is so pervasive that it has been associated with such public health problems as violence against women, car accidents, transmission of sexually transmitted infections and HIV/AIDS, unintended pregnancies, school failure, low work productivity, homelessness, and suicide (Blumenthal, 2002; Office of National Drug

1. Telsie A. Davis, School of Medicine, Emory University; Catherine Y. Chang, Department of Counseling and Psychological Services, Georgia State University. The authors would like to thank research assistants Danica Landry and Cassaundra Trimble for their diligent efforts in the coding of data. Correspondence concerning this article should be addressed to Telsie A. Davis, Emory University School of Medicine, Department of Psychiatry and Behavioral Sciences, 80 Jesse Hill Jr. Drive, Atlanta, GA 30303. E-mail: telsie.a.davis@emory.edu.

Control Policy [ONDCP], 2001). One in 14 hospitalizations are the result of substance abuse (Robert Wood Johnson Foundation [RWJF], 2009) and substance abuse-related problems have cost the United States an estimated $277 billion annually (U.S. Department of Health and Human Services [USDHHS], 2000; RWJF, 2009). Despite the indiscriminate nature of substance abuse, it has been traditionally conceptualized as a problem of men (Blumenthal, 2002; Kropp, & Banhal-Baugus, 1996); where men have been the focus of treatment and research despite historical evidence that American women have suffered substance abuse since before the Civil War (Blumenthal, 2002).

It is estimated that ". . . 200,000 American women will die of substance abuse-related illnesses this year—more than four times the amount who will die of breast cancer" (National Center for Health Statistics, 1993, p. 46, as cited in Blumenthal, 2002, p.13). Approximately one in three women in the United States has used an illicit drug at least once in her life, and among women of childbearing age (15–44 years of age), the rate is estimated at 45% (SAMHSA, 2003b). Moreover, an estimated 15% of all American women ages 15 to 44 are currently abusing alcohol or illicit drugs (SAMHSA, 2003b). Despite these alarming statistics, the plight of female substance abusers has been traditionally "masked by national denial" (Blumenthal, 2002, p. 13). In this article, the phrase "female substance abusers" is used to refer to women with substance use disorders.

Past denial of female substance abuse has perpetuated under-representation, and often, complete disregard of female substance abusers in the research literature (Brady & Ashley, 2005; Greenfield, 2002; Kropp & Banhal-Baugus, 1996). This disparity in the literature has resulted in male-designed and male-normed substance abuse treatment models being generalized to women (Blumenthal, 2002; Copeland & Hall, 1992; Kropp & Banhal-Baugus, 1996; Sterk, Elifson & Theall, 2000). Recently, researchers have argued that male-oriented substance abuse treatment results in poorer outcomes for female clients in comparison to men (Brady & Ashley, 2005); the consensus being that the male-oriented models are inadequately responsive to the needs of women (Arfken, Klein, di Menza & Schuster, 2001; Ghee, Johnson, Burlew & Bolling, 2009; Petry & Bickel, 2000).

SAMHSA (2003a) reported that in 2002, approximately one-third of substance abuse facilities offered gender-sensitive treatment programming for women. With increased efforts underway to expand the reach of

GSSAT, more studies of treatment efficacy are needed to identify whether it merits widespread policy changes and implementation. Thus, the purpose of this study was to explore the effectiveness of GSSAT. Specifically, this investigation sought to understand the impact of this treatment on women's recovery from substance use through the perceptions and lived experiences of the female clients served.

Gender and Sex Differences

In 1994, the research and treatment communities formally embraced a national focus on women's health and addictive disorders (Blumenthal, 2002). This new focus looked to redress past oversights and inequities, prompting critical examination of gender and sex differences research that indicated female substance abusers differed from their male counterparts in ways that may be relevant to their treatment (Blumenthal, 2002). To date, increased amounts of research concerning gender and sex differences among substance abusers has led to robust findings regarding the unique characteristics of women.

Researchers have documented that men and women differ in regards to precipitant causes of substance abuse; types of substances abused; patterns of use; and physiological, psychological and social modes of experiencing and expressing substance abuse (Brady & Ashley, 2005; Nelson-Zlupko et al., 1996; Weissman & O'Boyle, 2000). Women are more likely to have been exposed to drugs by men, and to use drugs to cope with emotional distress rooted in psychosocial problems and traumatic life events including sexual and physical abuse (Brady & Ashley, 2005; Nelson-Zlupko et al., 1996). Women report more frequent abuse of sedatives and tranquillizers (Blumenthal, 2002), but are more likely to enter treatment for heroin and cocaine use (SAMHSA, 2001). Women tend to use later in life, become addicted faster, and have a more rapid development of addiction-related medical problems (Nelson-Zlupko et al., 1996; Westermeyer & Boedicker, 2000). They are also more likely to use in isolation and have fewer social networks (Sanders-Phillips, 2002). Upon presentation to treatment, women are generally less educated, have fewer marketable skills, fewer financial resources, and are more preoccupied with daily survival issues and parental responsibility than are men (Nelson-Zlupko et al., 1996; Westermeyer & Boedicker, 2000).

Gender-Sensitive Substance Abuse Treatment

Gender-sensitive substance abuse treatment (GSSAT) is conceptualized as treatment responsive to empirically validated gender and sex differences (Marsh et al., 2000; Nelson-Zlupko et al., 1996; Sterk et al., 2000). There is no universally accepted definition of what constitutes GSSAT for women (Bradley & Ashley, 2005). However, gender-sensitive programming often includes one or more of the following core components: (a) interventions aimed at reducing barriers to treatment such as transportation and childcare, (b) admissions or services for women only such as women-only groups and female counselors, (c) ancillary services that address female-specific issues such as prenatal and gynecological care, and (d) a strength-based treatment philosophy that facilitates a supportive and empowering treatment environment (Bradley & Ashley, 2005; Marsh et al;., 2000; Moras, 2002; Nelson-Zlupko et al., 1996; Weissman & O'Boyle, 2000). Given the rationale for GSSAT is compelling and theoretically sound, and the benefit of implementation appears obvious, empirical investigation is warranted to measure its effectiveness (Kaskutas, Zhang, French & Witbrodt, 2005; Moras, 2002; Nelson-Zlupko et al., 1996).

Method

Design

Since the area of GSSAT remains largely unchartered in the research literature, Glaser and Strauss' (1967) grounded theory approach to qualitative methodology was chosen to generate a substantive theory about the effectiveness of gender-sensitive treatment that was derived from the data. The choice of methodology was also influenced by the researchers' desire to give voice to this historically silenced population's knowledge of their own treatment experiences and needs.

Participants

Participants included 10 women; eight who participated in individual interviews, and four (including two who participated in individual interviews) who participated in the focus group. Women self-identified as

African American (n = 4), Caucasian (n = 4), Latina (n = 1), and Mixed Race (n = 1). Ages ranged from 26 years to 47 years of age (M = 38 years). The average length of sobriety was 20 months. Five participants were married, two were divorced, two were single, and one did not report. Nine participants reported having children (M = 2.6). Two women lived alone with their children, five lived with their partner/spouse and children, and two lived with their children and a grandparent. Four participants earned a high school diploma, one had taken college classes, one had taken technical classes, and four did not complete high school. Seven participants received some type of government assistance and reported an income level of less than $10,000. Two participants received disability disbursements, and one participant reported spousal support. Alcohol, pain medications (e.g. oxycontin, percocet), and marijuana were abused by 50% of the participants. Cocaine, crack, heroin, and benzodiazepines were abused by 40% of the participants, followed by methamphetamine (30%), ecstacy (20%), and other drugs (20%). Poly-substance abuse occurred among all participants. Seven participants were prescribed methadone as a treatment for opiate dependence. Eight participants reported being diagnosed with a mental health disorder and taking psychotropic medications for co-occurring disorders. Eight participants reported being physically, emotionally, and/or sexually abused.

Setting

Data was collected in a community substance abuse treatment center in an urban area in the Southeastern United States. The center services adult men and women, 18 years of age and older, and provides both Methadone Maintenance and Drug-Free Treatment and Education programs. Fourteen treatment team members service both programs. Seven members of the treatment team are licensed and/or certified counselors, and five are female. Both the center director and medical director are male, and the clinical supervisor, who is also the principal investigator of this study, is female. The center provides GSSAT programming consisting of: transportation services; a children's play area; female individual counselors for women if requested; women-only therapy groups; a parenting group; and ancillary services such as obstetrics and gynecology, adult medicine, laboratory, eye and dental services, provided by the parent organization, a community primary care center.

Research Team

The research team consisted of the principal investigator, second author and two research assistants. The principal investigator is an African American woman and licensed professional counselor with 10 years of experience working with women with substance use disorders at the time of the study. She acknowledged the following assumptions prior to the investigation: (a) women thrive in a context of compassion and acceptance, (b) women feel more comfortable in settings where there are just women, and (c) the presence of men in group therapy inhibits women from being open and truthful about themselves and their issues. The second author is a Korean American woman who is a tenured associate professor of counselor education and licensed professional counselor with 14 years of experience specializing in multicultural issues in counseling, counselor education and supervision, and social justice issues. Both research assistants were African American female students in a Council for Accreditation of Counseling and Related Educational Programs (CACREP) accredited master's professional counseling program.

Procedure

Female participants actively enrolled in treatment, diagnosed as having a substance use disorder, and having a minimum of 30 days of sobriety were eligible for participation in the study. Participants were recruited using convenience sampling followed by theoretical sampling, wherein after the interview of the first three participants, the selection of participants was guided by a desire to include cases that could test and extend existing data and emerging theory (LeCompte & Shensul, 1999). Each participant discussed and signed a consent form and completed a demographic questionnaire prior to the start of the interview and/or focus group.

Each individual interview was conducted and recorded by the principal investigator, and lasted approximately one and a half hours. The interviews were semi-structured, moving generally from simpler to more complex topics as a means to facilitate respondent comfort, thereby eliciting meaningful responses (LeCompte & Shensul, 1999) and facilitating more discriminate coding (Strauss & Corbin, 1998). A focus group interview lasting approximately 1 hour and 30 minutes, composed of four participants, was conducted and recorded by the principal investigator.

Focus group participants were asked interview questions similar to those posed during individual interviews. They were also asked to provide feedback on the themes generated from the individual interviews.

Data Analysis

A grounded theory approach utilizing constant comparative analysis as described by Glaser and Strauss (1967) and Glaser (1992) was used to analyze interview data. Thus, data collection was intertwined with data analysis (Glaser, 1992; Glaser & Strauss, 1967; LeCompte & Schensul, 1999). Each interview was recorded and transcribed verbatim by the principal investigator. Transcripts of the interviews were submitted to the participants for review and to ensure participants felt heard and understood. No new information was received from the participants' feedback regarding the transcripts.

The principal investigator and second author began analyzing initial interviews using open coding methods so that all concepts and phenomena remotely relevant to the research topic were labeled (Brown et al., 2002; Glaser, 1999; Glaser & Strauss, 1967; Strauss & Corbin, 1998). To reduce the chances that personal biases of a single researcher would disproportionately influence the findings, the researchers coded independently and then came together for consensus after each interview. This process served to fulfill investigator triangulation as described by Denzin and Lincoln (1994). Each meeting concluded with the development of a codebook by which subsequent interviews were coded. Open coding of initial interviews produced key themes that formed the basis for more focused interviews. After the first six interviews, the researchers decided to conduct additional interviews in an attempt to reach saturation of the data. After two additional interviews, analyzed following the same protocol described above, the researchers agreed that the "informational saturation point" had been met (i.e. patterns of response began to replicate themselves and the data failed to generate new information) (Glaser, 1999; Glaser & Strauss, 1967; LeCompte & Shensul, 1999).

The principal investigator proceeded with axial coding on all eight interviews, which concerned refining core categories and identifying meaningful relationships between codes that offered preliminary explanations of the phenomena under study (Brown et al., 2002; Glaser, 1999; Glaser & Strauss, 1967). This concluded with the collapsing of themes and the formation of a condensed codebook that included three core categories corresponding to the three objectives of the study.

Two research assistants served as peer debriefers to ensure findings were grounded in the data (Brown et al., 2002; Lincoln & Guba, 1985). Both research assistants attended a joint-training session with the principal investigator before coding. Each reviewed a single transcript independently to assess the consistency between the raw data and the codebook. The principal investigator met jointly with the research assistants after each review to discuss discrepant findings and ensure high interrater agreement before moving to the next transcription. Decisions to amend, add, or eliminate codes were reached by consensus.

Next, the focus group interview was conducted to serve as an additional source of information, as well as, a source of validation of pre-existing themes. The recording of the focus group was coded collectively by the principal research and research assistants against the codebook. New information was used to amend the code book. In the final stage, data analysis consisted of selective coding of the data (Glaser, 1999; Glaser & Strauss, 1967) where the principal investigator scrutinized the dominant categories, and identified one core category that "pull[ed] all other categories together to form an explanatory whole" (Strauss & Corbin, 1990, p. 146).

Credibility

A number of steps were taken to ensure credibility. The effect of researcher bias was minimized through the practice of disciplined subjectivity wherein the principal investigator actively engaged in critical self-reflection through use of a reflexive journal (LeCompte & Shensul, 1999). Two member checks occurred when participants were given copies of their transcribed interviews to review, and through the use of a focus group to provide feedback on codes derived from individual interviews. Investigator triangulation was fulfilled in the use of two coders and two peer debriefers. Triangulation of data sources occurred in the analysis of multiple data sources (i.e. interviews and a focus group). Lastly, negative case analysis was performed on the transcription of the only participant to report having no preference for working with a female or male counselor.

Results

Data analysis of participant interviews revealed an overarching theme that GSSAT is effective and yielded two subthemes endorsed by all participants that provided an explanation for the perceived effectiveness. According to the participants, GSSAT is effective because it provides: (a) a supportive recovery environment for women comprised of five factors and (b) yields four positive treatment outcomes.

Supportive Recovery Environment for Women

Treatment effectiveness was significantly attributed to the presence of a supportive recovery environment for women. Data analysis indicated that the treatment environment was supportive of recovery because it encompassed five factors: (a) respect-of-person, (b) empowerment, (c) access to information, (d) women-only therapy opportunities, and (e) mixed-gender groups. Analysis did not reveal a hierarchy of the factors, nor did the factors always exist independently in the data. Factors were often found to intersect. For example, descriptions of women-only therapy opportunities often referenced the factor of respect-of-person and the factor of access to information often intersected with empowerment.

Respect-of-Person—Respect-of-person encompasses the idea that clients are valued and affirmed for their inherent worth as a person, irrespective of what they have previously done, said, or experienced. Participants reported that GSSAT afforded them respect-of-person, wherein they were treated in a nonjudgmental fashion and acknowledged as human beings.

> . . . I want just to be understood, you know, and so, in the women's group it's just, it's easy to be understood and understand, it's just a very comfortable atmosphere, that you know, you don't feel judgmental or judged or it's just really comfortable, and comforting, to know that I'm not crazy.

Another participant echoed the above sentiment.

> And can you imagine how much good that can do for a person that has done wrong, but the person that is helping you heal let's you know that even though you've done wrong, it's okay; don't just keep beating you upside the head about it all the time. Can you imagine?

Empowerment—The participants' verbatim descriptions included many references to empowerment, particularly related to their perceptions that treatment interventions instilled hope, acknowledged their strength and personal power, and positively targeted their self-esteem. Participants reported of the benefit of working with counselors who could see potential in them when they could not see it in themselves: "She could see, she could tell that I wanted to be a better person, and I think she saw that better person in me. And she knew where my heart was at and where I wanted to be." "You made me know that I could make it, you made me feel so worthwhile, you made me feel that I could ahh, continue on with life, and get my life back, you know." Another participant stated,

> I talk to her and she just knows how to say things that may get, that make me . . . not to make me feel bad, but just to feel good about myself, where I don't have to stay down, she keeps me happy.

Access to Information—Access to information refers to what participants described as having opportunities to gain new insights and obtain relevant and useful skills to support recovery. Mention of this element occurred in participant depictions of working with female and male counselors and peers, as well as participating in women-only and mixed-gender groups. Depictions of this factor often referenced empowerment, wherein the learning of new coping skills had a positive impact on self-efficacy. Participants reported:

> Uhm, just hearing other people's stories, and you know, they're, the things that they've been through and uhm, how they got honest and how they got off of drugs and you know, how they're staying clean, and just how they're, you know stories about their children, cause we've all got kids, so ahh, and stuff like that. Even about being with their husbands or live-in friends and just I don't know that's about the best way I can describe it. Just having them, just being there listening helps, to hear it, to compare my stories to some of the other people, and see that if they can do it, I can do it.
>
> This is giving me a great opportunity to learn how to feel comfortable . . . I guess I just learned I guess maybe different ways of dealing with those confrontations, instead of the same old you know running from it or hiding from it, avoiding the confrontation, uhm finding the positive out of it, and confronting it respectfully and finding out what is the real issue is and taking care of it, putting closure to it.

Women-only Therapy Opportunities—Participants articulated the value placed on having occasions where women could connect with other women, in the presence of women only. Participants asserted that women-only groups and individual counseling sessions with a female counselor were the only instances they felt safe to disclose sensitive, personal information. They also reported these two opportunities as being the most helpful components of GSSAT. Depictions of women-only therapy opportunities frequently referenced respect-of-person, wherein the opportunity to interact among women only often provided experiences perceived as non-judgmental. Elaborating on the importance of women-only therapy opportunities in general, one participant reported,

> I can't do men. I've tried. I have tried. It wasn't a good experience for me. Men tend to be judgmental you know, from my experience you know with my psychiatrist, he was judgmental you know. Uhm, he wanted me to see things from a man's point of view as well as from a woman's point of view, how can I do that, I'm a woman.

Women-only Groups—In conveying a preference for women-only groups, participants reported: "Well, uhm, if you're asking which one has done me the most good, I would have to say the group for the women-only. Because you know, we can be a little bit more open, ahh, than with the men . . ." "I've always liked more the women groups. With the women's group we can more be in tune with women's stuff because we are so much emotional." ". . . the women's group was so different, it was just, it just was like a sense of belonging, I belonged there, I needed to be there because I belonged there, you know. It gave me something to work around you know."

Individual Counseling with a Female Counselor—In conveying preference for working individually with a female counselor, participants reported: ". . . I just feel more comfortable with a female being that I'm a woman . . . especially, I guess, more so when it comes to personal issues that I think a woman can understand better because maybe she's been through it." "I don't know . . . , just like I say, I'm always more comfortable with a woman counselor because of me, I'm emotional, and I don't know, I just feel like women understand better."

Mixed-Gender Groups—All participants identified mixed-gender groups as contributing to the effectiveness of GSSAT; and all participants described these groups as less helpful than women-only therapies. The benefit of mixed-gender groups was largely attributed to its ability to recreate within treatment, the natural composition of society in which women have to live. This benefit is illustrated in the following quotes:

> . . . You know our lives are not conditioned that we only have to deal with women. You know, ahh, but we leave from here behind these doors, you know we go out to the world, and we deal with husbands, brothers, lovers, potential lovers, you know, boyfriends, fiancés you know, bosses on jobs.

> When you have a co-ed group going on, it's realizing what men go through and maybe men realize what women go through, and uhm, so it makes it you know, it's helpful.

All participants endorsed three main limitations of mixed-gender groups: disrespect, objectification, and harsh judgment. All three limitations referred to the treatment of women by male clients and male staff in mixed-gender groups. The following participant quotes illustrate one of the limitations. One participant described the disrespect she experienced in mixed-gender groups by saying,

> I've been in some groups where men were very disrespectful toward women too . . . Because women be crying, pouring their heart out and they [men] just be like, "Get over it." or "Let me tell you, let me tell you how to run this." or "tell you how to do this." And basically they ain't doing no work, they just talking.

Another participant depicted feeling objectified by male treatment staff and male clients. She stated,

> . . . I would feel a lot of times with uhm, with male counselors, you know, doctors, you know whatever, uhm, that it was just like they were looking at me like I was a thing, you know cause I was female. It was like I could see, it's horrible sometimes when you see them looking at your chest . . . It almost feels like sometimes, they weren't flirting or anything, it was just like hanging in the air you know . . . I can't explain, I don't have the words for it . . . a lot of times I felt like men looked at me as a sexual object, they didn't look at me as a person, you know, so that just made it, just harder, it was always a wall there.

In describing the harsh judgment of women she witnessed in mixed-gender groups, a participant stated,

> You know, see, men have issues with sex, alright, wanting sex, you know. Women, when a woman is putting herself out there as, "I was doing this and doing that," you know, they're always looked at as whores, you know. But when a man wants to go out and buy [sex], then they're not looked at like that, you know, it's clashing.

Positive Treatment Outcomes

In addition to offering a supportive recovery environment for women, participants reported that treatment effectiveness was also significantly associated with four positive treatment outcomes. Participants unanimously endorsed the following positive treatment outcomes as evidence of GSSAT's effectiveness: (a) insight, (b) positive coping skills, (c) empowered behavior, and (d) re-engagement with family.

Insight—Participants reported having increased self-awareness due to treatment. One participant stated, "So the difference in what's changed since coming to treatment is I've opened my eyes to what life really is, and not my illusion that I was trying to box myself in with, you know." Another participant discussed gaining an awareness of how she can continue to improve her life. She stated,

> I wanna learn how to be a better mother, I wanna learn how to be a better friend, you know, then on the job I wanna learn how to give it my all, and feel confident when I'm in that board room meeting or if I'm in the nurses station or wherever, I just, you know and I've gained a lot of, I guess insight on how I can do these things.

Positive Coping Skills—Participants reported gaining the use of new skills to help them cope with life stressors without the use of mood-altering substances. They reported of learning how to think and respond differently, and to participate in activities that are more positive and productive. One woman stated, ". . . I've attended church before, but I attend church more frequently . . . just, you know bowling, just trying to enjoy life, participating in different events with friends, things like that." Another said, "I'm getting a move on exercising, I'm more in healthcare. I'm more in taking

care of my health problems. Going to the doctor and see what way would
be the best for me to stay healthy. My eating have changed."

Empowered Behavior—Participants recounted stories of their newfound
ability to be responsible for and take charge of their lives since participating in gender-sensitive treatment. In discussing how she is responsible
as the result of treatment, a participant reported, ". . . it's just being accountable for who I am, for my actions, being responsible you know." In
discussing how treatment has aided in her taking charge of her life, one
woman shared,

> I'm going to be going to school . . . I'm thinking about CNA first,
> and while I'm working CNA, I can be thinking about what to do.
> Uhm, but just the doors that are opening that were, I didn't even
> see the doors before. You know just, I've just become somebody.

Re-engagement with Family—All participants reported experiencing a
lessening focus on themselves and an increasing focus on their loved ones
that came as a result of treatment. Participants noted that treatment presented an opportunity to focus on family members they neglected while
pursuing their addiction. One participant reported, "I'm very much more
involved in my children's life . . . just getting my son involved in like bas-
ketball camp, as was before, if we did something, it was just like oh god,
let's go ahead and go." Another stated,

> My family certainly, certainly like me more cause I'm there more,
> I can't, I can't rip and run like I use to cause I ain't got that ah, ah
> stuff in me you know . . . I'm just a, I'm a better mama, a better
> wife, just a better person . . .

Discussion

Findings support the theoretical argument that GSSAT is effective, and
its effectiveness is due to the supportive recovery environment it creates
and the positive treatment outcomes it yields. The supportive recovery
environment of GSSAT is achieved through the provision of five factors: (a) respect-of-person, (b) empowerment, (c) access to information,
(d) women-only therapy opportunities, and (e) mixed-gender groups.
The four positive treatment outcomes associated with GSSAT are:

(a) insight, (b) positive coping skills, (c) empowered behavior, and (d) re-engagement with family.

The finding that GSSAT fosters a supportive recovery environment for women supports previous findings and extends the literature. Four of the five factors that helped to create the supportive recovery environment found in this study (i.e. respect-of-person, empowerment, access to information, and women-only therapy opportunities) mirror the four core components identified by the literature, and reviewed earlier in this article, as necessary for any treatment programming to be gender-sensitive for women (Brady & Ashley, 2005). Findings for the fifth factor, mixed-gender groups, were novel. Mixed-gender groups have not been previously cited by the literature as a beneficial part of GSSAT. Thus, the finding that they are a contributing factor to the effectiveness of GSSAT broadens the literature and indicates mixed-gender groups warrant further study as a component of GSSAT. Participants' assertion that it was helpful to interact with men in group therapy given they would have to do so in their lives outside of treatment implies that traditional substance abuse programs may not have to completely abandon their co-ed structures to be responsive to the needs of women.

Consistent with the literature, participants unanimously noted that mixed-gender groups, although beneficial, were significantly less helpful than women-only therapies. Nelson-Zlupko et al. (1996) and Weissman & O'Boyle (2000) found that mixed-gender groups are less effective in meeting the needs of women in comparison to women-only groups. Based on the results of this study, we recommend that women should only participate in mixed-gender groups after they have gained sobriety, positive coping skills, and a sober support system in order to successfully deal with the disrespect, objectification, and harsh judgment of women that is routinely present.

The four types of positive outcomes (i.e. insight, positive coping skills, empowered behavior, and re-engagement with family) identified in this study parallel previous research findings. As a result of GSSAT, Baker (2004) found that women gained insight into their addictive, emotional, and parenting behavior, and demonstrated empowered behavior concerning their emotional health. Furthermore, Baker (2004) and Green et al. (2004) found that as a result of GSSAT, women gained positive coping skills, and also re-engaged with their children and family.

Implications

This grounded theory investigation provides practical knowledge of how to facilitate women's recovery in traditional substance abuse treatment settings. Our results suggest that treatment programs may not have to abandon traditional co-ed structures to successfully and appropriately serve women, but instead, can adopt women-sensitive treatment components (i.e. respect-of-person, empowerment, access to information, and women-only therapy opportunities) that are responsive to the needs of female substance abusers. Regarding research, this investigation adds to the paucity of empirical data on GSSAT and identifies treatment factors and outcomes that can be used to define and measure this treatment's effectiveness in comparison to other types of treatment for women. Currently, there is no universally accepted protocol of GSSAT (Brady & Ashley, 2005). Thus, gender-sensitive treatment can look very different from one treatment program to another. Given the core components included by most GSSAT programs were substantiated by these findings, we suggest that these components be a starting point for standardization and recommend quantitative inquiry of these factors.

Limitations

As we are aware of the benefits of this study, we are also aware of its limitations. All participants were clients at the principal researcher's agency of employment. Although the principal researcher processed informed consent issues with clients prior to their participation, including freedom to choose to participate and withdraw from the study at any point without fear of reprisal, it is unclear to what extent client participation and responses were affected by dual relationship issues. Moreover, the women that participated in this research may have felt more favorable about specialized women's treatment than those who did not, and thus, may have been more likely to agree to be interviewed.

Additionally, the results of this investigation are limited to a very specific population. However, of important note, generalizability is not a goal of grounded theory. Therefore, in lieu of aiming for widespread applicability, this study sought to gather a thick, rich description to explain client perceptions regarding GSSAT in one agency. Consequently, it was important to interview participants from one program to ensure the trustworthiness of the data. Nevertheless, the authors recognize that to protect against bias in participant responses, it may be helpful to have participants drawn from multiple agencies in future studies.

In closing, our examination of the effectiveness of GSSAT as perceived by women participants served to deepen understanding about the client's experience of gender-sensitive treatment, and endorses considerations of policy changes and widespread implementation of GSSAT. It is our belief that through the offering of respect-of-person, empowerment, access to information, women-only therapy opportunities, and mixed-gender groups once women have sobriety and support, women will be able to experience successful treatment outcomes such as insight, positive coping skills, empowered behavior, and re-engagement with family that have often alluded this underserved population.

References

Arfken, C. L., Klein, C., di Menza, S., Schuster, C. R. (2001). Gender differences in problem severity at assessment and treatment retention. *Journal of Substance Abuse Treatment, 20,* 53-57. doi:10.1016/S0740-5472(00)00155-0

Baker, P. L. (2000). I didn't know: Discoveries and identity transformation of women addicts in treatment. *Journal of Drug Issues, 30*(4), 863-880.

Blumenthal, S. (2002). Women and substance abuse: A new national focus. In C. Wetherington, & A. Roman (Eds.), *Drug addiction research and the health of women* (pp. 13-32). Bethesda, MD: U.S. Department of Health and Human Services, National Institutes of Health, National Institute on Drug Abuse. (Original work published 1998)

Brady, T. M., & Ashley, O. S. (Eds.). (2005). *Women in substance abuse treatment: Results from the Alcohol and Drug Services Study (ADSS)* (DHHS Publication No. SMA 04-3968, Analytic Series A-26). Rockville, MD: Substance Abuse and Mental Health Services Administration, Office of Applied Studies.

Copeland, J., & Hall, W. (1992). A comparison of women seeking drug and alcohol treatment in a specialist women's and two traditional mixed-sex treatment services. *British Journal of Addictions, 87,* 1293-1302. doi:10.1111/j.1360-0443.1992.tb02738.x

Denzin, N. K., & Lincoln, Y. S. (1994). *Handbook of qualitative research.* Thousand Oaks, CA: Sage Publications. doi:10.2307/2075820

Ehrmin, J. T. (2005). Dimensions of culture care for substance-dependent African American women. *Journal of Transcultural Nursing, 16*(2), 117-125. doi:10.1177/1043659604273549

Glaser, B. G., & Strauss, A. L. (1967). *The discovery of grounded theory: Strategies for qualitative research.* Chicago: Aldine Publishing Company.

Glaser, B. G. (1992). *Basics of grounded theory analysis: Emergence vs forcing.* Mill Valley, CA: Sociology Press.

Ghee, A. C., Johnson, C. S., Burlew, A. K, & Bolling, L. C. (2009). Enhancing retention through a condensed trauma-integrated intervention for women with chemical dependence. *American Journal of Psychology, 11*(1), 157-173.

Green, C. A., Polen, M. R., Lynch, F. L., Dickinson, D. M., & Bennett, M. D. (2004). Gender differences in outcomes in an HMO-based substance abuse treatment program. *Journal of Addictive Diseases, 23*(2), 47-70. doi: 10.1300/J069v23n02_04

Greenfield, S. (2002). Women and alcohol use disorders. *Harvard Rev Psychiatry, 10*(2), 76-85. doi:10.1080/10673220216212

Gordon, N. S. (2000). Researching psychotherapy, the importance of the client's view: A methodological challenge. *The Qualitative Report, 4*(3 & 4), Retrieved October 11, 2005, from http://www.nova.edu/ssss/QR/

Kaskutas, L., Zhang, L., French, M., & Witbrodt, J. (2005). Women's programs versus mixed-gender day treatment: results from a randomized study. *Addiction, 100,* 60-69.

Kauffman, E., Dore, M., & Nelson-Zlupko, L. (1995). The role of women's therapy groups in the treatment of chemical dependence [Abstract]. *American Journal of Orthopsychiatry, 65,* 355-363.

Kropp, F., & Banhal-Baugus, M. (1996). The association of personal-related variables to length of sobriety: A pilot study of chemically dependent women. *Journal of Addictions & Offender Counseling, 17*(1), 21-35.

LeCompte, M. D. & Shensul, J. J. (1999). *Ethnographer's toolkit.* (Vols. 1-7). Walnut Creek, CA: AltaMira Press.

Lincoln, Y. S., & Guba, E. G. (1985). *Naturalistic inquiry.* Beverly Hills, CA: Sage Publications.

Marsh, J., D'Aunno, T., & Smith, B. (2000). Increasing access and providing social services to improve drug abuse treatment for women with children. *Addiction, 95*(8), 1237-1247. doi:10.1046/j.1360-0443.2000.958123710.x

Moras, K. (2002). Behavioral therapies for female drug users: An efficacy-focused review. In C. Wetherington, & A. Roman (Eds.), *Drug addiction research and the health of women* (pp.197-236). Bethesda, MD: National Institute on Drug Abuse. (Original work published 1998)

Nelson-Zlupko, L., Dore, M., Kauffman, E., & Kaltenbach, K. (1996). Women in recovery: Their perceptions of treatment effectiveness. *Journal of Substance Abuse Treatment, 13*(1), 51-59. doi:10.1016/0740-5472(95)02061-6

Office of National Drug Control Policy (2001). *The Economic Costs of Drug Abuse in theUnited States,* 1992-1998. Washington, DC: Executive Office of the President (Publication No. NCJ-190636).

Petry, N. M., & Bickel, W. K. (2000). Gender differences in hostility of opioid-dependent outpatients: Role in early treatment termination. *Drug and Alcohol Dependence, 58*(1-2), 27-33. doi:10.1016/S0376-8716(99)00058-7

Robert Wood Johnson Foundation. (2009). Substance abuse policy research program releases five-year research roadmap. Retrieved from http://www.rwjf.org/public health/product.jsp?id=49188

Roberts, A. C., & Nishimoto, R. (2006). Barriers to engaging and retaining African American post-partum women in drug treatment. *Journal of Drug Issues, 36*(1), 53-76.

Sanders-Phillips, K. (2002). Factors influencing HIV/AIDS in women of color. *Public Health Report,* 117(Supplement 1), S151-S156. Retrieved from http://www.ncbi.nlm .nih.gov/ pmc/articles/PMC1913693/

Sterk, C., Elifson, K., & Theall, K. (2000). Women and drug treatment experiences: A generational comparison of mothers and daughters. *Journal of Drug Issues 30*(4), 839-862.

Strauss, A. L., & Corbin, J. (1990). *Basics of qualitative research: Grounded theory procedures and techniques.* Newbury Park, CA: Sage Publications.

Strauss, A. L., & Corbin, J. (1998). *Basics of qualitative research: Techniques and procedures for developing grounded theory.* Thousand Oaks, CA: Sage Publications.

Substance Abuse and Mental Health Services Administration, Office of Applied Studies. (2001). *The DASIS report: Women in substance abuse treatment.* Retrieved September 8, 2006, from http://www.oas.samhsa.gov/2k1/FemTX/FemTX.htm

Substance Abuse and Mental Health Services Administration, Office of Applied Studies. (2003a). *National survey of substance abuse treatment services (N-SSATS): 2002. Data on substance abuse treatment facilities, DASIS series: S-19* (DHHS Publication No. SMA 03-3777). Rockville, MD: Author.

Substance Abuse and Mental Health Services Administration, Office of Applied Studies. (2003b). *Overview of findings from the 2002 national survey on drug use and health, NHSDA Series H-21* (DHHS Publication No. SMA 03-3774). Rockville, MD: Author.

U.S. Department of Health and Human Services (USDHHS). (2000). *Healthy people 2010: Understanding and improving health.* 2nd ed. Washington, DC: U.S. Government

Printing Office, November 2000. Retrieved from http://www.healthypeople.gov/ Document/html/uih/uih_bw/uih_4.htm#subsabuse

Weissman, M. & O'Boyle, K. (2000). Women and addiction: treatment issues and innovative program models. *The Source, 10*(1), 17-20.

Westermeyer, J., & Boedicker, A. (2000). Course, severity, and treatment of substance abuse among women versus men. *American Journal of Drug and Alcohol Abuse, 26*(4), 523-535. doi:10.1081/ADA-100101893

11

Counseling the Female
Sexual Offender

Integrating a Trauma Focus into Treatment

MATTHEW J. PAYLO , STEPHANIE KINCH, VICTORIA E. KRESS[1]

Treatment issues associated with counseling female sexual offenders and the importance of integrating a trauma model are discussed in this article. Strategies for integrating trauma-focused cognitive behavioral therapy (TF-CBT) into female sexual offender treatment are provided. A case study example is provided to illuminate the concepts discussed.

As evidenced by the paucity of professional literature on this topic, female sexual offenders are a population that is underreported, undetected, and sometimes misunderstood (Sandler & Freeman, 2007). Although official reports have suggested that female sex offenders comprise approximately only 1-2% of the entire sex offender population (Vandiver & Walker, 2002), the actual rate may be significantly higher

1. Matthew J. Paylo, Department of Counseling and Special Education, Youngstown State University; Stephanie Kinch, Department of Counseling and Special Education, Youngstown State University; and Victoria E. Kress, Department of Counseling and Special Education, Youngstown State University. Additionally, we'd like to thank Marlana Robertson for aiding in the development of the manuscript's literature review. Correspondence concerning this article should be addressed to Matthew J. Paylo, Department of Counseling and Special Education, Beeghley Hall, Youngstown State University, Youngstown, OH 44555. E-mail: mpaylo@ysu.edu.

(Strickland, 2008). Sexual victimization by females often goes undetected because they engage in the behavior during routine, caretaking activities, and because people are often hesitant to believe that women are capable of sexually offending (Sandler & Freeman, 2007). An increased awareness of female sexual offenders combined with a proactive approach towards the detection and treatment of female offenders is needed (Strickland, 2008).

There is evidence to suggest that many professionals including police officers, child protection workers, and legal professionals have ambivalent, and at times dismissive, professional responses to allegations of female sexual offending behaviors (Denov, 2001). Contributing to this ambivalence, are cultural assumptions about the nature of femininity and women's sexuality: assumptions that have created barriers in the recognition of female sexual offenders. Traditional sexual scripts have been known to exclude the image of women as sexual aggressors, as sexually coercive, or even as sexually interested (Denov, 2001). Some argue that people are much less likely to recognize female sexual abuse because society finds it difficult to equate a nurturing, passive view of femininity with violence and sexual aggression, particularly when that aggression is directed towards children (Bunting, 2007).

Female sexual offenders may be especially under-recognized due to the traditional gender-related scripts attached to female interaction with children. Sexual abuse by females is often perceived by the general public to be less harmful and less serious than sexual abuse perpetrated by males (Denov, 2003b). The notion of male abusers and female victims has become paradigmatic within the field of child sexual abuse; this has obscured the recognition of female sexual abusers and their victims (Denov, 2003a). An additional barrier to recognizing and therefore reporting abuse by females is confusion around what constitutes sexually abusive behavior. Women are often permitted greater latitude around physical contact with children than are men, and as such, the boundary that would indicate a shift from non-abusive to abusive behavior is sometimes more difficult to distinguish (Hayes, 2008).

Numerous research studies have highlighted that female sexual offenders often have significant traumatic histories involving sexual and physical abuse in childhood, as well as an increased propensity to be involved in abusive romantic relationships in adulthood (Allen, 1991; Mathews, Hunter, & Vuz, 1997; Miller, Turner, & Henderson,

2009; Strickland, 2008). As such, women may benefit from a treatment model that integrates trauma treatment. The Center for Sex Offender Management, a branch within the U.S. Department of Justice, in their Female Sexual Offender Report (2007) acknowledged that clinicians need to appreciate the differences between male and female sexual offenders and consider the victim-offender duality that exist among many female offenders who have been sexually abused. Miller, et al. (2009) suggested that female sexual offenders do not fit neatly into the same typologies and risk patterns developed for male sexual offenders. In their review of noteworthy research on gender differences of sexual offenders, Miller et al. (2009) suggested that females are significantly less likely to recidivate sexually, violently, or generally when compared to male sex offenders, and are more apt to seek out assistance from professionals. The lesser rate of recidivism and the increased likelihood of seeking out treatment, combined with the increased exposure to childhood abuse and trauma, suggest that gender considerations are important in conceptualizing female sex offenders' treatment.

There is little known about the effectiveness of treatment programs for female sexual offenders (Oliver, 2007). A paucity of research and the lack of availability of grant funding have hindered a well-developed understanding of the effectiveness of various offender treatment interventions (Alexander, 1999). Traditional male sexual offender treatments seek to eliminate future sexual offenses (Grossman, Martis, & Fichtner, 1999) with the goals of addressing psychosocial adjustments, past trauma, and improved self-esteem as secondary. As outlined by Miller et al. (2009), limited results have been observed in large-scale meta-analyses of these treatments thus calling into question the overall effectiveness of traditional male sex offender treatments, as well as their effectiveness with the female sexual offender population. With a lack of well-documented, evidence-based approaches to treating sexual offenders, counselors must consider the existent differences between females and male sexual offenders when developing treatment considerations.

In this article, issues associated with counseling female sexual offenders and the value of integrating a trauma treatment focus into counseling will be highlighted. Additionally, strategies for integrating a trauma-focused treatment model, Trauma-Focused Cognitive Behavioral Therapy (TF-CBT), are provided. Finally, a case study example will illustrate the concepts discussed in the article.

Male and Female Offenders: Unique Considerations

Male sexual offending typologies usually involve the work of Groth (1979) that was later expanded upon by Berger (2000). According to Berger (2000), the four offender typologies are: compensatory (i.e., lack of ability to form relationships, feel socially inadequate, therefore offends to meet sexual needs and to reduce feelings of inadequacies), sadistic (i.e., achieving gratification through another's pain), power/control (i.e., non-sexual aggressive act desiring dominance over someone else), and opportunistic (i.e., situational offending; not originating out of anger but poor impulse control). When considering the motivations for male sexual offending, explanations for offending often involve either a need to meet one's sexual desire, a need to assert power and dominance over someone else, and even a lack of impulse control over one's actions in certain situations (Robertiello & Terry, 2007). Conversely, female sexual offenders usually use less physical force, know their victims personally, derive an emotional gain from the abuse, and are often unable to see their actions as abusive, but rather consider themselves to be kind, caring, and loving (Matthews, Mathews, & Speltz, 1991; Robertiello & Terry, 2007).

Research indicates there are different typologies of female and male sex offenders, and this suggests the need for gender differentiation in the treatment of sex offenders (Mathews et al., 1997; Robertiello & Terry, 2007). Mathews et al. (1997) found the following:

> Significant differences between the genders, especially in the degree of maltreatment, bringing into question whether some treatment approaches and programs developed for sexually assaultive males which are confrontational in nature, and focus primarily on accountability and behavioral changes, are adequate or sufficient for female offenders. (p. 197)

Some research has found that female offenders may hold onto self-resentment more readily than their male counterparts (Mathews et al., 1997). As such, women may respond well to a nurturing, safe, and non-judgmental environment during treatment where male focused treatment typically utilizes more aggressive, confrontational approaches. Thus, females appear to benefit from a treatment program which focuses on building self-esteem and female identity formation, while stressing healthy human sexuality, empathy, and relationship formation (Mathews et al., 1997).

The aforementioned research suggests the need for a female-sensitive treatment approach that is geared towards female specific experiences and offenses. As stated previously, women often have different motivations and respond to their offenses differently than men. Therefore women may respond differently to treatment. Kubik, Hecker, and Righthand (2002) suggested that female sexual offenders have experienced more severe sexual abuse, have been abused by more perpetrators, have been penetrated during their abuse more frequently, and are more likely to experience symptoms associated with posttraumatic stress disorder (PTSD) than their male counterparts. Therefore, the use of a traditional (i.e., offense only) treatment with females may heighten the likelihood of unsuccessful treatment outcomes, with little or no impact on the reduction of recidivism (Mathews et al., 1997). In order to further comprehend the female sexual offender, it is necessary to distinguish between the various typologies researchers have proposed. To aid counselors in their conceptualization of the female sexual offender, the demographic and typologies of female sexual offenders are provided in the following section.

Proposed Typologies

Although limited research has investigated attributes of female sex offenders, there is some evidence to suggest that female sex offenders are, on average, between the ages of 26 and 36 years old, and are likely to be Caucasian, single, of low socio-economic status, and struggle with substance abuse problems (Sandler & Freeman, 2007). They are more likely to be unemployed and to have been abused as children than are male sexual offenders (Sandler & Freeman, 2007). Matthews et al. (1991) offered a three-category typology of female sex offenders. These categories include: Teacher/Lover, Predisposed, and Male-Coerced. Additionally, Duncan (2010) contends that another category, Developmentally Delayed, is warranted.

The Teacher/Lover type of offender usually lacks insight into the power differential inherent in the abusive relationship. They often do not consider their "partner" to be a victim and they believe that, regardless of age or position, equality is present. The Intergenerationally Predisposed type includes women from families where sexual abuse has occurred and has been part of the culture for many generations. Turner and Turner (1994) suggested that these females suffer from the delusion that everyone is eventually abused. In their minds, they are aiding their victims by abusing them before anyone else has the chance to do so. The Male-Coerced type perpetrators are those who are coerced into sex offenses by a man with whom they are usually in a relationship, and are normally characterized as docile and lacking power in their relationship (includes both family and non-family members; Duncan, 2010). The Developmentally Delayed Offender type is described as an adult female diagnosed by a standardized test as having cognitive/intellectual impairment or diminished intellectual capacity. These offenders display the sexual mistreatment as a game, as appropriate caretaking, or as a family interaction that the child has been socialized to perceive as customary (Sandler & Freeman, 2007).

These four categories aid counselors in their conceptualization of the female sexual offender and provide a window into the offenders distorted rationale and cognitive processes. These cognitive distortions will ultimately become a focus of any female sexual offender treatment. A brief discussion of the unique difference in childhood trauma will provide the rationale for considering a trauma-focused treatment approach for working with female sexual offenders.

Role of Childhood Trauma

The severity of childhood trauma and sexual abuse are significant risk factors for the future development of sex offending behaviors (Strickland, 2008). A review of the research suggests that childhood trauma plays a prominent role in the lives of female sexual offenders (Mathews et al., 1997; Strickland, 2008; Widom & Ames, 1994). In reviewing the literature, it is also evident that there is a dearth of research on effective treatments for female sexual offenders.

Research has suggested that women who sexually abuse have suffered greater overall trauma as children, as well as more physical, emotional and sexual abuse, and more physical neglect, than have female offenders of nonsexual crimes (Strickland, 2008). Mathews et al. (1997) found that female sexual offenders are often exposed to more severe and prolonged abuse, are victimized at a younger age, are often abused by more perpetrators, and usually have reports of one or more of their assailants utilizing intense force or aggression during their molestation than their male counterparts. Widom and Ames (1994) stated that sexual abuse, physical abuse, and/or neglect occurring before the age of 12 increases the probability of arrests for adult sexual crimes regardless of gender. Therefore, in counseling female *or* male sexual offenders, therapeutic attention should be given to the trauma experiences and trauma reactions.

Trauma-focused treatments are demonstrated to be successful in treating trauma. There is a large body of research that supports the effectiveness of various trauma-based treatments in addressing trauma symptoms (Briere & Scott, 2006; Cohen, Berliner, & Mannarino, 2010). Therefore, incorporating a trauma focus into females' sex offender treatment introduces a unique therapeutic approach that may be conducive to supporting female sexual offenders in their change process, and aims to alleviate traumatic symptoms that may be contributing to offending behaviors.

Trauma-Focused Treatment

As female sexual offenders are frequently exposed to intense, prolonged traumatic events (Mathews et al., 1997), a trauma-focused approach may be valuable in counseling this population. While there is conflicting literature considering the notion that exposure to sexual abuse may invite future sexually deviant behaviors (Herman, 1992; Strickland, 2008), research suggests that intense traumatic events produce significant impairments on a woman's ability to monitor and manage her emotions, trauma related symptoms, and close relationships. While the cost of trauma-focused treatment and the time required to integrate or add trauma treatment onto regular offender treatment may be detriments, Briere and Lanktree (2012) contend that the long term impacts of untreated trauma far outweigh the cost of providing trauma -focused treatment. Briere and Lanktree (2012) suggested that these long-term impacts that are not addressed if the trauma isn't the focus of treatment include: anxiety, depression, cognitive distortions, PTSD, dissociation, identity disturbances, affect dysregulation, interpersonal problems, substance abuse, self-mutliation, eating issues, unsafe sexual behaviors, somatization, aggression, suicidality, and dysfunctional personality traits.

A Trauma-Focused Cognitive Behavioral Therapy (TF-CBT; Cohen & Mannarino, 2008) is one trauma-focused treatment that may be helpful when working with female sexual offenders. This evidence-based approach is aimed at assisting individuals in overcoming trauma-related difficulties. The goal of TF-CBT is to: (a) reduce negative emotional and behavioral responses to abuse, (b) correct the maladaptive beliefs related to the abuse, and (c) bring insight into the developmental impacts of the trauma, so that the client can make healthier decisions with regards to her inter- and intrapersonal relationships (Briere & Scott, 2006; Cohen & Mannarino, 2008).

It should be noted that TF-CBT is not intended to discount or replace other treatment approaches used with this population; rather this approach can complement other approaches that are more commonly used to treat sexual offending. Cashwell and Caruso (1997) contended that working with sexual offenders could be conceptualized as involving seven distinct stages: (a) addressing denial and increasing acceptance of responsibility of offense, (b) increasing the understanding of the impact of the assault on the victim, (c) developing insight into the motives and events that precipitated the event, (d) focusing on the clients own victimization experience, (e) increasing education on sexuality, sexual values, and sex roles, (f) altering arousal patterns, and (g) cognitive restructuring including addressing the client's distortions, which enable deviant fantasies and behaviors. While this traditional approach to sexual offending is often utilized, the authors contention is that by incorporating TF-CBT counselors can more comprehensively address the clients own victimization experience and how the subsequent trauma reactions have impacted them and their offending. TF-CBT refines the traditional approach to offender treatment by making it more applicable to the unique trauma considerations of female sexual offenders.

In this article, the TF-CBT (Cohen & Mannarino, 2008) will be discussed as an example of a trauma treatment approach that can be applied to working with female offenders. Utilizing an evidenced-based approach to trauma treatment, TF-CBT aids clients in forming connections between their thoughts, feelings, and behaviors, and is an evidence-based treatment for addressing the symptoms of PTSD and the associated related trauma problems (Foa, Keane, & Friedman, 2000). TF-CBT addresses trauma through the use of psychoeducation, stress management, affective modulation, addressing cognitive distortions, trauma processing, in vivo mastery of trauma reminders, and in the final stage, addressing safety and future personal development. Additionally, with a female sexual offender, even when addressing the trauma issues, the counselor needs to address the offender's sexual offense. While this can be done either concurrently (i.e., as part of the trauma treatment) or during the safety and future development section of the TF-CBT model of treatment, our model suggests addressing the sexual offense during the safety and future development section of the TF-CBT model. The following case will illuminate the TF-CBT model's treatment components and demonstrate the value of integrating a TF-CBT approach into treatment using a fictional female sexual offender who has experienced a significant trauma history.

Case Application

Shawna (i.e., a fictional case study based upon the authors' combined experiences with this population) is a 25-year-old incarcerated African American female recently referred for mental health services due to dissociative behaviors and having "meltdowns" in the general population (i.e., a prison housing wing). She candidly discussed the reason for her imprisonment: a sexual perpetration offense against a minor. She is currently participating in a group receiving mandatory treatment for her offense and states that she has received little to no benefit in this program. She is apprehensive as to "how talking" about her life can help her "deal with all the crap" she has experienced. She starts with presenting superficial material and then begins to discuss a romantic relationship she is having with a woman in the general population; this relationship is creating a great deal of anxiety for her.

Components of TF-CBT

Psychoeducation—Psychoeducation begins with the first contact with the client and will continue throughout the counseling process. Information about the diagnosis, trauma-related symptoms, the TF-CBT treatment plan, and information to normalize the client's situation should regularly be provided (Cohen & Mannarino, 2008). The essential aim in educating clients about the effects of trauma on their body, emotions, and their way of being, is to assist them in regaining power over their lives; lives in which they have often been powerless secondary to a lack of awareness. Psychoeducation can start with explaining the differences between stressful and traumatic events, and discussing the concept of PTSD. After this groundwork has been laid, a discussion of the problems that are often caused by these symptoms including difficulties in relationships, mood disturbances, and use of maladaptive behaviors to cope can be introduced. Psychoeducation can increase a client's level of knowledge, and his or her ability to tolerate further discussions of specific traumatic events (Pratt et al., 2005). Psychoeducational interventions may normalize a client's posttraumatic reactions to situations and relationships and may provide some meaning to behaviors that were previously misinterpreted as being aberrant (Pratt et al., 2005).

As Shawna began to feel more comfortable with her counselor and as her defenses diminish, she opened up more to the counselor. During the third session, Shawna began to dissociate. She curled up into the fetal position in the corner of the counselor's office. She talked with a child's voice and begged the unseen individual not to rape her. Through the use of psychoeducation, she began to see the connection between her current PTSD symptoms (i.e., dissociation, nightmares, avoidance) and her intense past sexual abuse. The counselor aided her by normalizing her current behaviors as being connected with her past trauma and indicated how the trauma effects her emotions, thoughts, and her present overall well being.

Stress Management and Affective Modulation—Relaxation skills are used to teach mastery over stressful experiences and provide a sense of control (Cohen & Mannarino, 2008). These skills may include deep breathing, progressive muscle relaxation, yoga, mindfulness exercises, music, sports, and so forth, and can be developed and adjusted with the client throughout treatment. Affective modulation skills are tailored to each individual client and are developed by first identifying areas where the client's difficulties reside (Cohen & Mannarino, 2008). The aim is to increase the client's ability to identify and express a range of feelings to improve affective modulation.

Shawna began to feel more comfortable with treatment as evidenced by her increase in attendance and willingness to discuss her experiences. She was taught a host of relaxation and stress management techniques and discussed the application of those techniques. She later reported using those stress management skills to help her manage and tolerate her ranging emotions and anxiety related to her past trauma. She readily identified her emotions and processed the origins of her frustration, discomfort, and anxiety. These skills began to lay the foundation for her increased tolerance to discuss her past abuse. She then reported that she was raised by her mother and father in a three-room apartment and doesn't remember much about her early childhood and development. She stated that what she does remember, she wishes she could forget. She displayed an ability to incorporate a greater sense of affect regulation and modulation. She was able to process how she felt in an anxiety-provoking situation in the present and utilized her learned stress management techniques, such as distraction and deep breathing. These skills helped Shawna to endure situations that emerged, and reactions to painful memories within the session, and then later outside of sessions.

Trauma Processing—Processing one's trauma can take many forms: sharing one's narrative verbally, the process of journaling, or even creative means such as poetry, songs, and biographies. All of these processes includes creating a trauma narrative which serves the purpose of (a) overcoming avoidance of traumatic/ difficult memories, (b) identifying distortions in the client's story, (c) contextualizing the client's traumatic experience into the scope of the client's entire life (the client is able to view themselves as more than just a victim of their experienced trauma; Cohen & Mannarino, 2008). Cognitive processing and challenging cognitive distortions are utilized during the client's trauma processing to assist in effective coping and thought changing.

Shawna began discussing her trauma narrative. She spoke of a turbulent household, with multiple episodes of domestic violence, neglect, and numerous accounts of abuse. Her abuse history involved physical, emotional, and sexual abuse. She recounted her past history with trepidation and caution, continually utilizing stress management and affect modulation techniques. She recounted over 300 hundred rapes that were orchestrated by her father as a fee-for-service business—"pimping out" his daughter for his own drug money. This happened over a three-year period (i.e., ages 10–13), until she became pregnant at the age of 13. She added that he was arrested for a drug violation at about the same time and since he was a repeat offender, was sentence to significant jail time. During this same time, Shawna had the baby and moved in with a distant relative to a new community. As she told her story, the counselor started to see a number of cognitive distortions that needed to be challenged.

Challenging Cognitive Distortions—Cognitive coping skills assist in recognizing connections among thoughts, feelings, and behaviors. The focus is to assist the client in identifying thoughts related to trauma or upsetting events, to determine the feelings and behaviors they have associated with those thoughts, and to evaluate whether these thoughts are accurate and helpful (Cohen & Mannarino, 2008). Cognitive distortions often contribute to negative affective states such as self-blame, shame, feeling damaged, and low self-esteem related to the trauma. This process is usually done in concert with the trauma processing.

With the aid of her counselor, Shawna continued to discuss her trauma narrative. Her story was littered with claims of her "worthlessness" and how she was "damaged." She did not verbalize it, but the theme that she did not deserve anything better was apparent. The counselor aided her in evaluating the claims being made and initially modeled a means to dispute these illogical accusations. Over the next few sessions, she was able to catch and correct her own language about her own worth and value. Her story began to take on a fuller context; not only as a victim, but as a resilient human being that desires and deserves to value herself and others. This treatment provides the groundwork needed to assist her in mastery over her trauma reactions.

In vivo Mastery—A counselor utilizes in vivo mastery to develop a graduated exposure program for clients who have developed debilitating avoidance tendencies in reaction to specific trauma reminders (Cohen & Mannarino, 2008). This technique allows clients to experience trauma reminders in a controlled, gradual process, which reduces generalizations and helps clients develop an ability to connect with a sense of security and safety. During this process, the client must confront traumatic memories and reminders of the trauma verbally or through written expression. In generating a mental image with the re-experiencing of the emotions associated with the trauma, a client can begin to overcome the gripping nature of these traumatic events.

As Shawna continued to recount the details of her trauma narrative, she continued addressing and challenging her emerging cognitive distortions. The counselor then began to introduce a graduated exposure program created to aid her in addressing her avoidance tendencies that seemed to emerge in her dialogue around present relationships and behaviors on the housing wing. Creating a sense of safety in the session, the counselor began to introduce some of Shawna's trauma reminders (e.g., feelings of powerlessness, being around a lot of unknown people, being in the presence of men). The counselor accomplished this through the use of guided imagery (GI). The counselor gradually and mentally placed Shawna, through the use of GI, in these re-experiencing situations, while physically still allowing her to remain in the safety of the counseling session. Shawna would later recount how she felt in those situations and processed how the gradual exposure slowly provided her with more and more perceived control.

Safety and Future Development—Many traumatized clients may require additional skills in order to make safe decisions and prevent future offending (Cohen & Mannarino, 2008). Examples of safety skills include developing a healthy sense of one's sexuality, developing the skills needed to prevent sexually inappropriate behavior, sharing one's story, processing with a trusted person, and utilizing skills taught during TF-CBT treatment. It is imperative that the counselor addresses the sexual offense of the female offender at least at this point in treatment.

The female sexual offender's rationale for sexual offenses can derive from a host of irrational thoughts and beliefs. These cognitive distortions can often be reflected in the types of offenses committed by the offender. These distortions can include normalizing her actions and related thoughts that the world is cruel and dangerous and that all individuals relate to others in this way. These cognitive distortions dilute the female offender's connection with reality, and justify her offending behaviors. The counselor can aid the offender in challenging these cognitive distortions; distortions on which the offending behaviors have been maintained.

The counselor will inevitably need to address these cognitive distortions, as this is an extremely important component of working with sexual offenders (Moster, Wnuk, & Jeglic, 2008). The process of addressing cognitive distortions involves challenging the attitudes and beliefs that maintain the behaviors, as well as confronting possible reactions of denial or minimizing the severity of the offense. The counselor must utilize cognitive restructuring, which includes (a) explaining to the client the role of their thoughts in their sexual offending behavior, (b) providing the client with the information on correcting these thoughts, (c) helping the client distinguish between appropriate thoughts from the inappropriate ones (e.g., thoughts that could lead to the violation of rights of others), and (d) helping the client challenge inappropriate thoughts (Moster et al., 2008). Theoretically, challenging these cognitive distortions will aid the female offender in reducing the frequency and urges of sexual offending behaviors by addressing the attitudes and beliefs that maintain and keep the offending behaviors in place.

Shawna began to understand the impacts of her trauma history on her thoughts about herself, her emotions, and on her past and present decisions with others. The counselor began to inquire about the connections between her sexual offense and her past abuse history. Shawna provided a more detailed discussion of her sexual offense, which involved a minor. She shared her belief that the world is corrupt and she was just creating a connection with that girl and "beating the world to the punch" by being "intimate" with her. The counselor and client processed how these cognitive distortions lead to the offending behavior(s). The counselor provided education to help her identify that her behaviors were not a demonstration of "intimacy" but could be better understood as abuse. The counselor worked with Shawna to aid in her understanding of how to self-impose her own ability to challenge those cognitive distortions that have led to her past offending behaviors. Challenging her cognitive distortions and reinforcing her own sense of responsibility to challenge those distortions, remained the focus of treatment until her eventual release/discharge.

After working with a female sexual offender via a trauma-focused approach, the client should, theoretically, have a better understanding of how her past experiences influenced and maintained her offending behaviors. A trauma-focused treatment approach enhances traditional approaches used to treat sex offenders in that it helps clients develop new ways of thinking about themselves, their actions, and their victims. By managing and diminishing trauma symptoms, the client may be less vulnerable to re-offend in the future.

Discussion

Counselors often treat female sexual offenders with a traditional approach, which focuses only on the sexual offense. This offense-only approach discounts or at least minimizes the impacts of a trauma history and its impact on the offending behavior (Strickland, 2008). A trauma-focus may be helpful in minimizing reoffending behaviors.

Due to the paucity of research, future studies are needed with this population, specifically to evaluate the effectiveness of TF-CBT with female sexual offenders. Furthermore, research is needed to examine whether addressing trauma symptoms leads to lower recidivism rates of sexually offending behaviors. Since the research in this area is emerging, qualitative research which investigates offenders' experiences of having a trauma-focused treatment integrated into their treatment, may also be helpful. Additionally, it may be beneficial for future studies to look at the long-term effectiveness of incorporating the trauma-focused elements discussed in this article into a comprehensive relapse prevention plan.

The authors' contention is that adequately dealing with the individual's trauma experience will provide that individual with the knowledge of trauma, the impact of the trauma, the coping skills, and the stability of the emerging therapeutic relationship to adequately deal with the intrusive nature of addressing sexual offenses. With an existent working alliance, a set of coping skills, and some understanding of the impact of trauma, the counselor can more effectively engage the individual in cognitive restructuring related to her offense(s)/victimization. The formulation of a comprehensive relapse prevention plan that incorporates the trauma-focused elements discussed in this article may ultimately reduce recidivism rates.

References

Allen, C. (1991). *Women and men who sexually abuse children: A comparative analysis.* Brandon, VT: Safer Society Press.

Alexander, M. (1999). Sexual offender treatment efficacy revisited. *Sexual Abuse: A Journal of Research and Treatment, 11*(2), 101-116.

Briere, J. N., & Lanktree, C. B. (2012). Treating complex trauma in Adolescents and young adults. Thousand Oaks, CA: Sage.

Briere, J., & Scott, C. (2006). *Principles of trauma therapy: A guide to symptoms, evaluation and treatment.* Thousand Oaks, CA: Sage.

Bunting, L. (2007). Dealing with a problem that doesn't exist? Professional responses to female perpetrated child sexual abuse. *Child Abuse Review, 16,* 252-267.

Cashwell, C. S., & Caruso, M. E. (1997). Adolescent sex offenders: Identification and intervention strategies. *Journal of Mental Health Counseling, 19,* 336-349.

Center for Sex Offender Management. (2007). Female sex offenders. Retrieved from http://www.csom.org/pubs/female_sex_offenders_brief.pdf.

Cohen, J. A., Berliner, L., & Mannarino, A. (2010). Trauma focused CBT for children with co-occurring trauma and behaviors problems. *Child Abuse & Neglect, 34,* 215-225.

Cohen, J. A., & Mannarino, A. (2008). Trauma focused cognitive behavioral therapy for children and parents. *Child and Adolescent Mental Health, 13,* 158-162.

Denov, M. S. (2001). A culture of denial: Exploring professional perspective on female sex offending. *Canadian Journal of Criminology, 43,* 303-329.

Denov, M. S. (2003a). The myth of innocence: Sexual scripts and the recognition of child sexual abuse by female perpetrators. *The Journal of Sex Research, 40*(3), 303-314.

Denov, M. S. (2003b). To a safer place? Victims of sexual abuse by females and their disclosures to professionals. *Child Abuse & Neglect, 27,* 47-61.

Duncan, K. A. (2010). Female offenders: Improving identification, reporting and prevention. Retrieved from www.theright2besafe.org

Foa, E. B., Keane, T. M., & Friedman, M. J. (Eds.). (2000). *Effective treatments for PTSD: Practice guidelines from the International Society for Traumatic Stress Studies.* New York, NY: Guilford Press.

Grossman, L. S., Martis, B. M., & Fichtner, C. G. (1999). Are sex offenders treatable? A research overview. *Psychiatric Services, 50,* 349-361.

Groth, A. N. (1979). *Men who rape.* New York: Plenum Press.

Hayes, S. (2008). The relationship between childhood abuse, psychological symptoms and subsequent sex offending. *Journal of Applied Research in Intellectual Disabilities, 22,* 96-101.

Herman, J. (1992). *Trauma and recovery.* New York, NY: Basic Books.

Kubik, E. K., Hecker, J. E., & Righthand, S. (2002). Adolescent females who have sexually offended: Comparison with delinquent adolescent female offenders and adolescent males who sexually offend. *Journal of Child Sexual Abuse, 11,* 63-83.

Mathews, R., Hunter, J. A., & Vuz, J. (1997). Juvenile female sex offenders: Clinical characteristics and treatment issues. *Sexual Abuse: A Journal of Research and Treatment, 9*(3), 187-199.

Matthews, J. K., Mathews, R., & Speltz, K. (1991). Female sex offenders: A typology. In M. Quinn (Ed.), *Family sexual abuse: Frontline research and evaluation* (pp. 199-210). Newbury Park, CA: Sage.

Miller, H. A., Turner, K., & Henderson, C. E. (2009). Psychopathology of sex offenders: A comparison of male and female using latent profile analysis. *Criminal Justice and Behavior, 36*(8), 778-792.

Moster, A., Wnuk, D. W., & Jeglic, E. L. (2008). Cognitive behavioral therapy with sex offenders. *Journal of Correctional Health Care, 14*(2), 109-121.

National Center for Women and Policing. (2000). *Successfully investigating acquaintance sex assault*. OJP: Berger.

Oliver, B. E. (2007). Preventing female-perpetrated sexual abuse. *Trauma, Violence, & Abuse, 8*(1), 19-32.

Pratt, S. I., Rosenberg, S., Mueser, K., T., Brancato, J., Salyers, M., Jankowski, M. K. & Descamps, M. (2005). Evaluation of a PTSD psychoeducational program for psychiatric inpatients. *Journal of Mental Health, 14*(2), 121-127.

Robertiello, G., & Terry, K. (2007). Can we profile sex offenders? A review of sex offender typologies. *Aggression and Violent Behaviors, 12,* 508-518.

Sandler, J. C., & Freeman, N. J. (2007). Typology of female sex offenders: A test of Vandiver and Kercher. *Sexual Abuse: A Journal of Research and Treatment, 19,* 73-89.

Strickland, S. (2008). Female sex offenders exploring issues of personality, trauma, and cognitive distortions. *Journal of Interpersonal Violence, 23*(4), 474-489.

Turner, M. T., & Turner, T. N. (1994). *Female adolescent sexual abusers: An exploratory study of mother-daughter dynamics with implications for treatment*. Orwell, VT: Safer Society Press.

Vandiver, D. M., & Walker, J., T. (2002). Female sex offenders: An overview and analysis of 40 cases. *Criminal Justice Review, 27* (2), 284-300.

Widom, C. S., & Ames, M. A. (1994). Criminal consequences of childhood sexual victimization. *Child Abuse & Neglect, 18,* 303-318.

12

Mental Health Court Goals and Practices

A Staff Perspective

Katie Ellis, Leanne Fiftal Alarid, and Michael Tapia[1]

Given that mental health courts (MHCs) employ personnel from two systems—criminal justice and mental health—it is unclear on how well this integration works with respect to program goals, supervision, treatment and continuity of care. Using best practice guidelines, this research examined MHC personnel from seven jurisdictions about their knowledge of court procedures and perception of MHC goals and effectiveness for persons with mental illness. Employees perceived that MHCs focused primarily on client recidivism reduction, medication stabilization, and obtaining timely treatment, in that order. However, employees felt that MHCs lacked adequate community treatment resources to meet these goals. A MHC team is multi-disciplinary and cross-training is important to allow team members to become familiar with each other's roles and responsibilities.

1. Katie Ellis, Leanne Fiftal Alarid, and Michael Tapia, Department of Criminal Justice, University of Texas—San Antonio. Leanne Fiftal Alarid is now at the University of Texas-Elpaso. Correspondence concerning this article should be addressed to Leanne Fiftal Alarid, University of Texas-Elpaso, Dept. of Criminal Justice, 500 West University Avenue, El Paso, Texas 79968. Email:Leanne.Alarid@utsa.edu.

Jails and prisons are now widely recognized as the largest mental health systems in the country (Slate & Johnson, 2008). Approximately 40% of the adult mentally ill population was estimated to have contact with the criminal justice system at least once in their lives (Berg, 2005). However, some persons with mental illness repeatedly cycle through correctional facilities, mental health treatment programs, and homeless shelters. Regulations and legislation limiting access and coverage of long-term mental health care for the insured, and especially for the uninsured, impact both the quality and duration of care in the health care and social services systems. Ineffective housing policies and lack of continuity of care have left people with mental illnesses socially disadvantaged and unable to cope with day to day activities, such as maintaining employment, housing, and managing finances. The problem can be exacerbated if clients lose access to or stopped taking their medications.

The criminalization of drugs since the 1980s has also been a major factor contributing to a significant increase of emergency room visits and incarcerations of mentally ill persons in jails, many of whom regularly use illicit street drugs (Slate & Johnson, 2008). Police often had no other option but to arrest persons with mental illness who have committed crimes, because no other facility would accept them. As jails became inundated with persons who were in a mental health crisis, the agencies attempted to stabilize individuals before release. However, limitations exist on the involuntary use of psychotropic medications without a court order (Berg, 2005).

Today, local jurisdictions are in dire need to simultaneously reduce the number of mentally ill offenders in their jails and find options for mentally ill offenders to have monitored psychiatric and substance abuse treatment in the community. The costs of keeping offenders with mental illness in jail strain county budgets and the facilities themselves which were not designed to offer necessary therapeutic regimens and stabilization. For example, inmates with mental illness cost twice the amount-- $160 per day versus $78 per day—in jail, when compared to offenders without mental health needs (James, 2006).

Larger urban areas began experimenting with various alternatives to long-term jail stays in the 1990s, and mental health courts (MHCs) were among those alternatives for offenders with mental illness and for dually diagnosed persons with mental illness. Modeled after the drug court concept, MHCs began in 1997 in Broward County, Florida as a jail diversion concept. By 2009, 250 MHCs in nearly every state were established (Almquist & Dodd, 2009). While most MHCs divert people with mental illness away from jails, concerns exist that the type of clients some MHCs accept may criminalize lifestyles of people with mental illness. In this case, the justice system then becomes the option for failure to provide adequate social services. Given that MHCs have personnel from two systems—criminal justice and mental health—it is unclear on how well this integration works with respect to the legal issues, supervision, treatment and behavior of individuals with mental illness. Some criminal justice and legal personnel, for example, feel inadequately trained to handle mental health treatment issues or may feel that a MHC is contradictory to their job to obtain the shortest possible sentence for their client (Waters, Strickland, & Gibson, 2009). Given these concerns, this research examined MHC professionals with varied backgrounds in law, criminal justice, and mental health about their knowledge of court procedures and perception of MHC goals and effectiveness for persons with mental illness.

Mental Health Court Characteristics

Slate and Johnson (2008) defined a MHC as:

> a specialized docket for certain defendants with mental illnesses that substitutes a problem-solving model for traditional court processing. Participants are identified through specialized screening and assessments, and voluntarily participate in a judicially supervised treatment plan developed jointly by a team of court staff and mental health professionals. Incentives reward adherence to the treatment plan and other court conditions, non-adherence may be sanctioned, and success or graduation is defined according to specific criteria." (p. 142)

The goal of MHCs was to provide community-based treatment to stabilize and reduce recidivism of mentally ill offenders. The intervention consisted of a non-adversarial court proceeding, whereby dispositions were decided by the treatment team, who met before every court hearing, and the participants were supervised weekly or bi-weekly, depending on risk. MHCs typically use a team-based model of case management that directly links to psychiatrists, nurses, counselors and social workers to provide individual treatment plans and services (National Alliance on Mental Illness, 2007). Professionals who work in MHC programs typically include judges, MHC managers or coordinators, prosecuting attorneys, defense attorneys, probation officers, case managers, and various counselors and clinical practitioners who are contracted by a local mental health agency to provide court-ordered treatment.

The court manager/coordinator primarily ensured the court was operating as intended and resolved any operational issues that arose. The role of the attorneys and judges were typical of a traditional court, in that the prosecuting attorney represented the state, the defense attorney represented the defendant, and the judge assumed the role of directing the activities in his/her court. However, unlike the adversarial nature of traditional court proceedings, the process was a cooperative effort to pursue the client's best interests (Thompson, Osher, & Tomasini-Joshi, 2008). Probation officers monitored the clients' adherence to the program guidelines (i.e., staying drug free, attending treatment services, medication compliance, etc.). Case managers were responsible for assisting the clients in their treatment plans and serving as a link between the client and community mental health agencies. The counselors and clinical practitioners met with defendants throughout the duration of the MHC, so treatment practitioners met with clients who fulfilled specific eligibility criteria.

Eligibility for MHC

MHCs differed on clients deemed eligible for the program based on three characteristics: clinical diagnosis, legal status, and type of offense committed.

Clinical Diagnosis—Most jails across the country evaluate the mental status of every individual at time of booking. Inmates who have visible symptoms of mental illness (e.g., bizarre behavior, hallucinations, etc.) or who report a history of mental health problems are further screened by licensed counselors, clinical social workers, psychiatrists or psychologists (Temporini, 2010). The American Psychiatric Association classifies mental disorders into five axes in the Diagnostic and Statistical Manual of Mental Disorders (DSM-IV). For example, Axis I disorders include schizophrenia, mood disorders such as Bipolar Disorder and Major Depressive Disorder, anxiety disorders, and dissociative disorders (formerly called multiple personality disorder). While most MHCs required that clients have an Axis I diagnosis for admission, others had a broader definition that included diagnosed mental illnesses under other axes, organic brain injury or trauma to the head, and/or developmental disabilities (Bureau of Justice Assistance, 2000; Erickson, Campbell, & Lamberti, 2006). In a study by Steadman, Redlich, Griffin, Petrila, and Monahan (2005) in which over half (53%) of the sample were women aged 35 and older, Schizophrenia was the most common diagnosis (29%), followed by Major Depression (22.5%), and Bipolar disorder (19%). For offenders with mental illness, case processing time is critical to get them the help they need. A study of seven MHCs revealed that the average time from referral to disposition was 27.5 days, ranging from 1 to 45 days (Steadman et al., 2005).

Legal Status—MHCs also differed in the types of supervision, which was affected by the client's legal status. For example, King County, Washington originally allowed only guilty pleas, but now allows deferred adjudication probation terms for misdemeanants for no longer than two years. Broward County, Florida allowed for one year of diversion supervision for misdemeanants only. In contrast, Anchorage, Alaska required a guilty plea with probation terms that extended up to ten years, but MHC supervision terms of up to five years. In San Bernardino, California, the probation period was limited to two years for misdemeanors, and six years for felony offenses (Bureau of Justice Assistance, 2000). Steadman et al. (2005) found that most cases were referred either by the Public Defender's Office or judges in other courts within the jurisdiction, primarily because six of the seven programs were post-adjudication.

Offense Types—Some of the first generation courts were more specific, such as Broward County that accepted only misdemeanors but denied all driving under the influence and domestic violence charges. Programs have since broadened to include felony crimes but still screen an individual's history for violence (Fisler, 2005; Redlich, Steadman, Monahan, Petrila, & Griffin, 2005). About 46% of accepted clients had committed felonies, and 54% for misdemeanors. While drug offenses were the most common, the types of offenses (drugs, property, and violent) were split fairly evenly (Steadman et al., 2005). San Bernardino, California is unique in that it requires that the offender have a criminal history (Bureau of Justice Assistance, 2000).

MHC Studies

The bulk of the initial literature on MHCs consisted of program descriptions as a condition of federal grant funding to get programs operational. A review of available literature on outcomes of MHCs uncovered a small number of published outcome studies, in which there was a treatment and comparison group design (Boothroyd, Mercado, Poythress, Christy, & Petrila 2005; Cosden, Ellens, Schnell, & Yamini-Diouf, 2005; McNiel & Binder, 2007). McNiel and Binder (2007) utilized propensity score weighting to match, and found that the MHC group had longer time to a new arrest compared to the control group. The probability of MHC graduates committing a new offense 12 months after graduation was 31% compared to a 47% probability for the comparison group. In a randomized trial, Cosden and colleagues (2005) found an increase in the number of bookings for the MHC group, but no change in the number of days spent in jail, or in the amount of convictions. The authors concluded that the MHC program did not help all participants, but it did make a difference in most. When they removed the participants who continued to engage in criminal activity from both samples, (which was approximately 20%), the remaining MHC participants averaged fewer days in jail post-intervention than the control group. In regards to the psychosocial functioning hypothesis, both groups made improvements on independent functioning, quality of life, psychological distress, and drug and alcohol abuse. Boothroyd and colleagues (2005) compared MHC defendants with mentally ill defendants who went through regular magistrate courts and found no significant differences between groups in change in psychiatric symptoms. The authors attribute this finding to possible insufficient quality of treatment in this particular study.

MHC Challenges

More recently, discussions have emerged in the literature to address the criticisms challenging some court procedures used that undermine voluntariness, privacy, confidentiality, and potential for effective treatment. These problems were not found in every court, but in a study of 20 courts by the Bazelton Center, about half had one or more of the following problems: lack of client choice in the referral process, lack of transparency, and restrictions of client withdrawal (Seltzer, 2005). While half the courts required that the client plead guilty, only some courts suspended the sentence. Upon successful completion, less than half of the MHCs dismissed or allowed for expungement of the charges, but it was not automatic, so the client had to file a separate request to the courts. Critics question whether treatment is really voluntary or coercive, since the penalty for not adhering to treatment is jail. There is a lack of written policies specifying consistent treatment duration, as many courts decided treatment on an individualized basis per client (Seltzer, 2005). Additional concerns include the lack of accountability that mental service providers have to the court-ordered services. Solutions include building trust, ensuring client comprehension, ensuring confidentiality, while at the same time, managing risk and carrying out court-ordered treatment in a timely manner (Erickson et al, 2006; Fisler, 2005; Redlich, 2005; Redlich et al., 2005).

Staff members are in an advantageous position to know how the program is operating because they have firsthand knowledge of the program's operations and goals (Bouffard, Taxman, & Silverman, 2003). Only one published study was found that directly asked MHC professionals about procedures and concerns. McNeil and Binder (2010) interviewed 43 MHC employees or service providers for one pre-plea court in San Francisco that accepted nonviolent felons and misdemeanants. The employees included judges, attorneys, case managers, probation officers, psychiatrists, and administrators. The survey asked about MHC goals, selection process, legal issues, treatment access, advantages and how the program could be improved.

Recidivism reduction, improvement of public safety, improved client function, and cost savings were identified by employees as the main purposes of MHC. One main issue was that contracted treatment services had long waiting lists because of limited space availability, and employees recommended expanding resources. While the staff supported MHC over traditional court for persons with mental illnesses, some employees' observations were not consistent with the intent behind a particular policy. For example, clients in the program signed a release to allow the sharing of information, yet staff said that privacy was protected. Another example was that employees insisted that the program was voluntary, but mentioned that the "choice" was between MHC treatment or going through traditional court and likely getting sentenced to jail (McNeil & Binder, 2010).

In order for a program to operate fluidly, staff from a variety of backgrounds must know what the goals of the program are, and how their collaborative relationships are or are not effectively contributing to these goals (Bouffard et al., 2003). This research examined MHC personnel about their knowledge of court procedures, perception of MHC goals, and perception of MHC effectiveness for persons with mental illness.

Methods

The program survey utilized in this study asked questions that were related to best practices in MHC implementation and operationalization. Email was the preferred method of establishing contact with the court because the contact person would be able to read the cover letter and the questionnaire at their convenience. A total of 28 MHC programs from around the U.S. were selected for participation based on a list maintained by the Bureau of Justice Assistance. Program selection was not random, as it was based on whether the program listed a coordinator or manager with an email address. Given the nonprobability sampling method used in this study, we consider the findings to be exploratory. Initial email contact requested participation of their entire staff in this study, and included the questionnaire, asking for them to pass it along to the key personnel in the MHC. Of the 28 courts contacted via email, three emails were returned for bad addresses. Therefore, the response rate was based on 25 MHC programs with valid e-mail addresses. Employees from nine different programs replied, with usable surveys from seven different programs across the country. This response rate is consistent with previous studies which report that email surveys conducted in the same manner average between 24–31% (Sheehan, 2001).

MHC employees that completed the survey, including a Deputy Prosecuting Attorney, a Pretrial Services Officer, a Program Analyst, a Licensed Clinical Social Worker, a judge, a MHC Coordinator, and a MHC Program Manager. Most of the professionals were previously employed in the public sector or had related experience, such as being part of drug court team or a mental health agency. The judge volunteered her court as a pilot MHC, and used her administrative time for the docket.

The questionnaire consisted of open-ended questions and one question that asked for a rating of perceived MHC goals. Questions consisted of three themes: professional experience, knowledge of procedures, and perception of MHC's goals and effectiveness. The questions for the survey were derived from ten elements of the best practices model developed for MHCs by Thompson and colleagues (2008), in collaboration of the Council of State Governments. The questions measuring each element can be found in Table 1.

The survey questions were also derived from the lead author's 10-month experience observing court proceedings and staffing with one MHC team and community mental health service providers. Collectively, these elements sought to eliminate arbitrary operationalization and serve as a roadmap to determine whether or not MHCs are operating as intended. The survey responses were coded by two different people to ensure interrater reliability in a systematic approach.

Findings

Findings emerged from the research questions and themes in the survey responses, which included MHC program goals, client referral/acceptance, client treatment, continuity of care, family support, and agency collaboration and communication barriers.

Goals of the MHC

Respondents were asked to rank order the importance of four MHC program goals: prevent recidivism, stabilize clients through medication/treatment, decrease number of days in jail, and save taxpayer money. The most important goal of MHCs was to prevent recidivism by decreasing the rate of return to the criminal justice system. Another respondent mentioned enhancing public safety as an additional goal to reducing recidivism. One respondent interpreted recidivism reduction as "keeping persons with mental illnesses out of prison." The recidivism goal was the most easily measured through re-arrests, which all programs reportedly tracked. A pretrial services officer stated that the purpose of MHC was:

> To connect clients to the services needed in the community to treat their mental health and keep them from getting new criminal charges. Yes, I think we are very successful at this. We have stats to show the decrease in number of jail days our clients have and we see very big changes in the clients as they go through the year with us.

A close and related second goal was to stabilize clients through continuing medication and treatment. Staff respondents reiterated the significance of sobriety, connecting clients with appropriate community-based mental health treatment services and to "help people get better." The judge felt it was the responsibility of the MHC to correct whatever situation it was that led the client to commit the crime. The two main goals were interrelated, in that a clients' instability related to their mental illness (e.g., substance use, violence, etc.) contributed to a higher likelihood of contact with the criminal justice system, a finding supported in other studies (Baillargeon, Binswanger, Penn, Williams, & Murray, 2009; Banks, Pandiani, & Boyd, 2009). The Pretrial Services Officer offered a broader response:

> The assumption is that if our clients had been getting treatment for their mental health in the first place they wouldn't be in trouble with the law. The purpose is to get them connected to resources in the community and make sure they are following through with treatment goals.

Decreasing the number of days spent in jail was third in importance, and saving the government money was the least important goal of MHC programs. Overall, the respondents chose measures that related to client success as more important than cost efficiency for MHCs. No common ratings were detected based on occupation (criminal justice or mental health employees).

Referral and Acceptance of Clients

Each of the respondents provided an overview of how the MHC clients were referred and accepted within their respective MHCs. In three of the courts, the prosecuting attorney and/or defense attorney made the referral. In other courts, the list was much broader to include judges, attorneys, clinicians, and family members. Once the case was referred, an individual or a group met to review the case and decided whether to accept to the MHC or refer the case elsewhere. In two courts, the District Attorney's (DA's) office reviewed the criminal history of the referrals to determine if the defendant met the legal criteria and make the final decision. Clients in two jurisdictions were not eligible for the program if they were already on probation. Five of the seven respondents reported that a MHC team made the final decision about who would be accepted into the program. In one of those courts, the DA's office reviewed each referral to ensure the defendant met the legal criteria.

Once the client was accepted into the program, every client was fully evaluated, assessed, and/or screened to ensure that participation was voluntary on the client's part. Once the client demonstrated that he or she was willing to participate, the defendant was formally accepted to participate in the MHC. The Program Manager offered a more in-depth response:

> I was told in advance that the goal was to make sure we matched applicants to the resources of the program, aka "creaming the sample," but I have come to see the process as two-pronged, first, correlation between offense and diagnosis and second, prognosis for change.

It seemed that the Program Manager was saying that the offender's crime needed to be examined to establish that mental illness contributed to the offense. Overall, each of these respondents knew about referrals, screening for acceptance, and about probation supervision. Staff members seemed knowledgeable about the inner-workings of the court as it related to the client population.

Treating MHC Clients

Every respondent mentioned therapy or counseling being offered to the MHC clients. Four of the respondents reported a full range of services, including mental health services, housing assistance, medication monitoring, vocational services, and residential care housing. Three employees reported that initially policies and procedures did not exist to guide the MHC operation and treatment delivery. Despite the fact that MHCs were modeled after drug courts, the clientele of MHCs were unique and required a different response. When policies were lacking, program staff took it upon themselves to create them. For example, the Clinician researched treatment approaches, while the Program Manager implemented the necessary operational policies and procedures.

Three of the seven respondents did not have direct contact with MHC clients. The four staff members who had first-hand client contact said that the biggest challenge was the heterogeneity of the client population. More specifically, clients had varying mental health diagnoses, and even within the same diagnosis, clients had vastly differing levels of day-to-day functioning, stability, and insight into their own illnesses. Related to that was the high number of clients with co-occurring disorders who abused illegal substances along with having a diagnosis of mental illness. One respondent stated that "trying to keep their clients off of street drugs" was by far the biggest challenge. She stated that her staff utilized both in-patient and outpatient treatment options in the community to help clients with addiction.

Another major challenge was the long waiting list before the client could receive treatment by a community-based agency. MHC teams agreed on the treatment protocol for a defendant, but the lengthy period of time that passed before the client could actually begin treatment con-tributed to the illness, thus exacerbating the problem that the MHC was hoping to stabilize. Lack of treatment services funding was also the biggest problem in another program which had few treatment options for clients.

Respondents were asked to assume that they could make any chang-es in the MHC, and mention as many changes as they wished. Without any prompting on examples of such changes, six out of seven respon-dents mentioned funding for treatment services or increased employees resources. The following quotes are examples:

> More funding would be huge for us. The local mental health center and its case managers have requested emergency funds for medi-cations or housing needs. Also, we are only allowed to have 30 participants at one time . . . it would be nice to be able to take more people."—MHC Coordinator

> More treatment options- money for housing, transportation, den-tal work, health care . . . If we had these resources, we could actu-ally become a prevention court.—Program Manager

> I would have more staff!—Pretrial Services Officer

> More community based treatment programs, particularly residen-tial programs—programs for individuals with co-occurring dis-orders, programs for individuals with children, and programs for older adults. The shortage of these resources often forces clients to wait in jail for weeks and even months before they can be released to appropriate treatment.—Program Analyst

> I would have more resources available—both in terms of services
> and more caseworkers so they didn't have such high caseloads.
> Not only does this challenge them in trying to work with and
> monitor the defendants, it also results in burnout that causes a
> high turnover. It is difficult for these defendants to be moved from
> caseworker to caseworker.—Judge

A third challenge was overcoming the traditional way of thinking between the legal community and the mental health staff. One of the differences was client confidentiality. On the one hand, attorney-client privileges assured confidentiality. However, most conviction records are publicly available. In the mental health community, a clients' record is more extensively protected through HIPAA. However, MHCs rely on clinicians to provide updates and progress reports that extend the knowledge to other non-clinical workers. It seemed from the surveys that criminal justice professionals overall were less attentive to the clients' confidentiality rights than mental health employees who regularly worked with clients with special needs. For social workers and clinicians, clients' confidentiality was central and common in daily practice.

Another example of differences in thinking between the legal community and the mental health employees occurred when clients violated the terms of their MHC participation. Criminal justice employees tended to revert back to traditional responses of revocation, or by defense attorneys being "too quick" to defend clients that had violated the terms of their MHC participation, as if they felt the need to prevent their client from being sent to jail like in a traditional criminal court. The judge offered an insightful look at working with defendants with mental illness from her position:

> I have found that for whatever reason, defendants will respond to a
> judge's requirements more readily than they will a case manager's-
> possibly because positive feedback from an authority figure is a
> new experience for them.

Overall, the respondents believed that individuals in a MHC environment can change and resume living productive lives.

Continuity of Care

A continuity of care plan was important to ensure that services would still be available to the client even after completing the MHC program. Only one court did not have a formal continuity of care plan, but intended to start one in the future. Courts with continuity of care plans seemed to implement them differently. The biggest differences were who supervised the client after graduation from MHC and what type of treatment was offered during aftercare. For example, one court decreased the level of treatment services in aftercare, but the client simply continued with the same community case manager after he/she graduated from the MHC program. In another court, the clients continued to receive the same services and treatment after graduation. This same court also required participation in treatment to enter the MHC program. Two other courts changed both the level of service and the case managers. One MHC assisted clients in getting connected to a community treatment clinic or agency, while the other transferred the clients to another case management program with a local mental health agency. One jurisdiction had a specific aftercare plan that the clients were required to complete with their service coordinators prior to graduation, but the change in the level of service was unclear. One respondent reported that the continuity of care merely consisted of encouraging clients to continue with mental health services. Overall, the respondents reported that it was important for the clients to continue receiving mental health services after completion of MHC.

Family Support

Six of seven respondents reported that most of the MHC clients did not have family support, which is consistent with the literature showing that persons with mental illnesses who have contact with the criminal justice system have few resources to turn to for help (Slate & Johnson, 2008). Three respondents estimated that between 50-65% of MHC clients completely lacked family support. A fourth respondent clarified that having family support was not always positive if family members regularly abused illegal drugs, and perceived that clients who had family members who used drugs had the opportunity to use themselves, which ultimately contributed to the client's program failure. Only the Program Manager reported that their MHC court had a "large percentage of family involvement, and many attended court with their loved ones."

Inter-Agency Collaboration and Communication Barriers

Communication is vital in situations involving multiple collaborating agencies. One MHC had "great communication" and the respondent attributed program operational success to communication quality. Our findings showed that misconceptions and communication barriers were common, such as that held by the Public Defender's office and the local Solicitor's office. Five out of seven respondents mentioned at least one communication barrier that existed with an agency or with particular people. In response, a training seminar for attorneys was held that seemed to correct the misconceptions.

Another barrier was due to the size of the team. In large teams, pertinent information did not always get passed on to the clinicians and treatment providers who needed this information. One reason for this, we believe, was failure to assign accountability for this communication to one particular position. MHCs with good communication had a liaison (such as a regional mental health provider), who monitored the work of the case managers and kept everyone informed. This point person was the one to whom the judge or anyone on the team could go if there was an issue with one of the defendants' treatment and progress.

Respondents recognized that collaborating with team members of different backgrounds meant that the team had different perceptions on how to handle issues, based usually on either a legal or a mental health viewpoint. While not a barrier, differing viewpoints was one of the outcomes of interagency collaboration. These differences were handled by encouraging an open atmosphere at weekly team meetings. To overcome interagency communication problems, respondents engaged in stakeholder communication, training, and on-the-job learning.

Policy Implications

The "best practices" approach has been widely recognized as a valid way to measure the implementation and operationalization of various programs in criminal justice including MHCs. Program implementation is crucial to a program's longevity. If a program is not carefully and methodically

204 Annual Review of Addictions and Offender Counseling

implemented, unanticipated problems could arise for which there is no ready solution. While staff cannot anticipate every obstacle, they must have solutions ready. Program implementation studies are important early in the process because they can detect potential problems, resulting in further policy formulation and/or intervention to change what may not be effective (Birkland, 2005). In this exploratory study, surveys were obtained from seven MHC programs to analyze how MHCs have been implemented in the United States. We found that all respondents were able to communicate how the MHC clients were referred and accepted into the MHC program. The respondents felt properly trained to deal with the targeted population.

All of the programs examined were made up of multi-disciplined teams in some combination of mental health employees and criminal justice personnel. MHC staff worked with a variety of different community agencies, with a primary focus on recidivism/risk reduction and public safety, which was consistent with McNeil and Binder's (2010) research. MHCs in our sample concentrated secondarily on treatment goals such as clients' stabilization on medication and obtaining treatment for their condition.

Useful policy information can be derived from this study. First, clients in MHC programs needed access to more community-based treatment resources to increase the focus on treatment and truly differentiate MHC courts from traditional programs. Limited treatment resources were also consistent with McNeil and Binder's (2010) research. Jurisdictions seeking to implement a brand new MHC program should consider that referring eligible clients to a MHC program will take time, as program staff does not want to risk bringing in clients who do not fit the criteria and don't need to be there.

As expected, MHCs in our study differed in the manner of monitoring each client based on a case-by-case basis, which was also observed by staff in McNeil and Binder's research. The individualized treatment plans and discretionary responses to incidents is a hallmark of MHCs. However, the staff cautioned that individualized treatment plans also have a tendency to be inconsistently implemented, keeping some offenders under court supervision much longer than they would have been had they gone through a traditional court. Furthermore, not all courts had a continuity of care plan to link clients with community mental health services after they graduated. A continuity of care plan is essential to stabilization of this population (Baillargeon et al., 2009).

Courts with a liaison point person reported fewer communication barriers among the staff team and increased informational flow between agencies. Policies on protecting clients' confidentiality and adhering to all regulations are necessary before releasing such information. Liaisons were also important to bridge the gap between criminal justicians and clinicians. Not all criminal justice professionals were trained in mental health issues or social work practices. Similarly, not all clinicians have in-depth knowledge of the criminal justice system or criminal law. Lamb and colleagues (2004) assert that a successful treatment program is contingent upon the input and expertise of "professionals who are knowledgeable and accepting of the tenets of both the criminal justice system and mental health treatment" (p. 121). Similarly, it has increasingly become more desirable and common to expect community correctional staff to possess both humanistic and supervisory qualities (see Deering, 2010). Employing someone who has background in both of these fields would be an efficient way to solve some inter-agency work environment issues. This type of information should be useful for any jurisdiction preparing to implement a MHC, or MHCs that are currently having communication problems.

This study also reinforced the importance of cross-training all MHC staff. Because a MHC is comprised of a multi-disciplinary team, it is recommended that team members become familiar with each other's roles and responsibilities. Also, team members need to be accurately informed of the goals of the MHC program and how those goals are intended to be met. A general, new-hire training could be utilized for any and all positions to inform the new team member(s) of the goals and procedural aspects of the MHC. For cross-training purposes, court and legal training could be offered for clinicians and social workers, and mental health training could be offered for the legal and criminal justice professionals.

Limitations

One limitation of this study was the lack of depth of responses. We were unable to follow-up with the responses due to our study protocol restraints. The study also lacked client outcome data. While this study examined seven different programs, another limitation was the single contact person who responded from each court. It is certainly possible that staff perspectives differ within the same court. Given that each MHC seems to be unique, findings here are not necessarily generalizable to other jurisdictions (Waters et al., 2009). Future researchers may wish to gather in-depth perspectives from multiple staff in courts from several jurisdictions. Recommended program parameters include: pre-adjudication vs. post-adjudication courts; felony vs. misdemeanor courts; and the referral process. Client parameters might include the target population Axis-1 diagnoses only vs. other forms of serious mental illness, criminal history, and treatment services provided. Finally, it is possible that the sample is biased toward courts that had very few problems, and were more likely to share their successes. Courts which may not be staffed adequately or if the court had too many problems might have been less likely to share their experiences.

In conclusion, future research regarding MHC staff may wish to consider the referral process, quality staff communication between agencies, providing timely access to treatment services, and providing that treatment for a long enough duration so that, ultimately, clients remain stable long after the MHC experience ends.

References

Almquist, L., & Dodd, E. (2009). *Mental health courts: A guide to research-informed policy and practice.* New York, NY: Council of State Governments Justice Center.

Banks, S. M., Pandiani, J. A., & Boyd, M. M. (2009). Measuring criminalization/diversion of adults with serious mental illness. *Best Practices in Mental Health, 5* (2), 62-70.

Baillargeon, J., Binswanger, I. A., Penn, J. V., Williams, B. A., & Murray, O. J. (2009). Psychiatric disorders and repeat incarcerations: The revolving prison door. *The American Journal of Psychiatry, 166* (1), 103-109.

Berg, M. (2005). Mental health courts: A new solution to an old problem. *Behavioral Health Management, 25* (4), 16-21.

Birkland, T. A. (2005). *An introduction to the policy process: Theories, concepts, and models of public policy making.* M.E. Sharp.

Boothroyd, R. A., Mercado, C. C., Poythress, N.G., Christy, A., & Petrila, J. (2005). Clinical outcomes of defendants in mental health court. *Psychiatric Services, 56* (7), 829-834.

Bouffard, J. A., Taxman, F. S., & Silverman, R. (2003). Improving process evaluations of correctional programs by using a comprehensive evaluation methodology. *Evaluation and Program Planning, 26,* 149-161.

Bureau of Justice Assistance. (2000). Emerging judicial strategies for the mentally ill in the criminal caseload: Mental health courts in Fort Lauderdale, Seattle, San Bernardino, and Anchorage. Retrieved from http:// www.ojp.usdoj.gov/BJA.

Cosden, M., Ellens, J., Schnell, J., & Yamini-Diouf, Y. (2005). Efficacy of a mental health treatment court with assertive community treatment. *Behavioral Sciences and the Law, 23,* 199-214.

Deering, J. (2010). Attitudes and beliefs of trainee probation officers: A new breed? *Probation Journal, 57,* 9-25.

Erickson, S. K., Campbell, A., & Lamberti, J. S. (2006). Variations in mental health courts: Challenges, opportunities, and call for caution. *Community Mental Health Journal, 42* (4), 335-344.

Fisler, C. (2005). Building trust and managing risk: A look at felony mental health courts. *Psychology, Public Policy, and Law, 11,* 587-604.

James, D. V. (2006). Court diversion in perspective. *Australian and New Zealand Journal of Psychiatry, 40,* 529-538.

Lamb, H. R., Weinberger, L. E., & Gross, B. H. (2004). Mentally ill persons in the criminal justice system: Some perspectives. *Psychiatric Quarterly, 75* (2), 107-126.

McNiel, D. E., & Binder, R. L. (2007). Effectiveness of a mental health court in reducing criminal recidivism and violence. *The American Journal of Psychiatry, 164* (9), 1395-1403.

McNiel, D. E., & Binder, R. L. (2010). Stakeholder views of a mental health court. *International Journal of Law and Psychiatry, 33* (4), 227-235.

National Alliance on Mental Illness (2007). Assertive community treatment: Investment yields outcomes. Retrieved from http://www.nami.org

Public Law 106-515, November 13, 2000, 106th Congress. Retrieved from http://www.gpo.gov

Redlich, A. D. (2005). Voluntary, but knowing and intelligent: Comprehension in mental health courts. *Psychology, Public Policy, and Law, 11,* 605-619.

Redlich, A. D., Steadman, H. J., Monahan, J., Petrila, J., & Griffin, P. A. (2005). The second generation of mental health courts. *Psychology, Public Policy, and Law, 11,* 527-538.

Seltzer, T. (2005). Mental health courts: A misguided attempt to address the criminal justice system's unfair treatment of people with mental illnesses. *Psychology, Public Policy, and Law, 11*, 570-586.

Sheehan, K. (2001). Email survey response rates: A review. *Journal of Computer Mediated Communication, 6* (2).

Slate, R. N., & Johnson, W. W. (2008). *Criminalization of mental illness: Crisis and opportunity for the justice system.* Durham, NC: Carolina Academic Press.

Steadman, H. J., Redlich, A. D., Griffin, P., Petrila, J., & Monahan, J. (2005). From referral to disposition: Case processing in seven mental health courts. *Behavioral Sciences and the Law, 25*, 215-226.

Temporini, H. (2010). Conducting mental health assessments in correctional settings. In C.L. Scott (Ed.), *Handbook of correctional mental health (2nd ed.,* pp. 119-148). Arlington, VA: American Psychiatric Publishing.

Thompson, M., Osher, F., & Tomasini-Joshi, D. (2008). *Improving responses to people with mental illnesses: The essential elements of a mental health court.* New York, NY: The Council of State Governments Justice Center.

Waters, N. L., Strickland, S. M., & Gibson, S. A. (2009). *Mental health court culture: Leaving your hat at the door.* The National Center for State Courts.

Table 1: Employee Perception Measures of MHC Best Practices

1. *"Planning and Administration"* recommends that MHCs be developed by a multi-disciplinary team between mental health and criminal justice. Professional experience was measured through staff position in the MHC, along with how they became involved in the MHC, and what experience they had that led them to be chosen for that position.

2. *"Target Populations"* involves whether the program is serving the clients for which it intended. Staff were asked to explain their current perceived goal of the MHC, and whether or not they perceive the court as achieving the goal(s).

3. *"Timely Participant Identification & Linkage to Services"* recommended that the MHC identify the participant at the earliest time, in regards to minimizing the person's jail stay. One question asked how MHC participants were referred and accepted into the court.

4. *"Terms of Participation"* recommended clearly defining all conditions of the individual's participation such as plea arrangements, duration of involvement, and services. One survey question asked how the MHC participants were supervised in the MHC program.

5. *"Informed Choice"* is ensuring the defendant was able to give consent and was aware of what the program entailed, including possible sanctions should the participant violate the conditions. One survey question asked staff how the MHC participants adhered to the conditions of their probation or involvement in the MHC program.

6. *"Treatment Supports and Services"* was defined as individualized treatment services and case management to assist and follow client progress. Employees were asked what mental health services were offered or court mandated for participants. They were also asked about outside support network by estimating the percentage of participants who lacked family or a support network.

7. *"**Court Team**"* described the importance of criminal justice staff being able to work with the mental health staff. Employees were asked about the ability to solve problems as they arise, as well as how they have overcome the obstacles in this area. The respondents' experience in working in an inter-agency environment and their experience working in general with persons with mental illness were also taken into account here.

8. *"**Monitoring Adherence to Court Requirements**"* noted the importance of staff working to monitor the participants' progress and adherence, ensure public safety, and offer sanctions and incentives. Employees were asked if there was a continuity of care plan, and if so, to describe the continuity of care plan (i.e. what happens when the MHC participant graduates from the program).

9. *"**Sustainability**"* recommended collecting data to determine whether or not the court is achieving its goal of reducing recidivism. Since the courts were already doing this, we asked staff to comment on any improvements that could be made to prevent or reduce the likelihood of relapse. A second question asked what changes the respondent would make (if they could) to improve and sustain the mental health court program.

10. *"**Confidentiality**"* refers to regulations that protect clients' confidential medical and mental health records, and recommended that clients sign a release of information to allow limited information flow between agencies.

11. *"**General Questions**"* asked how staff overcame any identified obstacles in program implementation. Finally, survey respondents were asked to rate four general goals of a mental health court: recidivism, positive clinical outcomes, saving the jurisdiction money, and freeing up jail space.

www.ingramcontent.com/pod-product-compliance
Lightning Source LLC
Chambersburg PA
CBHW061731270326
41928CB00011B/2196